I0810161

IMAGES
of America

STANTON COUNTY

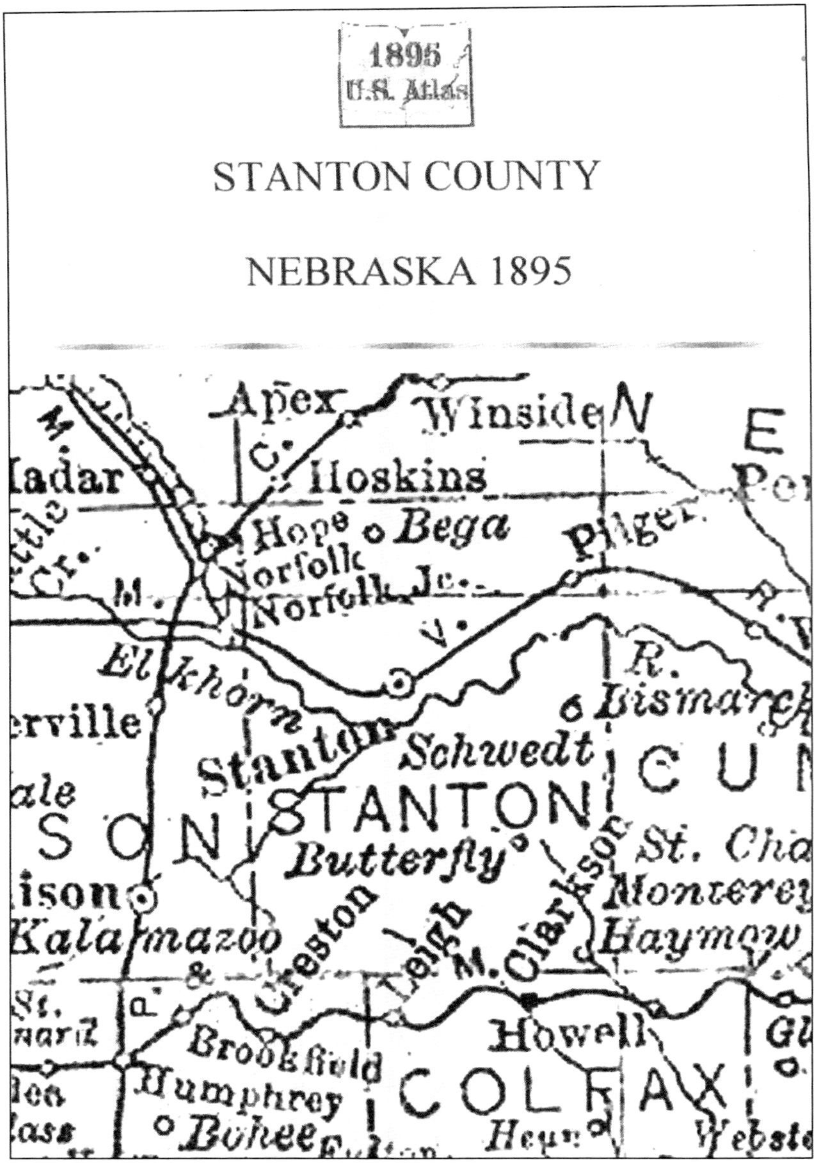

This 1895 map of Stanton County indicates the outline of the county boundaries and the location of the towns of Stanton and Pilger. The county is rectangular and measures 18 miles wide by 24 miles deep. A number of the communities and counties adjoining Stanton County are visible. Those which are contiguous to the Stanton County lines are Colfax County and Platte County to the south; Cuming County is on the eastern border; Wayne County is on the north boundary; and Madison County adjoins on the west. (Courtesy of the Historical Society of Stanton County.)

On the cover: In 1916, Company G troops march south through downtown Stanton to board the train at the Chicago and North Western Railway train depot. The troops are headed for the Mexican border. A Stantonite, Alwin Axen, is in the troop formation. John Hakl's Shoe Store sign can be seen behind the troops. (Courtesy of Marci Poeschl.)

IMAGES
of America

STANTON COUNTY

Mary L. Maas

ARCADIA
PUBLISHING

ISBN 978-0-7385-6127-1

Published by Arcadia Publishing
Charleston SC, Chicago IL, Portsmouth NH, San Francisco CA

Printed in the United States of America

Library of Congress Catalog Card Number: 2008929028

For all general information contact Arcadia Publishing at:
Telephone 843-853-2070
Fax 843-853-0044
E-mail sales@arcadiapublishing.com
For customer service and orders:
Toll-Free 1-888-313-2665

Visit us on the Internet at www.arcadiapublishing.com

This is dedicated to those who have helped save our history with the preservation of photographs. It is a tribute to those who recorded the anecdotes and experiences of our forefathers to share with our children, our grandchildren, and all future generations to come.

CONTENTS

ACKNOWLEDGMENTS

This book has been created with the help and encouragement from so many people in the community and my family. Members of the Historical Society of Stanton County provided many of the photographs, in addition to the pictures used from the Pilger Historical Museum and the Stanton Historical Museum archives.

A sincere thank-you goes to those who shared their private collections for the book. Laura Forker, editor and publisher of the *Stanton Register*, gave unlimited access to her newspaper archives, equipment and expertise to help make this project a success. A majority of the photographs for Pilger's history were taken from the private collection belonging to Marian Klima and the town's history researched by Roland Jensen. Marci Poeschl, Art Catlin, Larry Belz, Milford and Gloria Koch, Richard Kuehn, Inez Barth, and Mason Moritz were instrumental in providing help with the research and many of the photographs for Stanton's history. Carol Armbruster, head librarian at the Stanton Public Library, opened those stored records for my research.

I want to express my deepest gratitude to Ted Gerstle, editor, and John Pearson, publisher, at Arcadia Publishing, who provided their time, their encouragement, and their patience to make this project the best it could be.

All these people and many others shared their knowledge and records of history so they could be made available in a snapshot journey through Nebraska's Stanton County.

INTRODUCTION

Stanton County, located in northeast Nebraska, was first known as Izard County. It was named in honor of Mark W. Izard, the territorial governor from 1855 to 1857. After a change in boundary definitions in 1862, the county name changed too. It became Stanton County to honor Edwin M. Stanton, the American secretary of war who served under Abraham Lincoln from 1862 to 1867.

Stanton and Pilger are the two incorporated communities located in the county. Stanton was platted by S. L. Holman in 1871. One attribution to the origin of the city's name was to Holman, who named Stanton in honor of his wife's family name. In another version, the town was also named after Edwin M. Stanton. The City of Stanton is the county seat of Stanton County and incorporated in 1881. Pilger, located in Humbug Precinct, incorporated in June 1887. Pilger received its name from John Peter Pilger, who owned the land upon which the town was platted. In 1932, the precinct's name, Humbug, was dropped, and the precinct's name became Pilger.

On the western edge of the county, near the city of Norfolk, is a residential subdivision called Woodland Park. The community has an elementary school, affiliated with the Norfolk Public School district, and a convenience store, but it is in close proximity to Norfolk for most other shopping and services.

The first settlers, Charles and Mitchell Sharp, arrived in the summer of 1865 to stake their claims on land along Humbug Creek. The Sharps immediately returned to Omaha. On the way back, they met Jacob Hoffman and Francis Scott, who traveled north with their families and possessions. The Hoffmans and Scotts built their cabins, the first buildings erected in the county, near the Humbug Creek.

Although Stanton County is one of the smaller counties in Nebraska, having 428 square miles, much of it is located in the beautiful Elkhorn River valley. When settlers came to the valley, they found herds of antelope, buffalo, deer, and elk, which grazed on lush prairie grasses and along the river. The river and creeks teemed with channel catfish, perch, bass, and bullheads, which gave a welcomed variety to sparse diets. The abundance of wild game included prairie chickens, quail, grouse, wild duck, and geese, which all provided food for trappers, hunters, and early pioneers. Raccoon, otter, beaver, muskrat, and mink fed along the river. Coyotes and wolves had dens in the bluffs and hills.

Before the white settlers came to the region, Pawnee Indians lived and hunted along the Elkhorn River. As the settlers pushed the tribes out of their territories, the Pawnee had to fight rival tribes of Omaha, Sioux, and Ponca Indians for the hunting and food supply in the Elkhorn Valley. Archaeological research has found evidence of a Native American battleground along the river banks east of Stanton. In 1854, the Kansas-Nebraska Act opened the territory, of what is now Nebraska, to homesteaders who could claim a quarter section of "free" land with a $10 filing fee. Those with capital could opt for the outright cash purchase of land.

The people who decided to put down their roots and establish farms, towns, schools, and churches came from many ethnic backgrounds. Germans settled the Pilger area along the Humbug Creek and in the Union Creek area south of Stanton. Bohemians populated the southern area of the county near Haymow Precinct, spreading further south into Colfax County. Swedes, Danes, and Norwegians sprinkled throughout the county with a concentration of Swedes in the Bega settlement north of Stanton.

They came by wagon and oxen. They came on foot and horseback. Some came with little more than the dream of a new life and success on the virgin prairie.

Stanton County is an agricultural and a major livestock feeding area. Pasture land and feed lots hold dairy and beef cattle. Confinement units contain swine operations in several locations in the county. Corn and feed grains are grown for cattle and hog production and soybeans are grown for a cash crop. Green Fiber recycling plant is located in the western part of the county. Nucor Steel mill is a major industry established in Stanton County since 1970.

Industrious entrepreneurs have lived and built businesses since the first settlers arrived. They invested their time, energy, capital, and vision unsparingly. They built mills, brick factories, shops, and stores to fulfill the needs of the developing communities. They built churches, schools, roads, railroads, elevators, and bridges with their labor and sacrifice. They faced prairie fires, grasshopper plagues, floods, tornadoes, drought, and crop failures with the determination to persevere. They shared with their neighbors and children their love of the soil and their connection to the community and pledged allegiance to their country. Their pioneer quest and courage is a proud legacy for future generations to build upon, and they set the bar high to make all descendents reach up, reach out, and pass it on.

One

When It All Began
1865

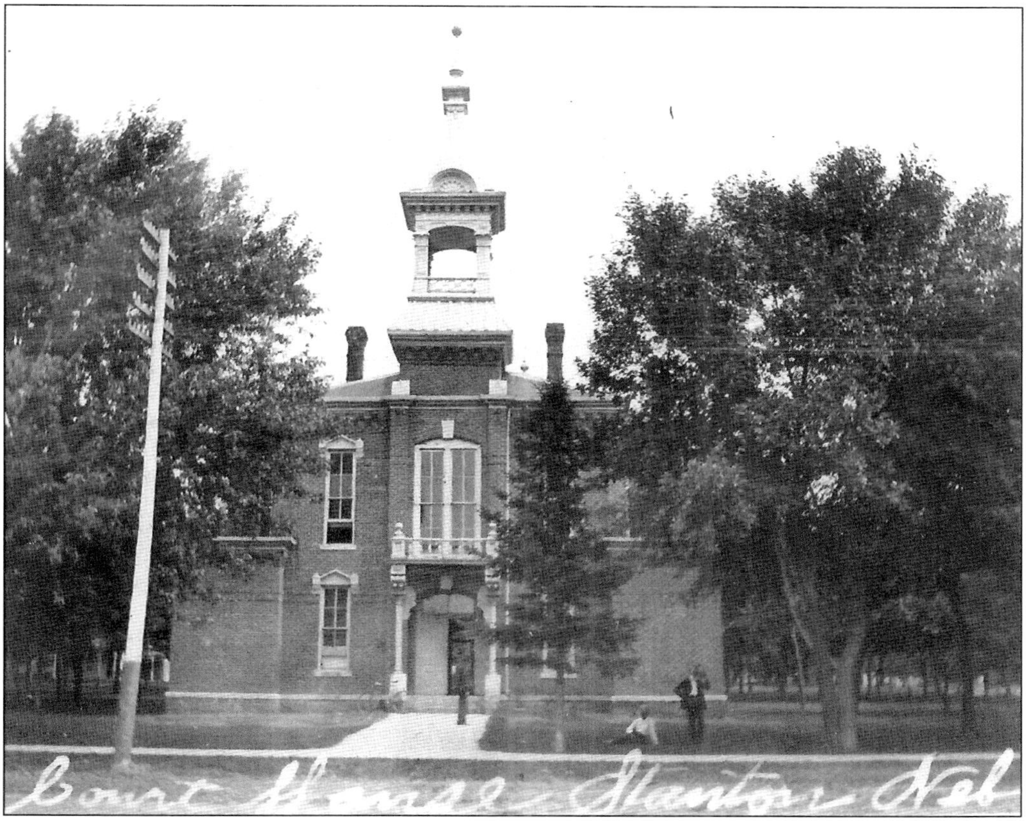

This is the second Stanton County Courthouse built on the east end of Stanton's main street, then known as Pacific Avenue. The first was a small wood frame building built at a cost of $475 in 1871. The construction of the two-story brick courthouse was completed in 1883 at a cost of $10,624. In 1976, a modern, one-story structure was built at the same street location. (Courtesy of the Historical Society of Stanton County and Art Catlin.)

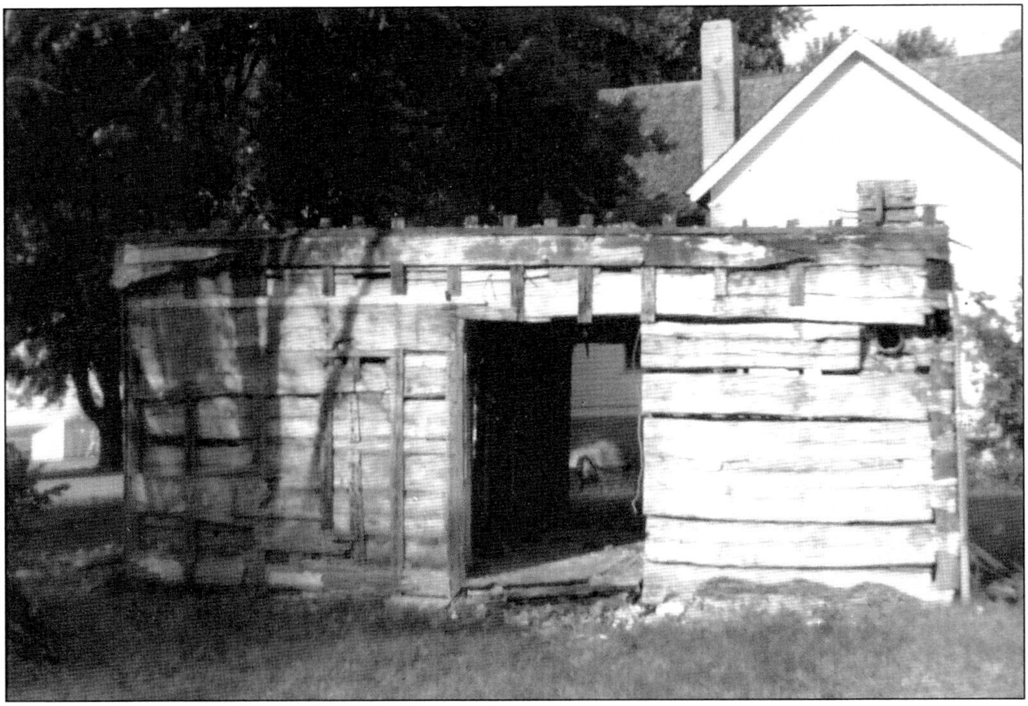

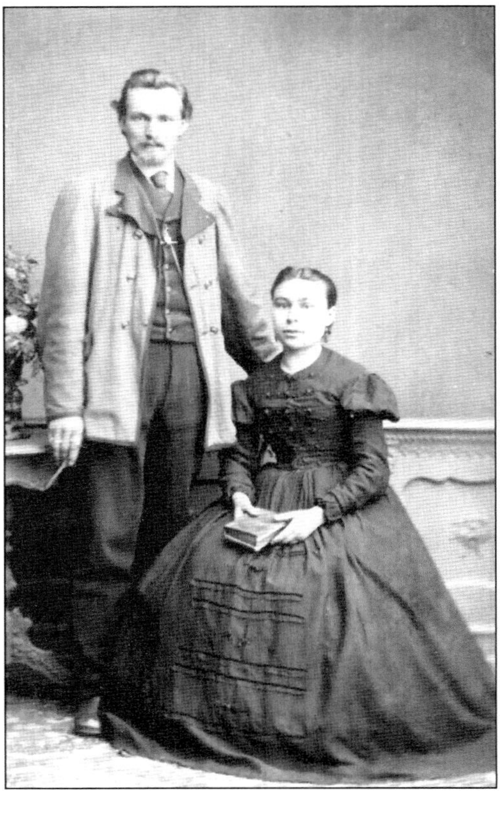

A portion of the first log cabin, built in Stanton County in the 1860s by Andrew Schauble, has been restored and is on display in the Pilger Museum Annex. The log cabin was purchased by Joseph and Francis Klima and moved into Pilger. They occupied the cabin with their three children, Joseph Jr., Francis (Fanny), and Lige, until 1886, when their house was finished on their farm two miles northwest of Pilger. During that period of time, Joseph worked for the Fremont, Elkhorn and Missouri Valley Railroad. During his spare hours after working on the railroad, Joseph carried lumber and supplies on his back to build the house and outbuildings on the farm. (Above, courtesy of the Pilger Museum; left, courtesy of Marian Klima.)

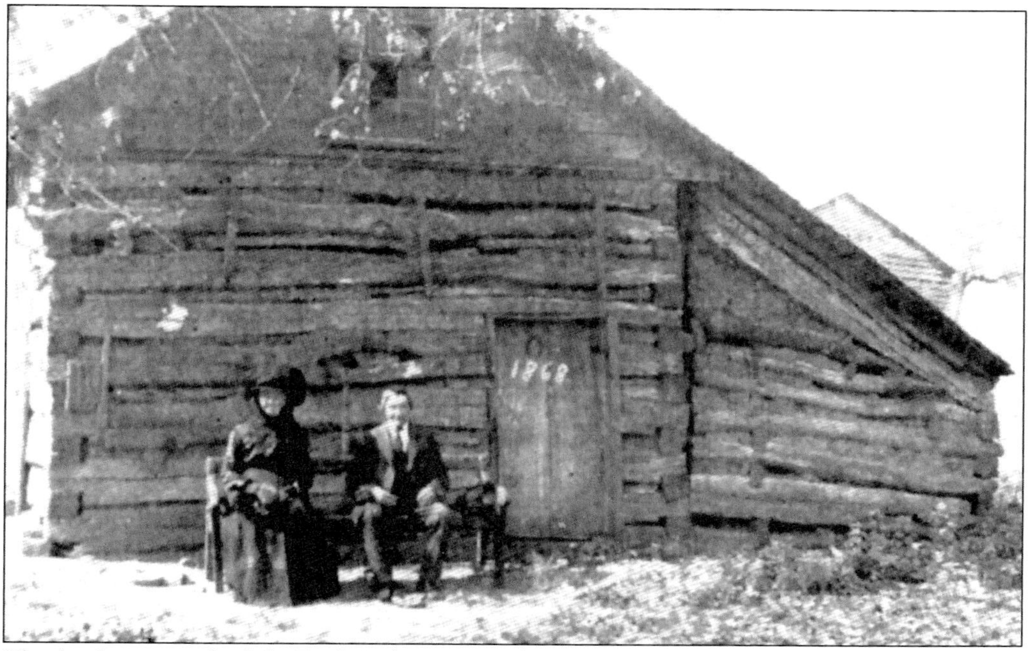

This log house was built by Fred Koch in 1869. The Koch cabin was 12 feet by 16 feet. The walls were plastered with clay and sand mortar and then whitewashed with a mixture of milk and ashes on the inside and out. It was later used as a granary until Koch's son Herman Koch tore it down in 1935. (Courtesy of the Historical Society of Stanton County.)

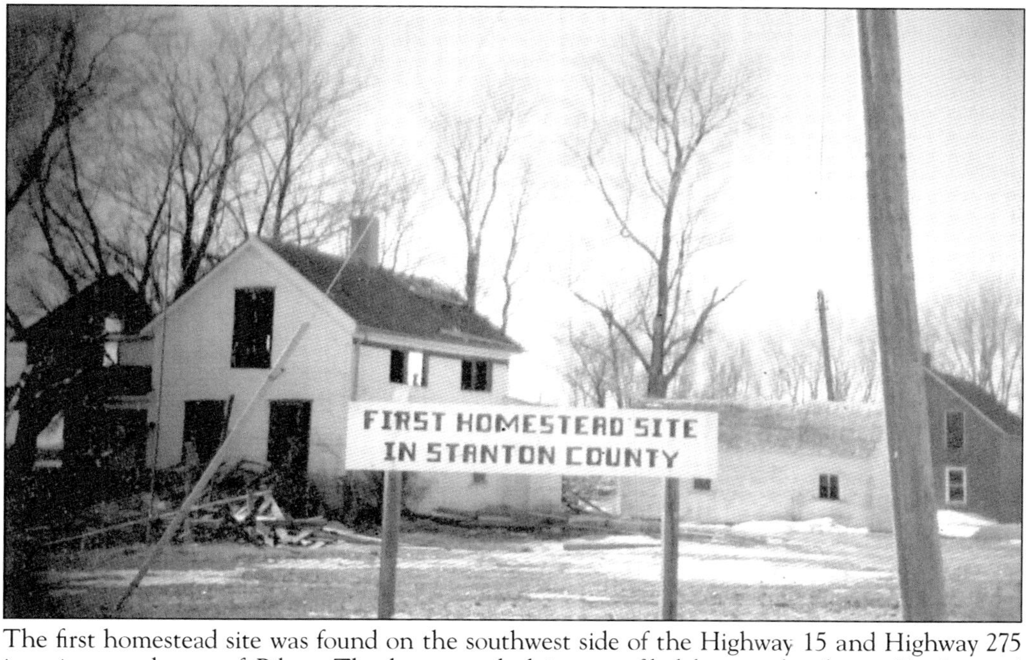

The first homestead site was found on the southwest side of the Highway 15 and Highway 275 junction northwest of Pilger. The homestead claim was filed by two brothers, Charles and Mitchell Sharp, in 1865. They were the first pioneer settlers to "prove up" their homestead claims in Stanton County. (Courtesy of the Pilger Museum.)

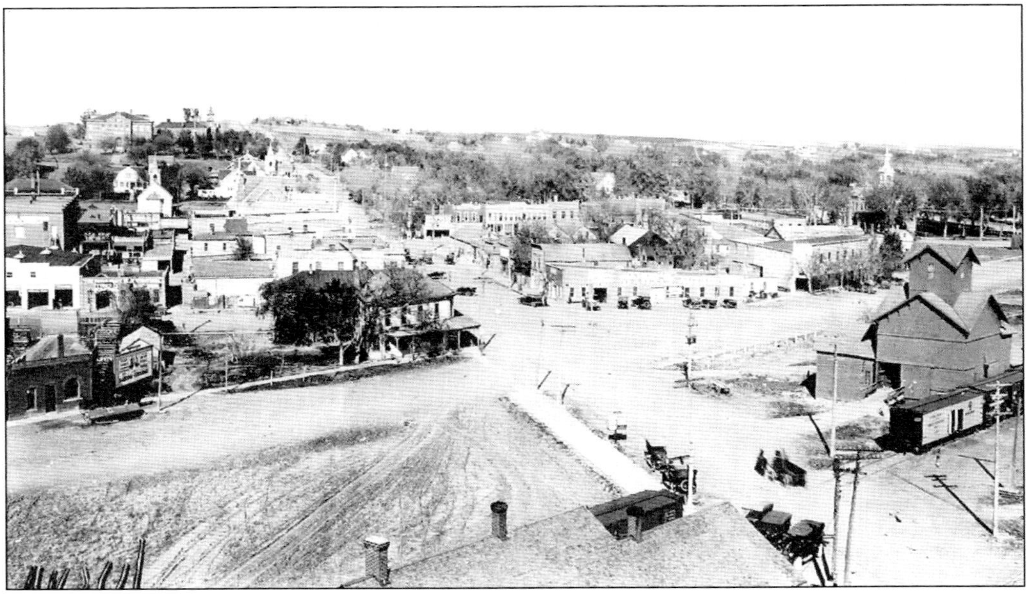

This bird's-eye view shows Stanton at the dawn of the 20th century. This was taken from on top of the Stanton mill looking north. Directly below the mill is the depot roof. The two school buildings are seen at the top left side. The courthouse spire is to the right. The large white building directly north from the depot is the Elkhorn Hotel. (Courtesy of the Historical Society of Stanton County.)

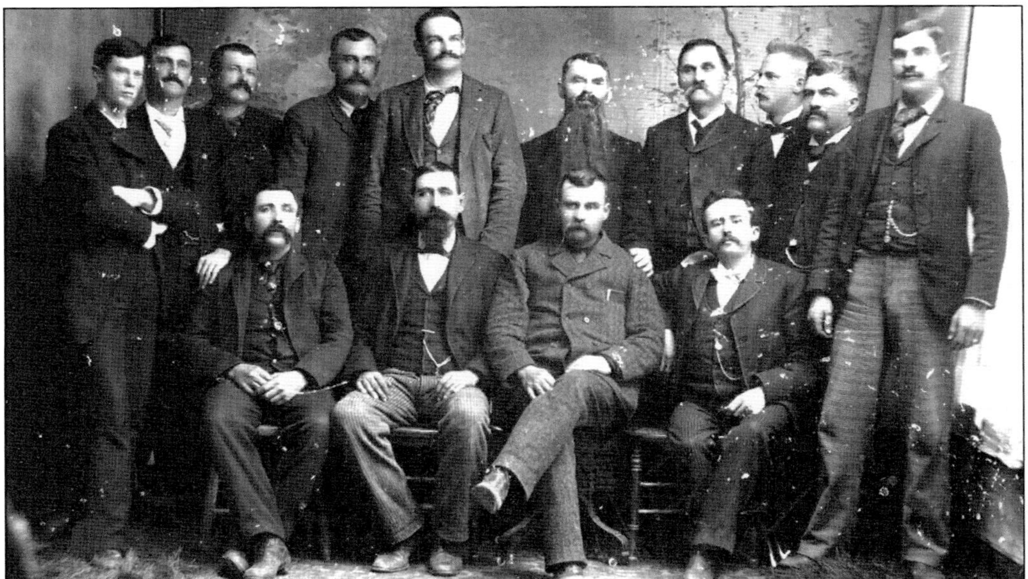

Stanton County officials posed for this photograph taken in 1888. Seen are, from left to right, (first row) Frank Canroll, John Tyler, Dave Owne, county commissioners; and J. N. Vining, county coroner. The second row includes Bob Appleby, county clerk; Robert Loerke, county assessor; Alex Peters, sheriff; George Young, county attorney; J. W. Mackey, judge; Dr. W. L. Bowman, physician; Frank Laomer, deputy treasurer; Adam Pilger, treasurer; and Eugene Resseguie, bridge foreman. (Courtesy of the Historical Society of Stanton County.)

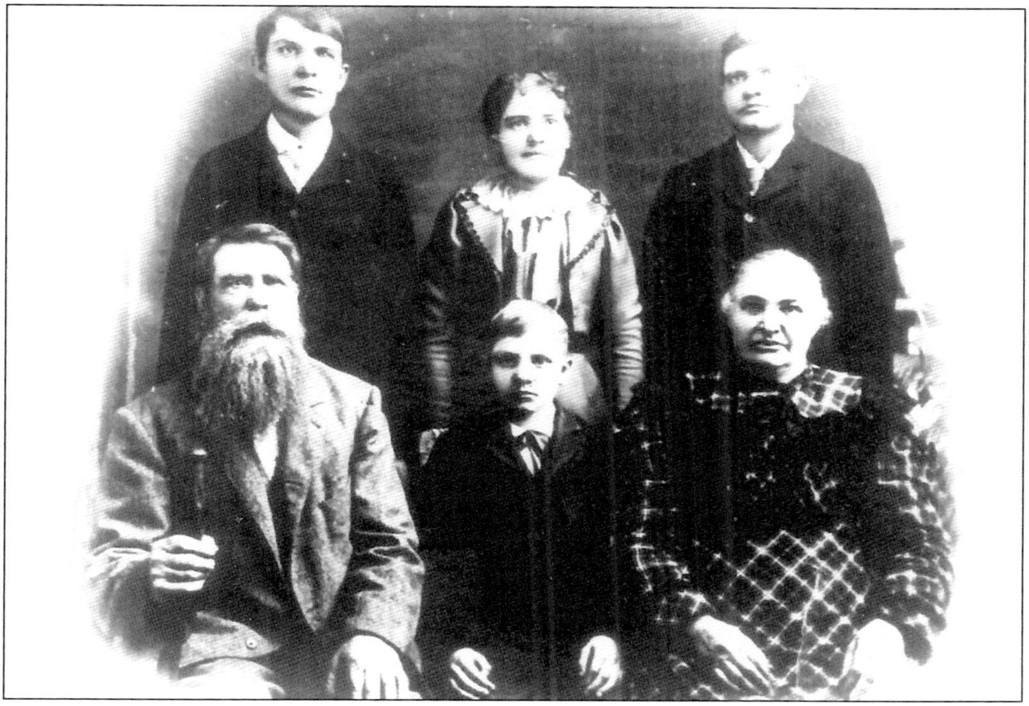

John Peter Pilger was the original owner of the land upon which the village of Pilger was named and platted. He is shown with his family in this photograph, and they are, from left to right, (first row) John Peter, Julius Pilger, and Elizabeth Jung/Young Pilger; (second row) unidentified, Katharine Pilger, and August Pilger. (Courtesy of Marian Klima.)

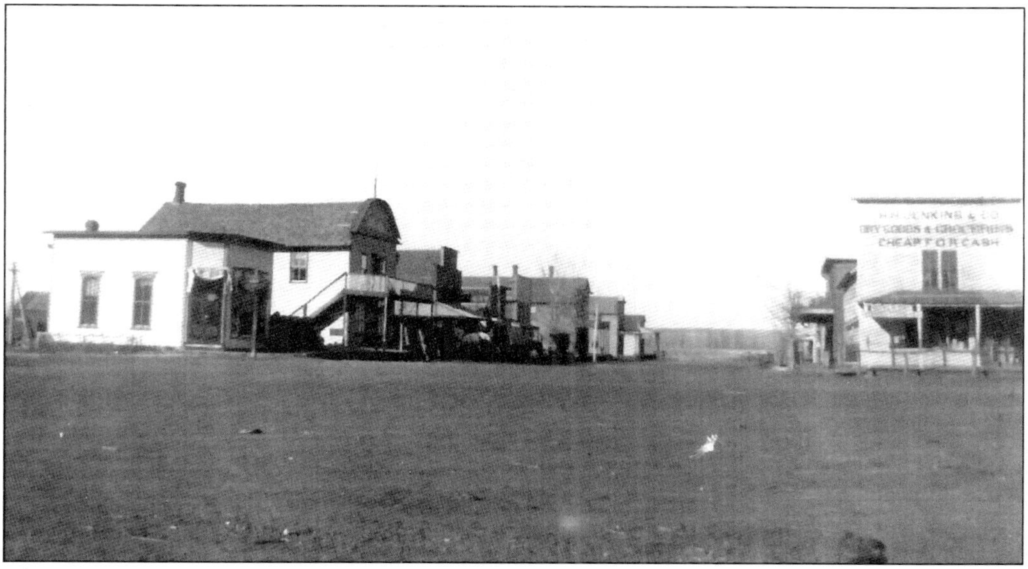

This is an 1896 view of one of the first streets developed in the village of Pilger. The small, white wooden frame bank building was replaced by a two-story brick building in 1906. On the right side, the store sign advertises "H. H. Jenkins & Co., Dry Goods and Groceries, Cheap For Cash." (Courtesy of Marian Klima.)

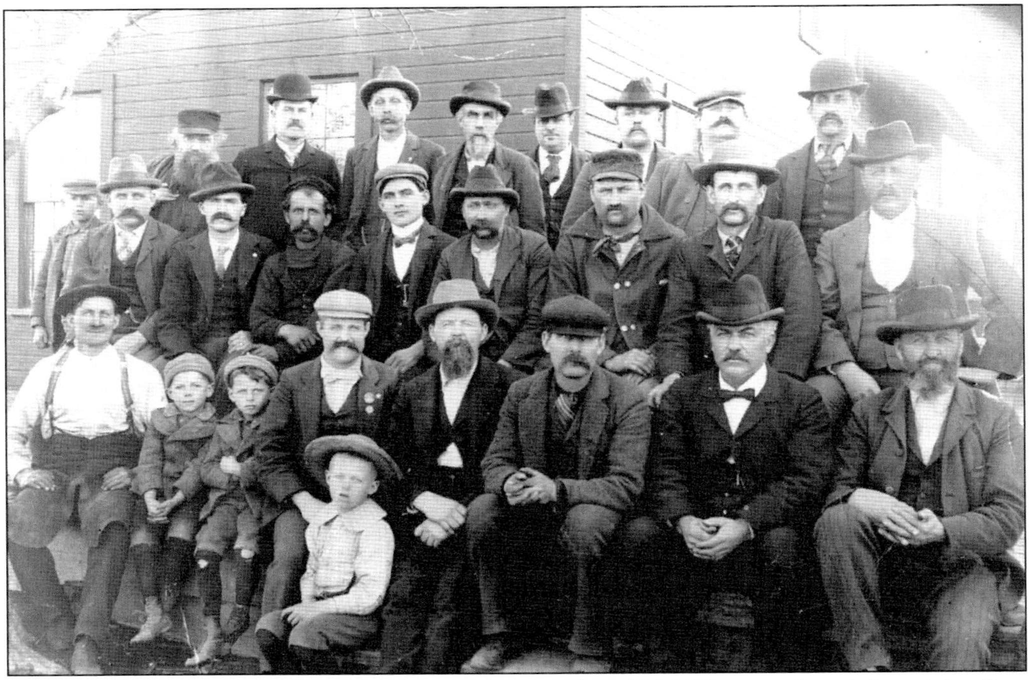

The Pilger businessmen gathered for a group photograph in 1900. They are, from left to right, (first row) Henry Grovejohn, Bill and Otto Olk, Fred Husbands and son Earl, John Matheson, Charley Tinney, Adam Pilger, and I. R. Layton; (second row) an unidentified boy, Karl Koplin, Charley Davidson, Jake Olk, Paul Schneider, Louie Petersen, Herman Koplin, Louis Koplin, and George Munger; (third row) John Rustemeyer, B. H. Schaberg, John Petersen, William Church, I. B. Jeffries, Carl Axen, August Schellpeper, and Sam Bordner. (Courtesy of the Pilger Museum.)

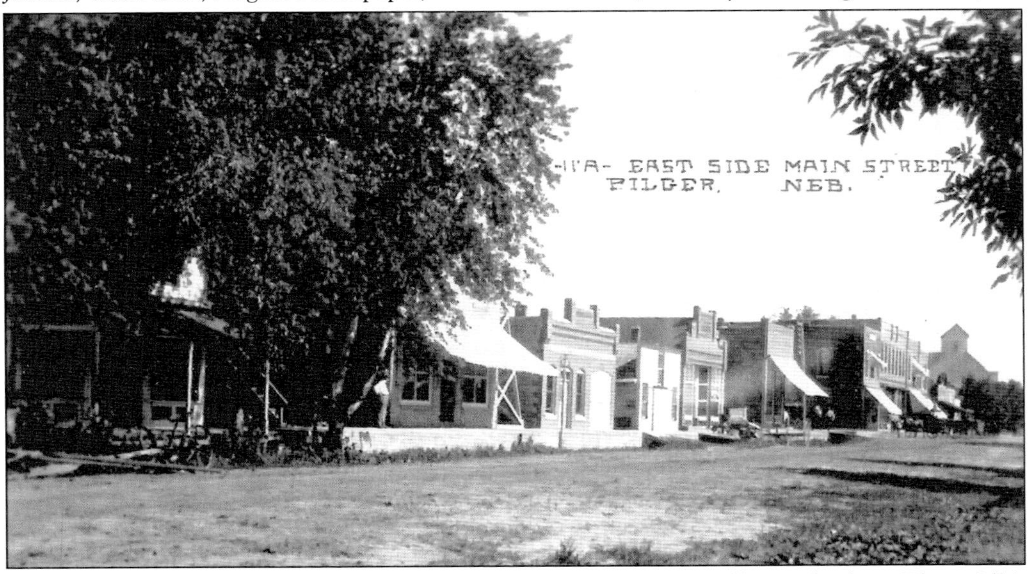

This view shows the east side of Main Street in the fledgling village of Pilger. Theo Olk's Woodworking Shop is located next to the village hall on the left side of the photograph. The Pilger elevator is on the far right side. (Courtesy of Marian Klima.)

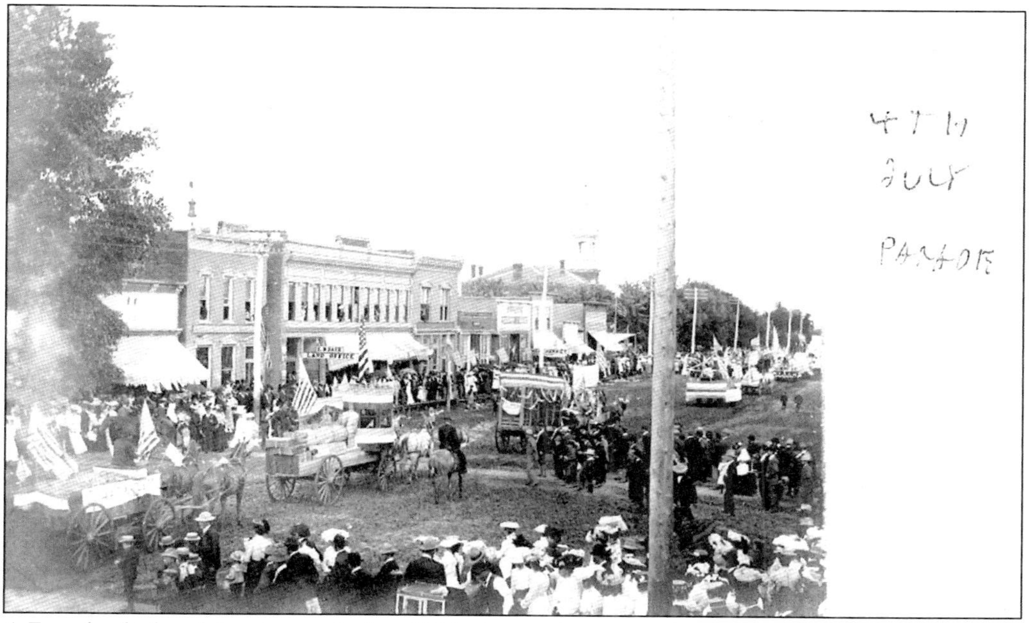

A Fourth of July celebration in the late 1800s draws a large crowd in downtown Stanton. Everyone is dressed in their Sunday best. Flags wave on floats and along the street. Signs on storefronts advertise E. B. Baer Land Office and the Meat Market. The last float at the bottom left has a Horton and Chace banner. They owned one of Stanton's elevators at that time. (Courtesy of Art Catlin.)

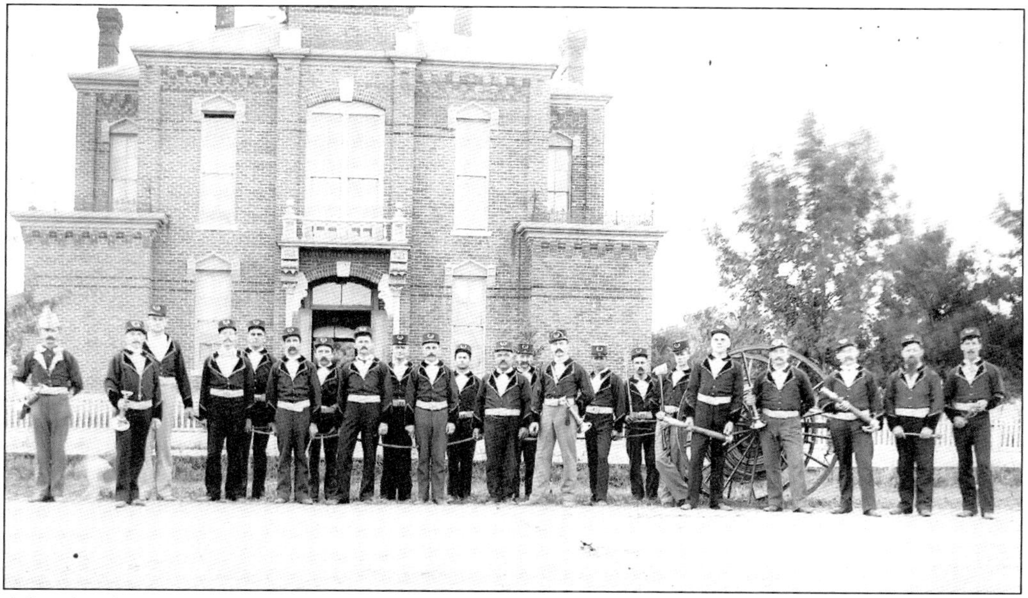

After fire destroyed the Wilson and Company elevator in Stanton in 1886, there was a concerted effort to organize a fire department. On August 17, 1893, the Stanton Volunteer Fire Company was recognized as a hose team. The hose house was located on the triangular block with the bell tower and jail. These firemen are lined up in front of the first Stanton Public School building in 1894. (Courtesy of the Historical Society of Stanton County.)

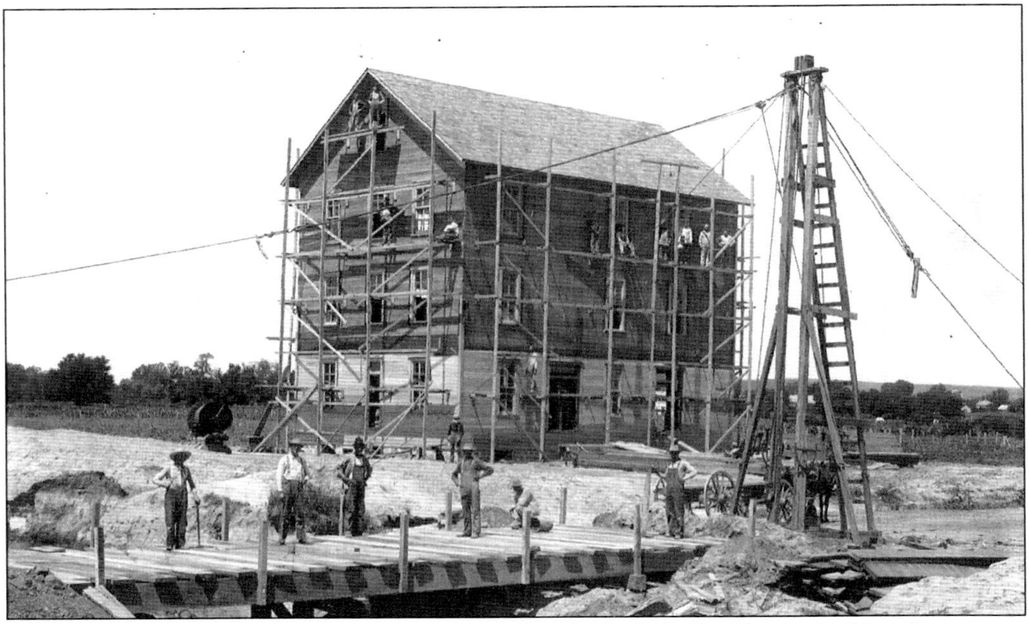

The Stanton Water Power Company contracted with Frank L. Sanders to build and operate a mill on the Elkhorn River cutoff south of town. Excavation began in April 1901. In the above photograph, workers are building the mill. In June 1902, a flood tore out the east end of the milldam. When the milldam failed and gave way again in 1905, the mill was moved near the Chicago and North Western Railway station uptown. E. A. Marshall acquired the mill in 1925, and it burned down in January 1931. The photograph below shows the interior of a mill. On the left are stacks of flour-filled bags. On the right the sign posted on the wooden panel states "no smoking allowed" and below that the written command "don't spit on the floor." (Above, courtesy of Larry Belz; below, courtesy of the Historical Society of Stanton County.)

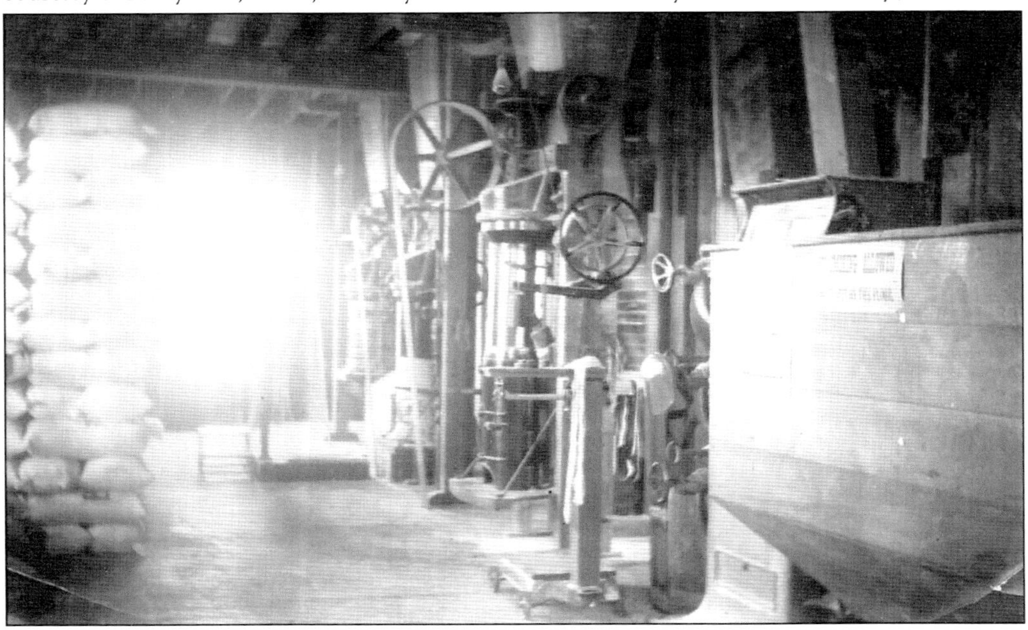

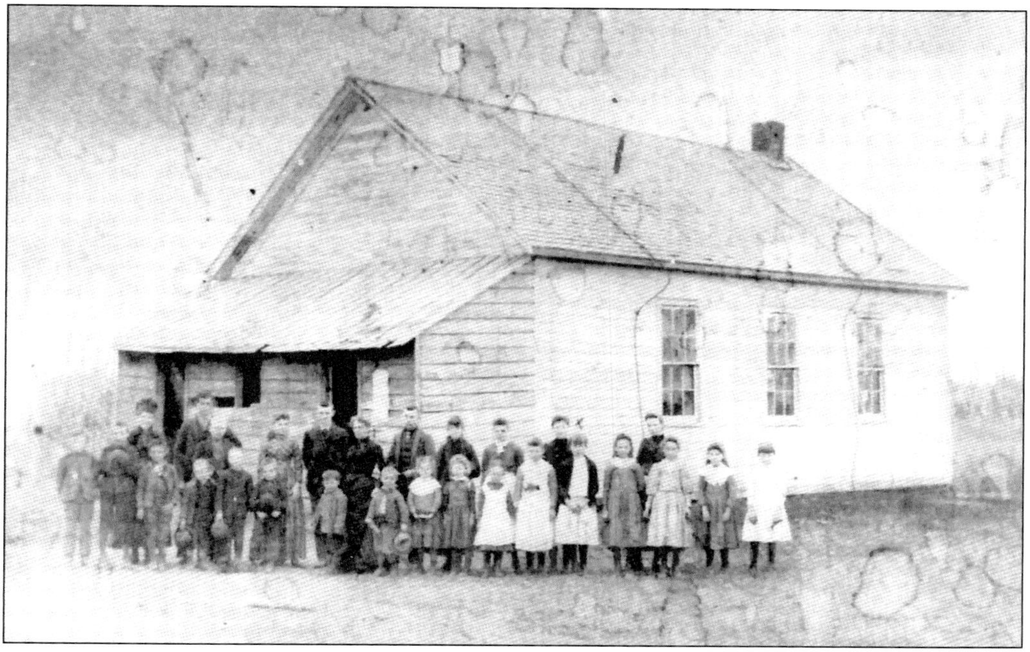

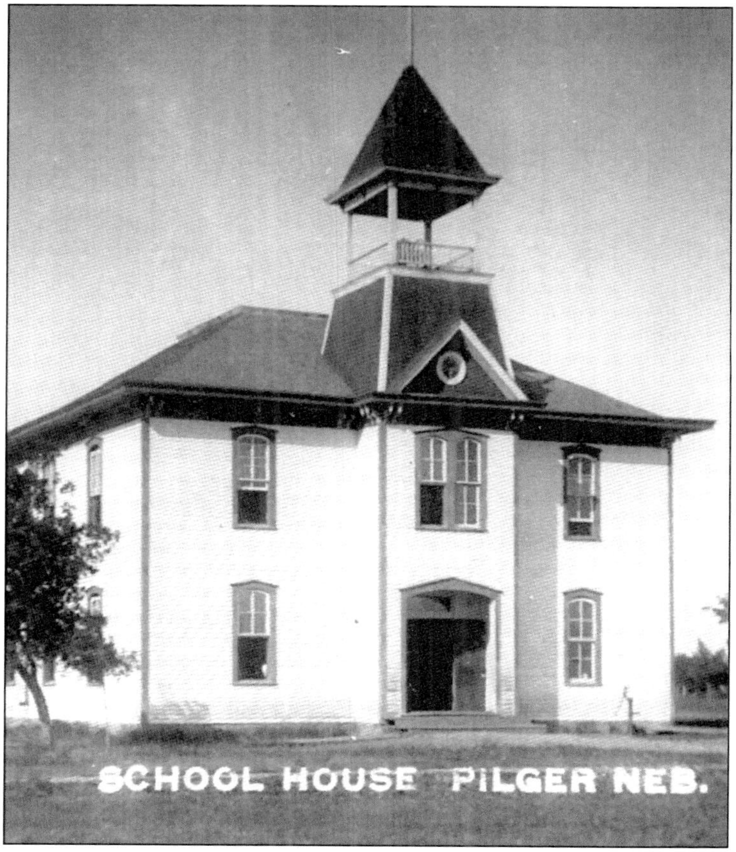

Pilger had the first schoolhouse to be built in Stanton County. Pilger District No. 1 was organized in 1868. The original school building was 24 feet by 28 feet. In 1890, enrollment numbers needed more room, so a new four-room school was erected at a cost of $2,675. The school had an upper story for public use. In 1903, a wing was added to accommodate 10 grade levels with three rooms on each floor. By 1904, the school had 11 grades and 167 students in attendance. The original school building was sold to J. G. Matheson for $105. (Courtesy of the Klima Collection.)

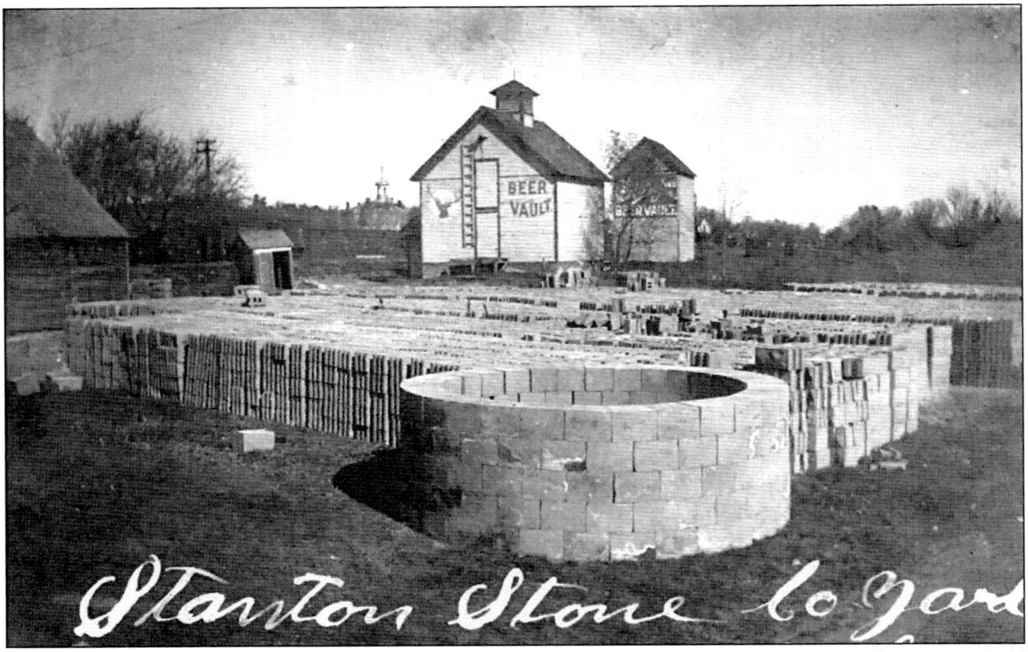

The Stanton Cement Stone Company plant was located on the Perry Kinney farm, one-half mile east of Stanton in May 1903. A. W. Forbes and R. Porter owned the plant, which had the capacity of making 25 "stones" (cement blocks) per hour. The plant was in operation until 1907. J. V. Robinson, plant manager, laid many sidewalks and foundations for businesses in the city. (Courtesy of Art Catlin.)

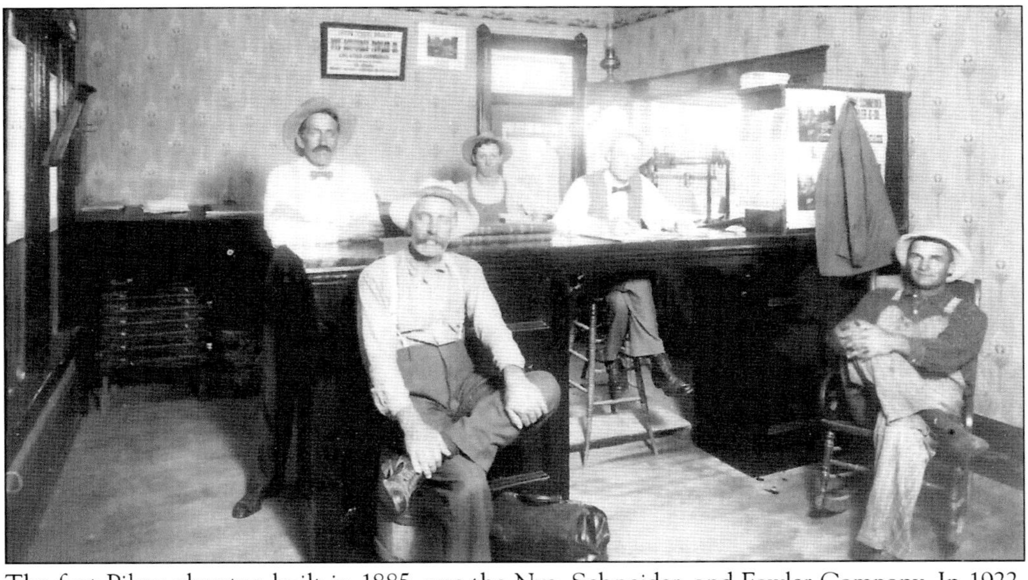

The first Pilger elevator, built in 1885, was the Nye, Schneider, and Fowler Company. In 1922, the name was changed to the Nye-Jenks Grain Company. It later became a part of the Farmers Union. The men shown in the Nye, Schneider, and Fowler scale office are, from left to right, (first row) Isaac Bordner and unidentified; (second row) Sam Bordner and two unidentified. (Courtesy of Marian Klima.)

This is one of the earlier new elevators, the Nye-Jenks elevator, which was built on the east side of the main street in Pilger. Notice should be taken of the gentleman standing at the top window on the roof of the building. (Courtesy of Marian Klima.)

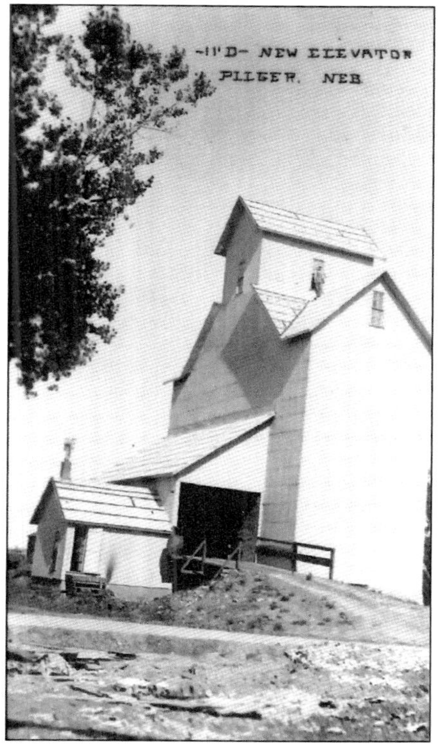

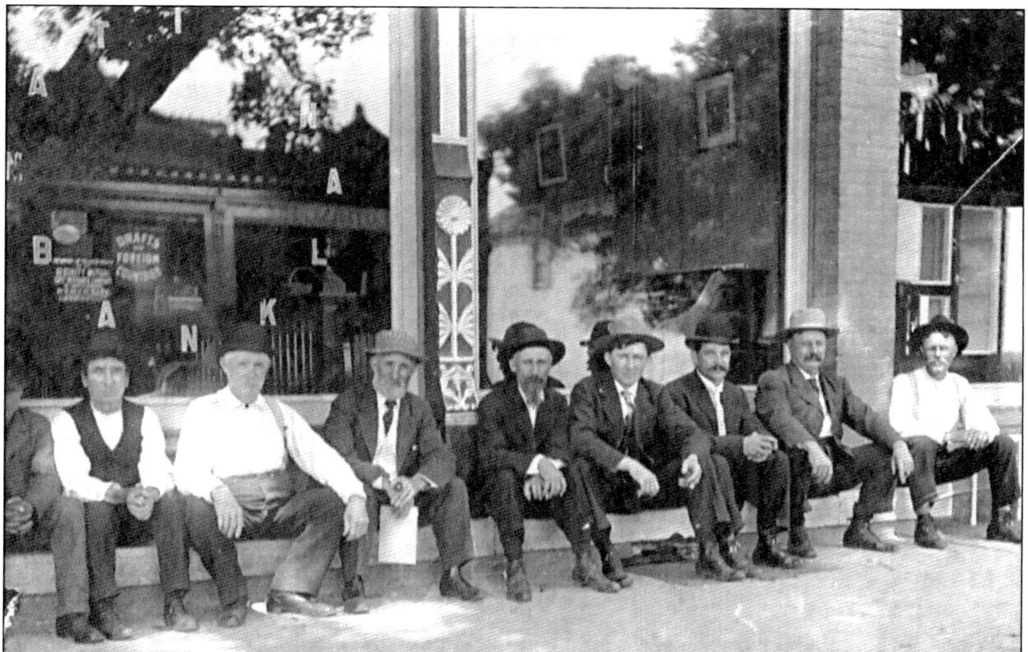

A group of Stanton County pioneers sits on the ledge of a storefront. Those identified are, from left to right, Louie Armbruster, Levi Miller, Judge Mackey, ? Schulz, ? Mewis, Dale Chamber, ? Esswein, and two unidentified. (Courtesy of the Historical Society of Stanton County.)

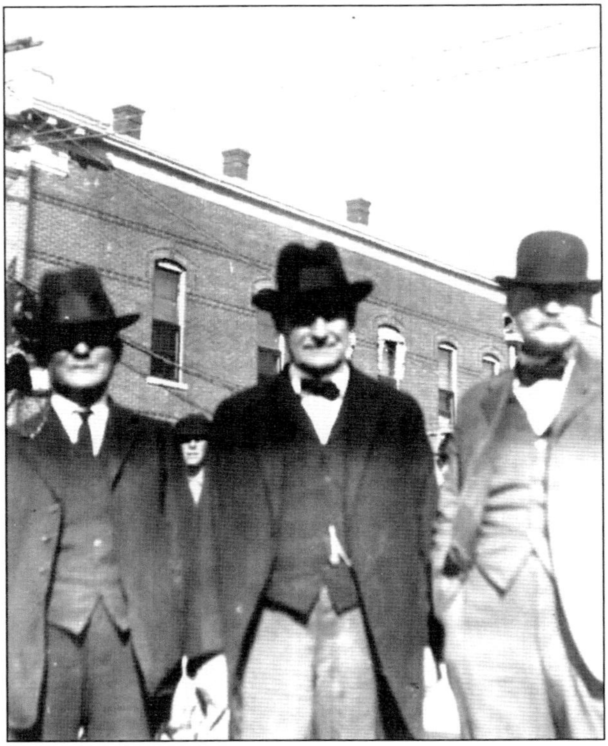

Three pioneer businessmen pose for a photograph. Robert Grattan (left) was the co-owner of Grattan General Store in Stanton. He served in the capacity of Stanton county treasurer for eight years and for an additional eight years as the deputy county treasurer. The other two are W. J. Bryan (center), whose business association is unknown, and John Matheson, a farmer and agricultural implement business owner in Pilger. (Courtesy of Marian Klima.)

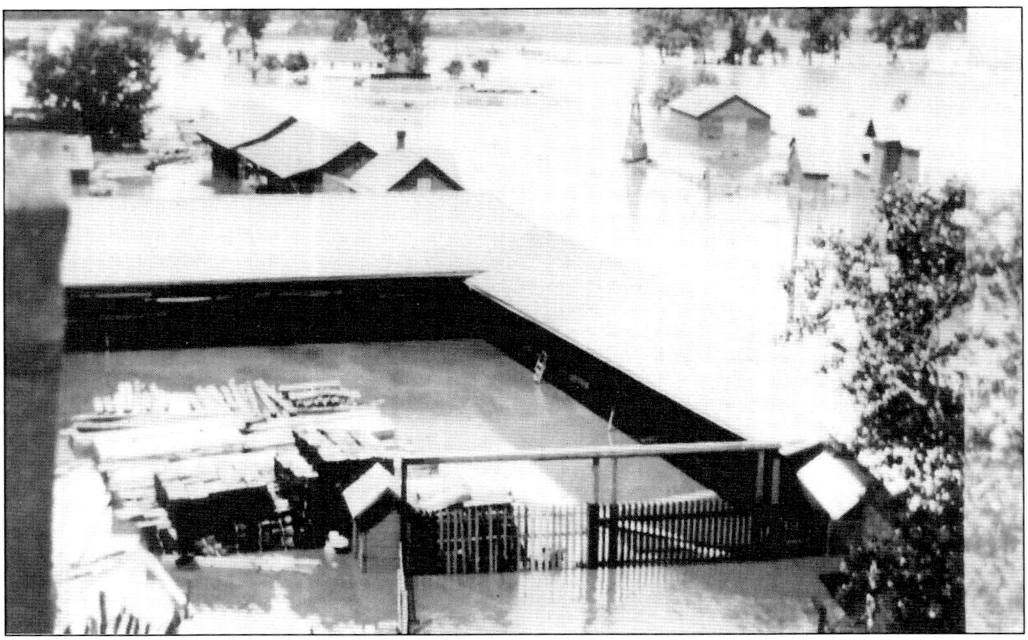

One of many floods, which plagued Pilger for a number of years, is surrounding the businesses in this photograph. The Nye-Jenks Lumberyard is in the foreground. The Farmers Co-op Lumber is in the rear. L. D. Watson Hog Buying Company pens and windmill are to the right with a portion of the Pilger Livery barn also visible on the front right side. (Courtesy of Marian Klima.)

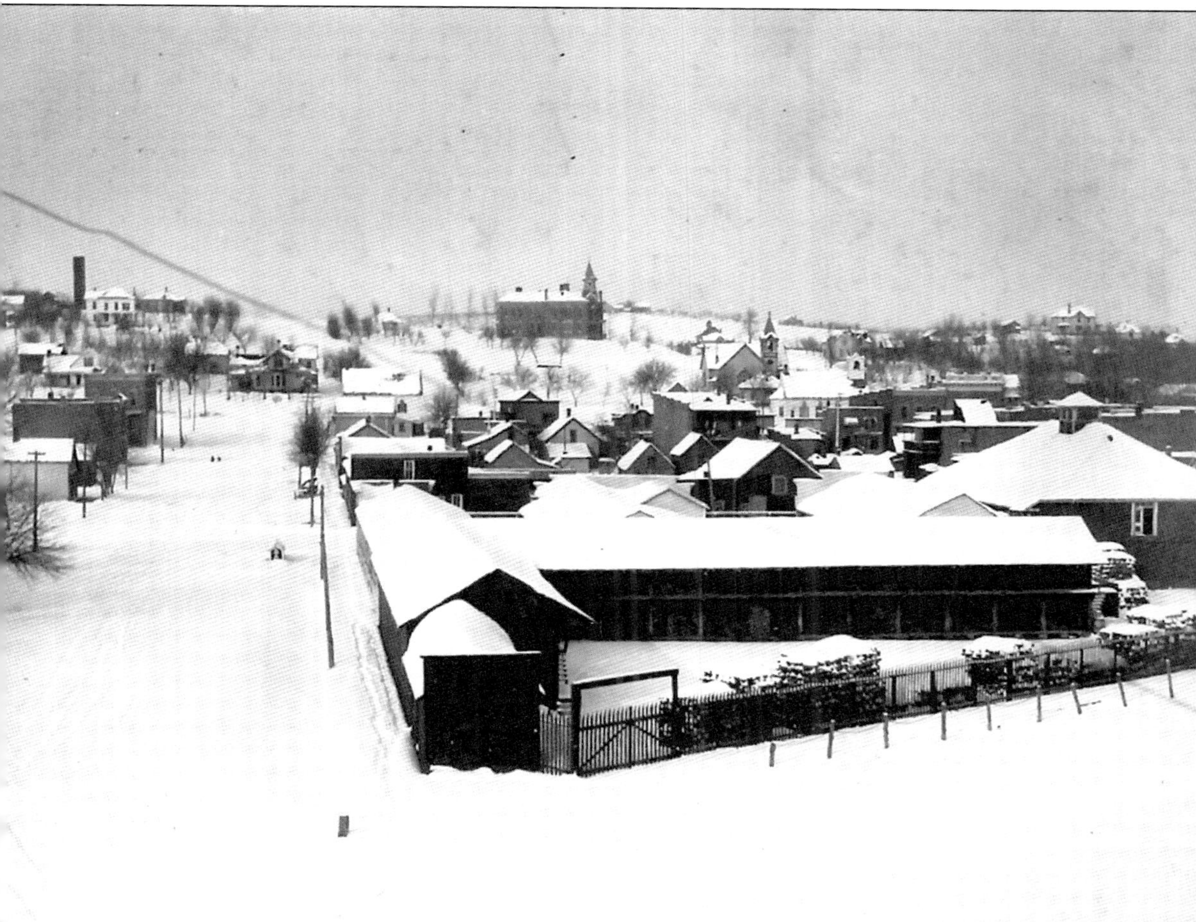

This is a snowy picture of the Stanton Lumber Yard. The three storage sheds run to the north and south in direction. Avenue E travels from the northeast to the southwest. The Stanton Public School is in the top center portion of the photograph. To the left is the Stanton standpipe for the town's water supply. This is taken from the upper floor of possibly the mill, which would have been high enough to provide the lens angle to see as far to the west and also to the northeast in that area. To the north and slightly east, the steeple on the Methodist church is visible. Just below that is the steeple of the first Congregational church, before it was moved a half a block west and sold to the St. Lucas congregation. This would date the photograph prior to the building of the new brick Congregational church in 1905. (Courtesy of Art Catlin.)

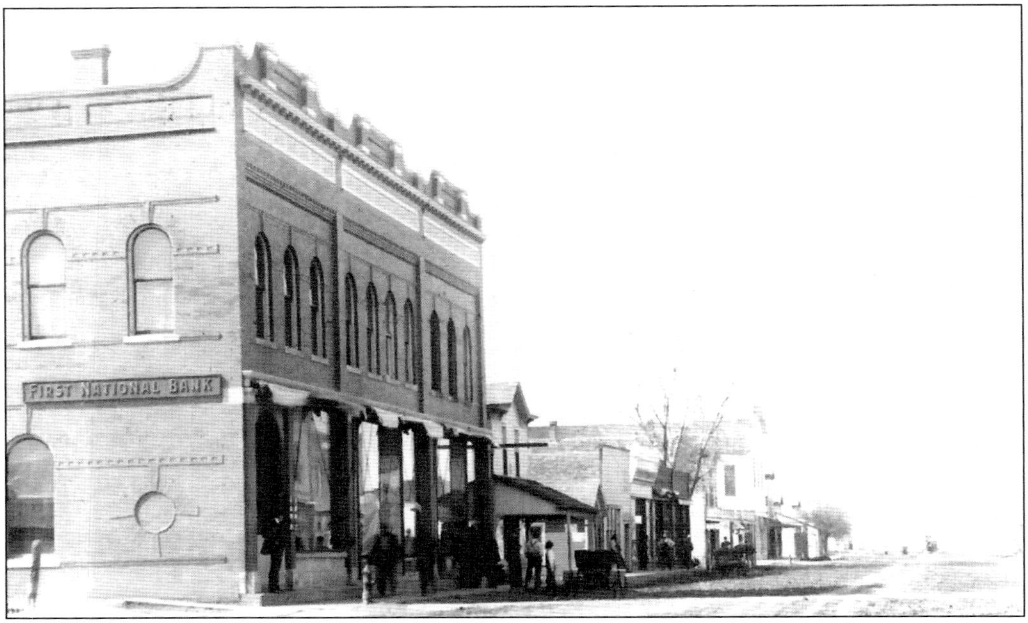

The First National Bank of Pilger is one of the earliest banking institutions in the county. It was established around 1900. It is the large two-story brick building on the left in the above photograph. It was located on the west side of the main street in Pilger. Farther up the street, in a northerly direction, the white two-story building is the Pilger Opera House. Frank Young stands in the teller's cage at the First National Bank. The gentleman standing in the background is unidentified. In 1924, the Pilger State Bank was organized by the Folda banking group from Colfax County. They acquired equipment from First National Bank and occupied this building. By 1929, the Folda banks were reputed to have $4.5 million in assets. (Courtesy of Marian Klima.)

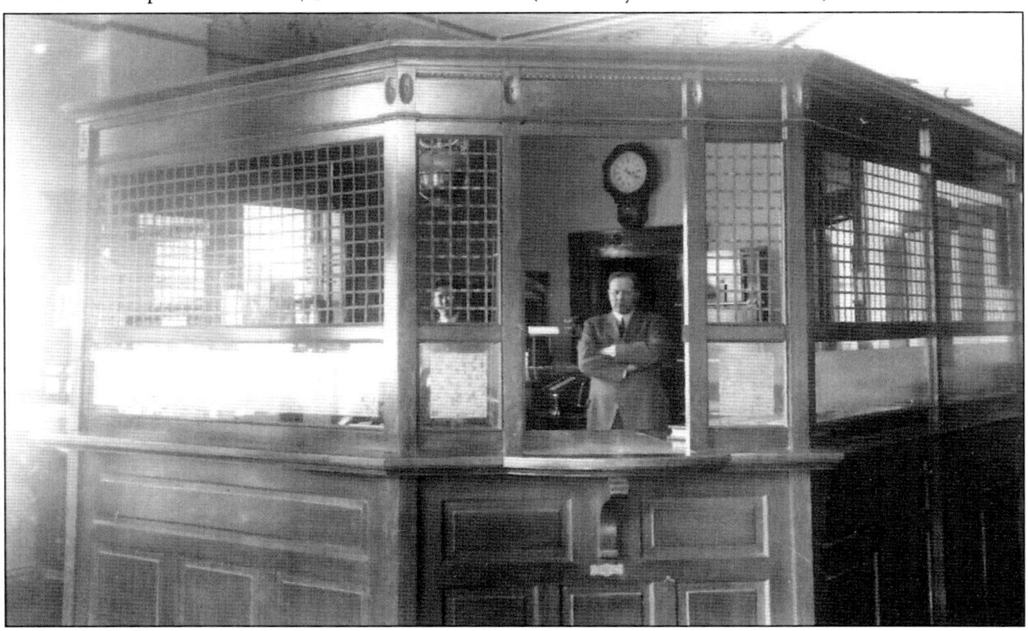

Two

A GOOD EDUCATION
1868

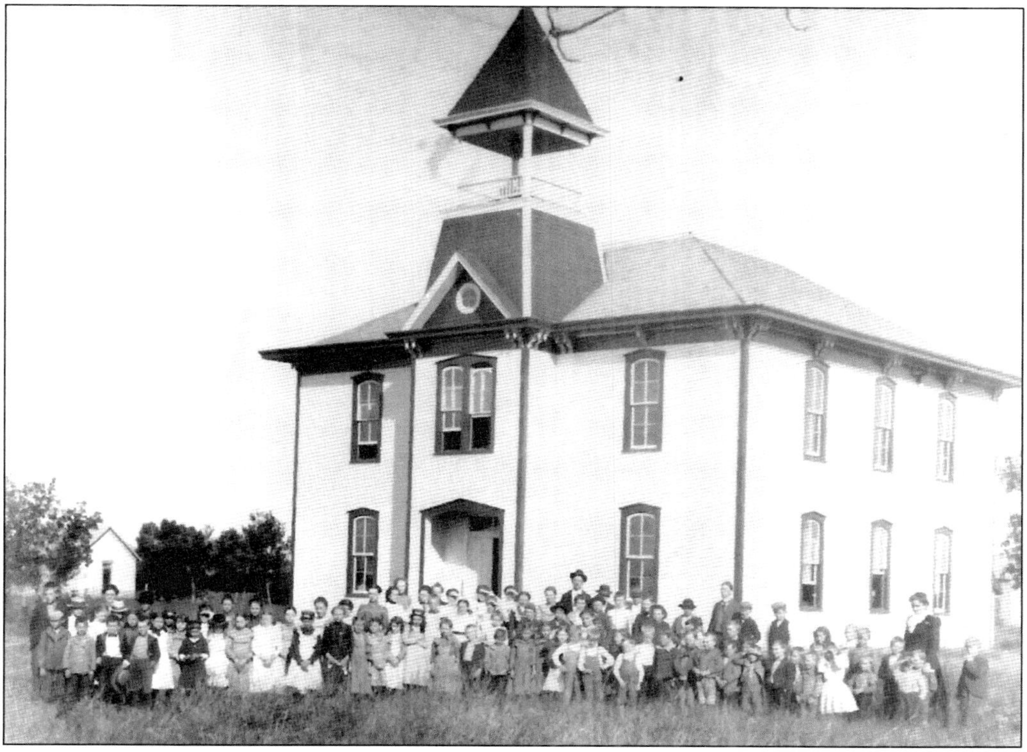

This four-room, two-story frame building, constructed in 1890, was the second built for students of the Pilger District No. 1 at a cost of $2,675. An added wing in 1903 would provide two more rooms for the 10 grades. The curriculum in 1882 followed textbooks from McGuffey's *Readers*, *Ray's Arithmetic*, *Harvey's English Grammar*, *Goodrich's United States History*, *Cutters Physiology*, and *Guyot's Geography*. Wood was used for heat until 1884, when the railroad made coal more available. (Courtesy of Marian Klima.)

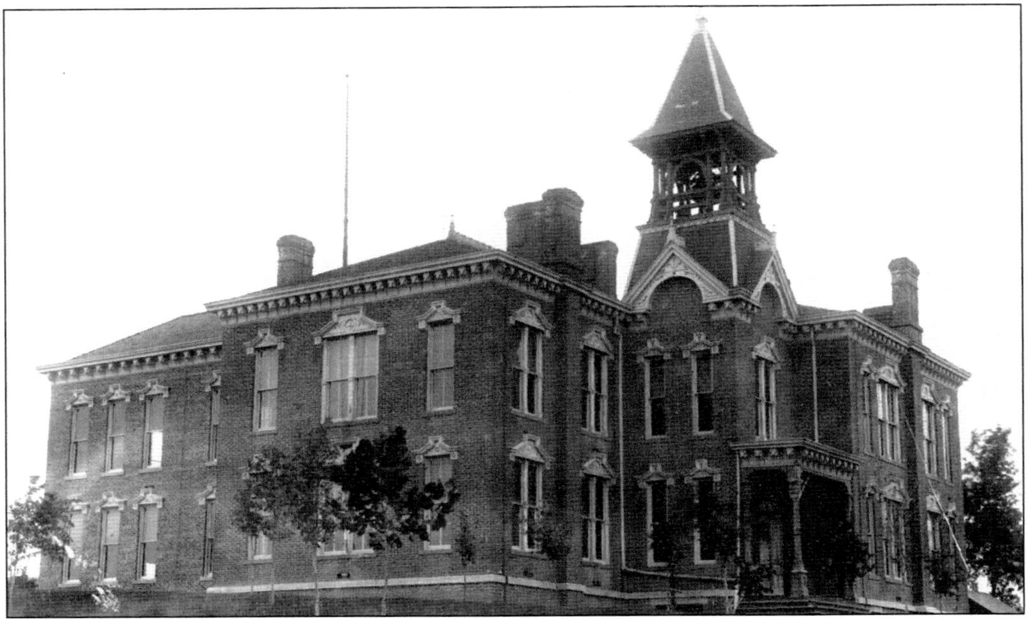

Stanton's District No. 3 students moved into this schoolhouse in the fall of 1885. Christine Maskethine Matthes sold the parcel of land, homesteaded by her deceased husband, to the district for $55. Situated on top of the hill, north of Stanton proper, the school provided a magnificent view across the hills and valley. The two-story building had eight rooms and a bell tower at a cost of $9,000. (Courtesy of Art Catlin.)

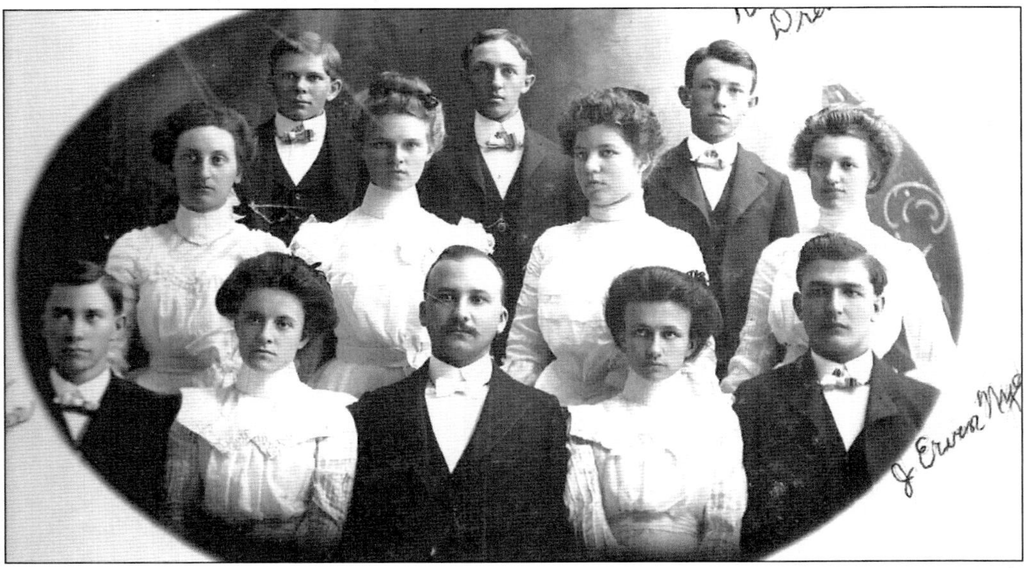

Shown here with Prof. H. E. Mason, the school superintendent, are 11 of the 12 Stanton High School 1901 graduates. Several handwritten names indicate those identified on the photograph: Blanch Barnett (first row, second from right), J. Ervin Nye (first row, right), and Richard Drewelow (third row, right). The additional classmates listed in the alumni book are Flonnie Ackerman, Edwin Chace, Frank Giacomini, Anna Johnson, Josie Johnson, Charles Kearney, Fred Rhodes, Alta Underburg, and Nina Young. (Courtesy of the Historical Society of Stanton County.)

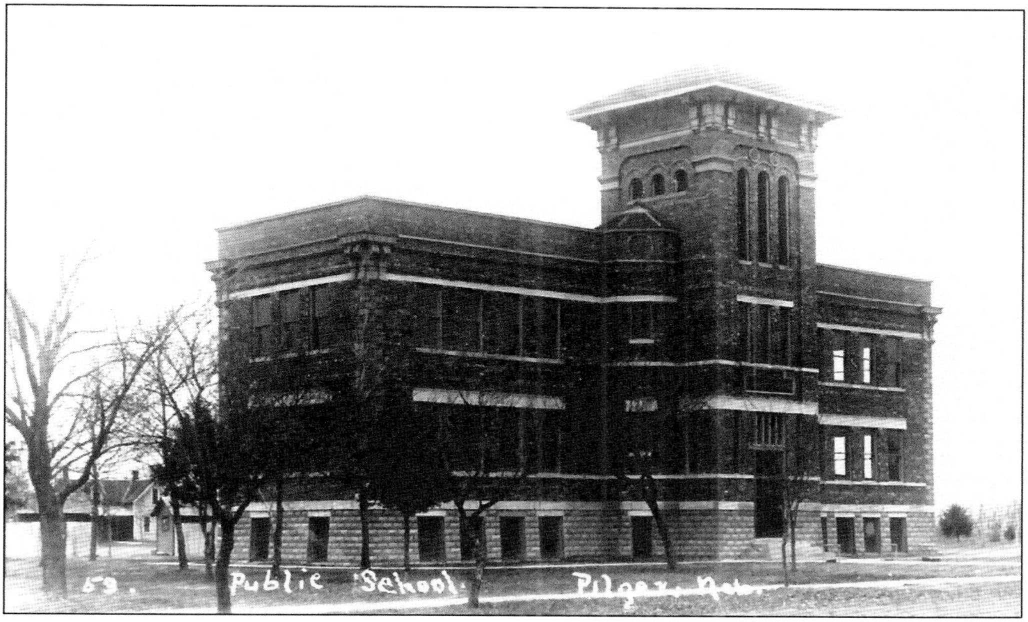

Pilger District No. 1 built a new six-room brick school in 1909 at a cost of $15,000. In 1925, a gymnasium with an assembly hall on the second floor added to the dimensions shown above. A fire in January 1931 destroyed the inside of the building, leaving only a partial shell for rebuilding. The fire ignited in the basement and burned through the roof. Fortunately there was little additional replacement cost to the district due to sufficient insurance coverage. Classes continued in churches and halls around town until instruction could resume in the restored brick structure. The Pilger District petitioned to dissolve in 1967. On March 19, 1968, a merger with Wisner District No. 30, Cuming County, took effect. A new building for grades 9 through 12 opened for the students in the combined districts in Wisner in September 1969. Pilger retained a school for the lower grades. (Courtesy of the Klima Collection.)

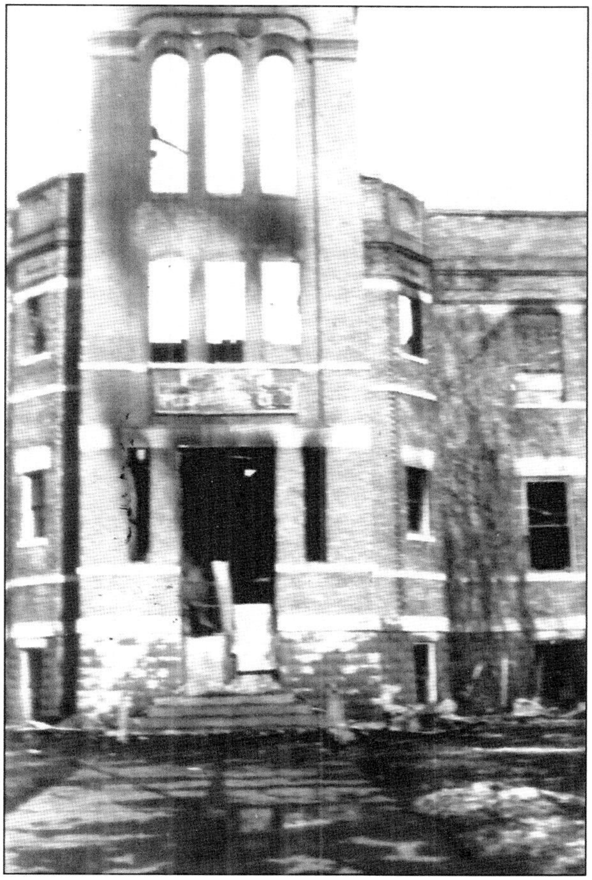

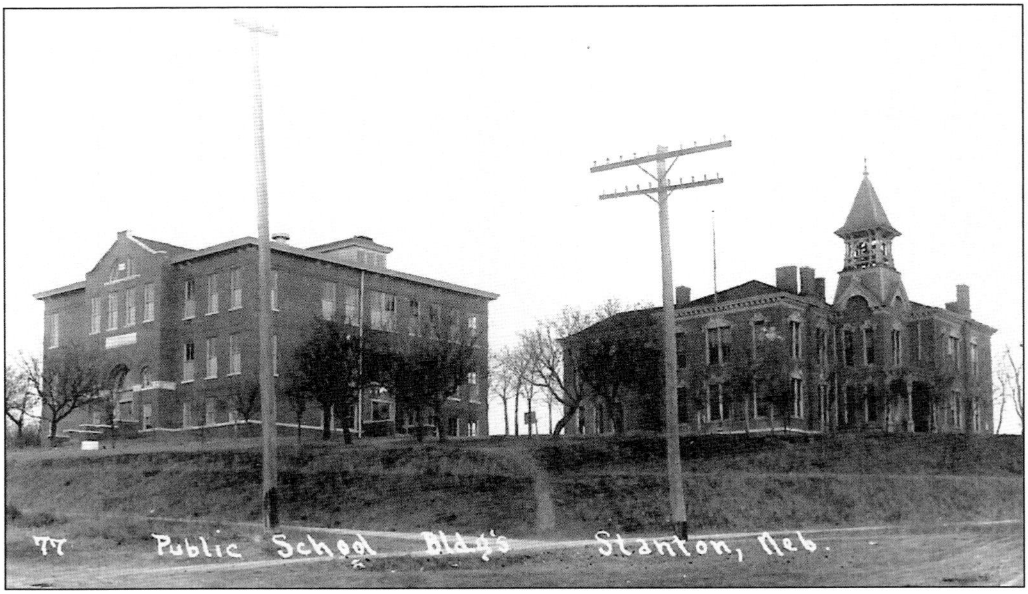

The increased enrollment of students necessitated construction of a second large brick school in Stanton. A 1901 two-story addition extended the west side on the original schoolhouse and provided two additional rooms. However, the capacity was still inadequate. The new building fronted to the south (the original faced east) and was built for the four high school grades. (Courtesy of Art Catlin and the Historical Society of Stanton County.)

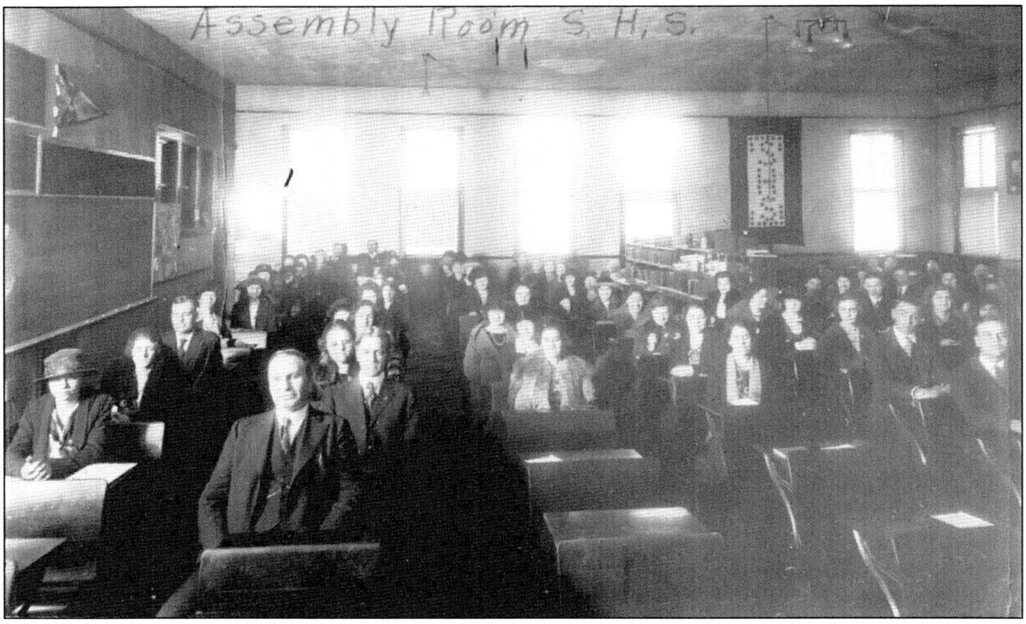

The assembly hall in the Stanton High School was almost filled to capacity in this photograph taken sometime between 1915 and 1920. Adele Krenzien, a teacher, is the lady in the first seat on the left side of the room. Superintendent of schools William Flake is the gentleman in the seat to the right of her in the front row. (Courtesy of the Historical Society of Stanton County.)

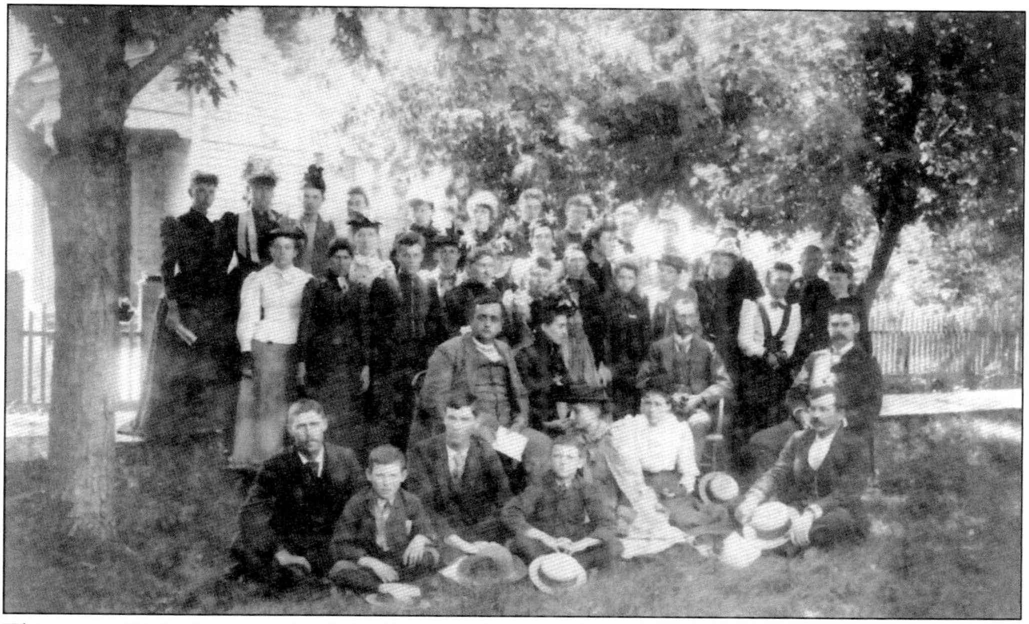

This is an 1888 photograph of the Stanton County Teachers Institute A four-day session was held, during which time Gov. John Milton Thayer spoke for a fee of $3. It was noted that Charles Coney was the superintendent of schools in Stanton County. This picture was taken while he was appointed from 1887 to 1895. Fanny Klima is one of the ladies in the photograph. (Courtesy of Marian Klima.)

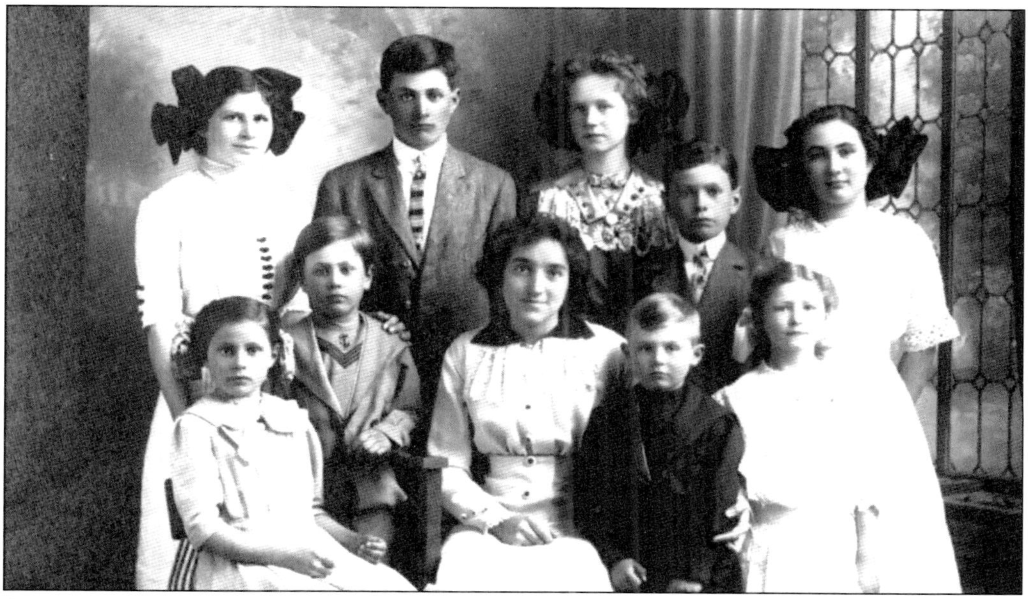

Stanton County rural school District No. 5 was organized in 1874. It was known as the Armbruster school. The students and teacher in this photograph taken in 1911 are, from left to right, (first row) Angie Armbruster, Bert Armbruster, teacher Vera Baker (Chilcoat), Art Kuehn, and Frieda Kuehn; (second row) Kate Armbruster, Bill Armbruster, Opal Colbert, Sigmund Armbruster, and Ann Armbruster. The district dissolved in 1961. (Courtesy of Richard Kuehn.)

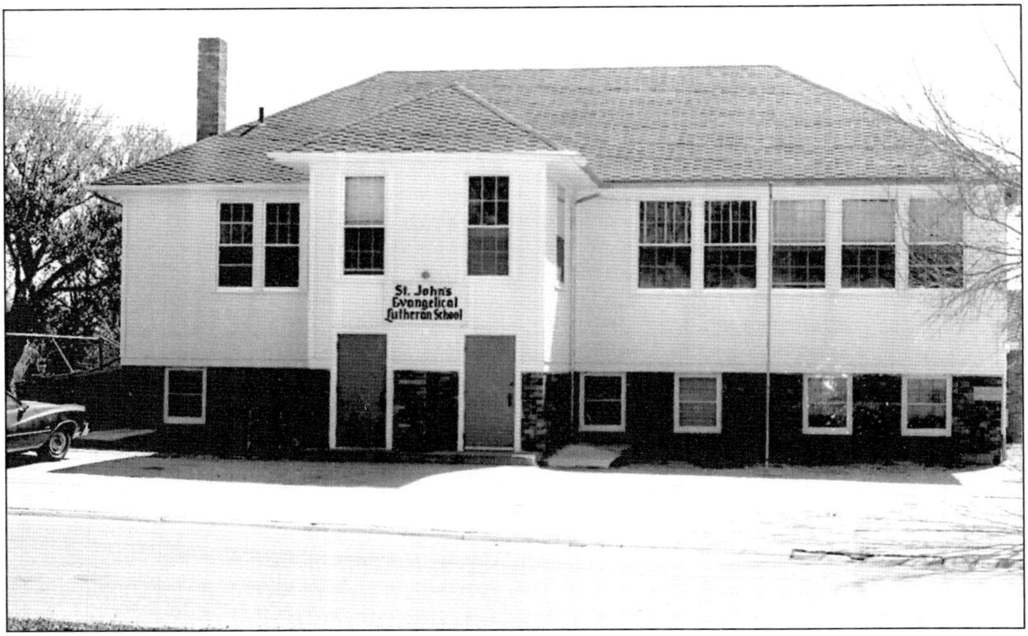

The original St. John's Evangelical Lutheran School was built in 1885 at a cost of $450. In the beginning, the children were instructed by the pastors. "Called" teachers have instructed the students since 1889. Classes were taught in German until 1918 when the anti-German sentiment grew during World War I. Some 68 students enrolled for the 1919–1920 school year. This school was built in 1931. (Courtesy of the Stanton Register.)

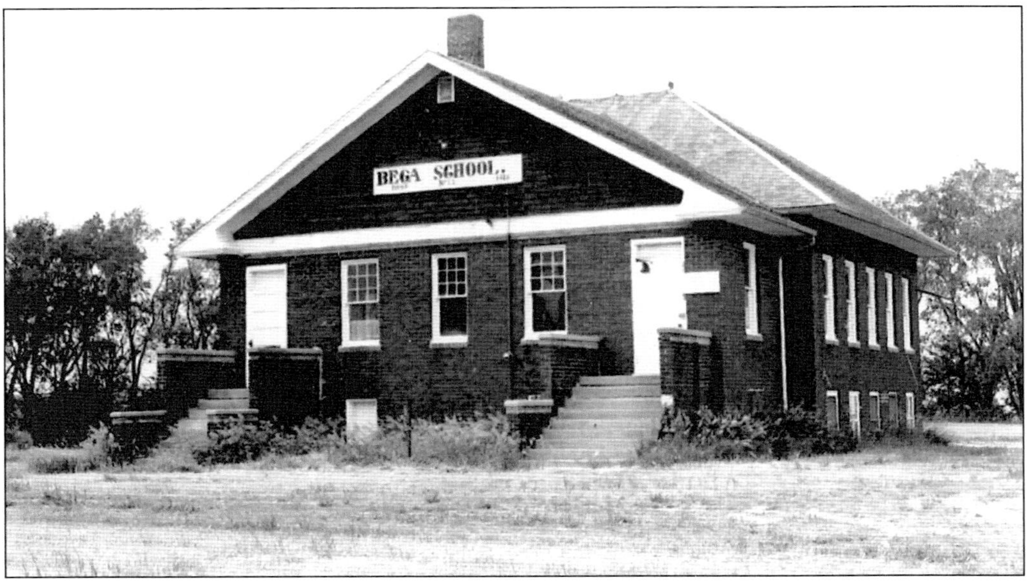

Bega District No. 12 began in Mattie Olson's granary until a dugout was available in 1873. The first wooden frame building was a typical one-room school. This schoolhouse was built in 1919. It held two classrooms for kindergarten through grade 10. It had a stage, a basement, and a Delco Electronics lighting plant. The students were contracted out from 1948 until the district closed in 1970. (Courtesy of the Stanton Register.)

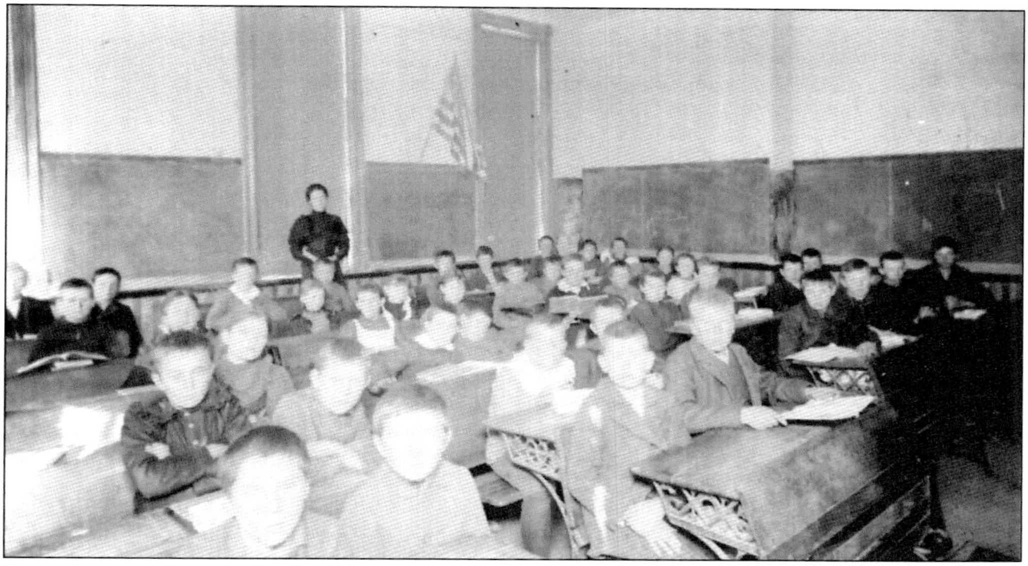

A teacher stands at the back of the classroom, watching a large number of students in the Pilger Public School. Identities are unknown for this early-1900s photograph. The desks had bench seats that folded up. Each seat connected to the desktop, which was used by the student seated in the row behind. The desktop had an open shelf beneath for books and paper storage. In the picture below, a young group of students at the Pilger Public School poses outside the front entry. Most of the boys sport bibbed overalls, and the girls wore dresses in that era, however, not many appear to wear a smile for the camera. (Courtesy of Marian Klima.)

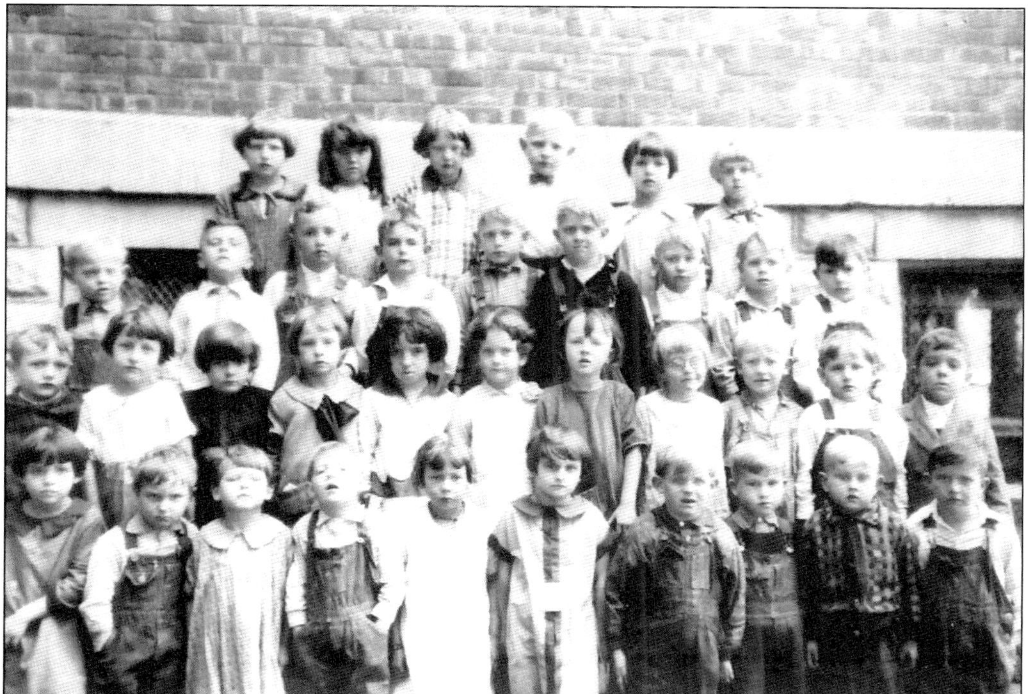

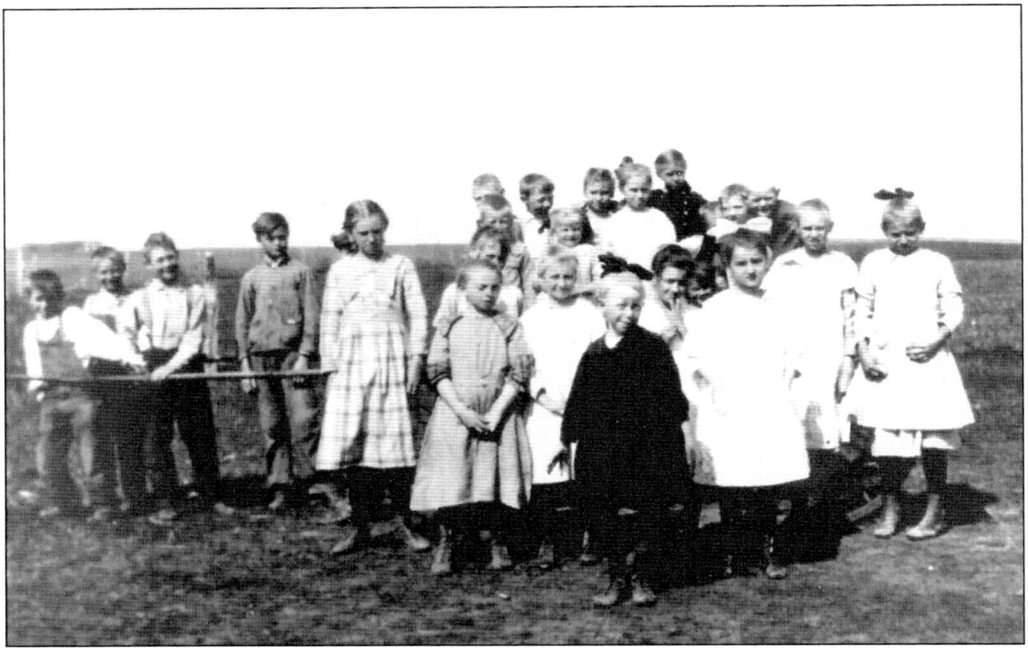

The Patterson School District No. 18 formed in 1875. Most of the teachers were local girls who had graduated high school with two years of normal training qualifications. A special note should be made of the high-top shoes worn by the girls and the young lady posing for the camera in the front row. The school was destroyed by a tornado in 1854. (Courtesy of Marian Klima.)

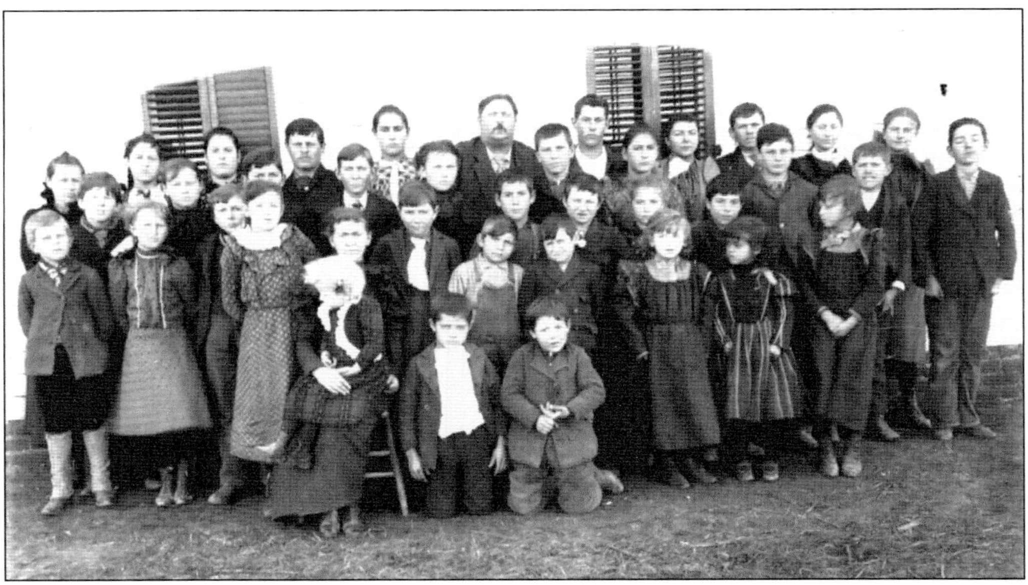

Haymow District No. 32 students line up with their teacher, William Woodruff (center in back row), for a group photograph around 1900. The teacher salaries ranged from $25 per month in 1925 to $650 per month in 1976. The district closed its doors in 1981. The students ranged in ages from kindergarten to 21 years old. The highest enrollment number was 46 in 1901. (Courtesy of Art Catlin.)

This souvenir school photograph card was handed out in honor of Mae Woodruff, who taught at Haymow District No. 32 during the school year 1900 to 1901. A second page listed the names of the students she taught. (Courtesy of Art Catlin and the Historical Society of Stanton County.)

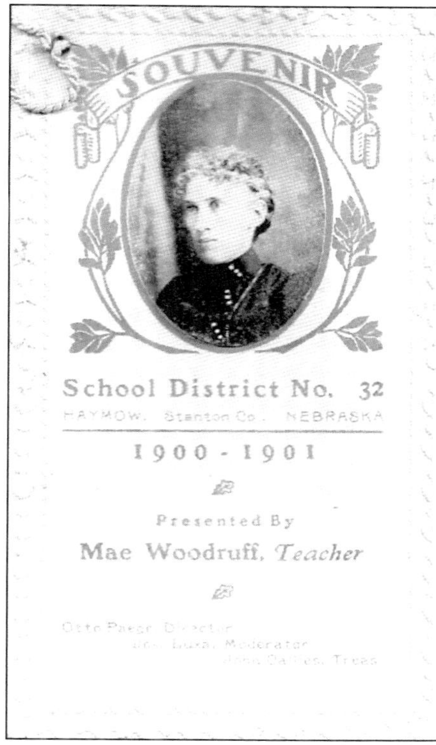

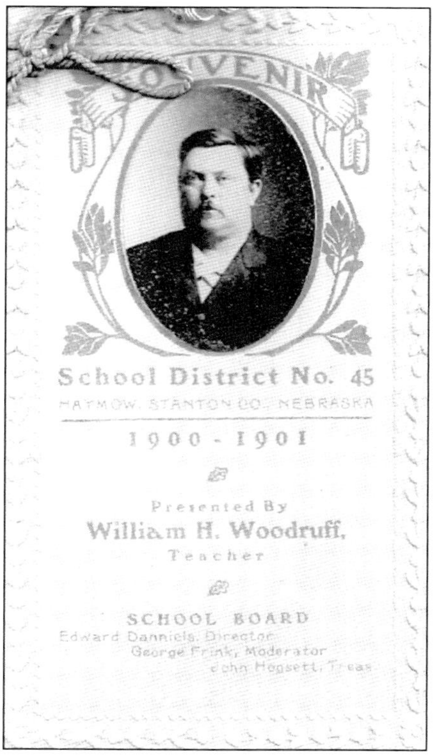

William Woodruff taught students in District No. 45 also noted as Haymow, Stanton County, Nebraska. A souvenir school photograph card was presented in his honor during the school year 1900 to 1901. (Courtesy of Art Catlin and the Historical Society of Stanton County.)

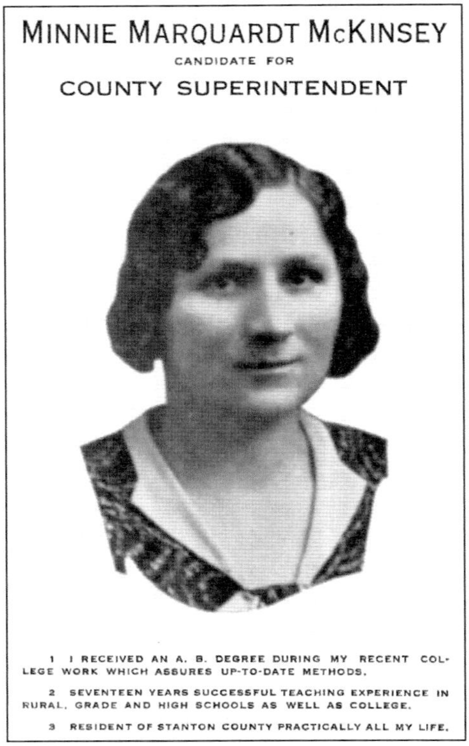

Minnie Marquardt McKinsey distributed these postcards listing her credentials during her county superintendent campaign in the 1930s. She was elected in 1931 and served in that capacity until 1939. She was a teacher at Stanton High School once again in the 1950s and 1960s. (Courtesy of the Historical Society of Stanton County and Art Catlin.)

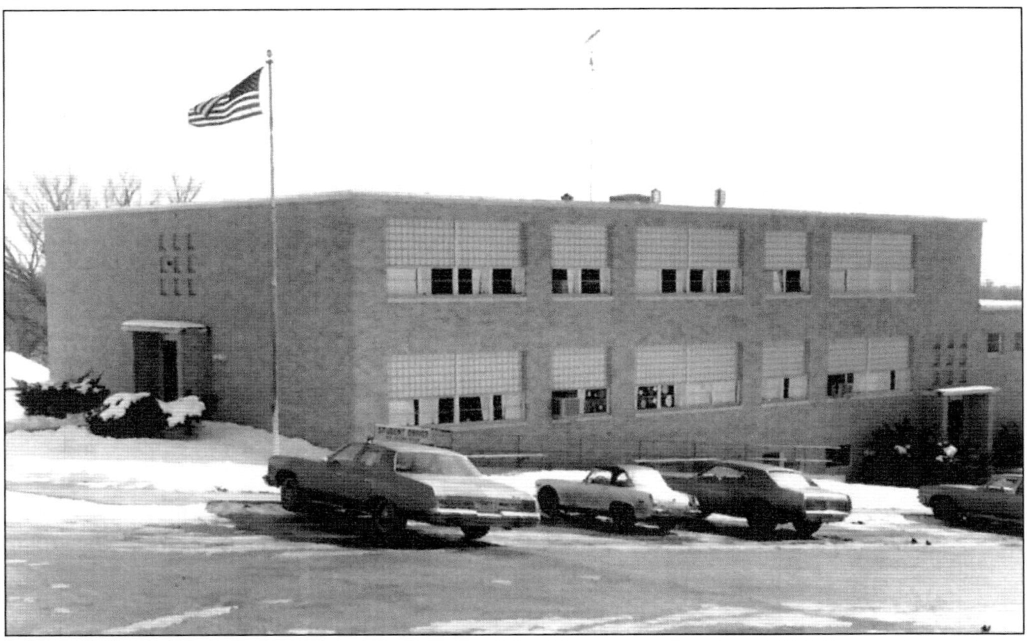

This is the north side of the new high school building completed in 1953. It was located just down the slope from the former public school buildings. This shows the north entrance of the high school in 1974, prior to the two-story construction project to add a large library and office on the top floor and a music room below. (Courtesy of the Stanton Register.)

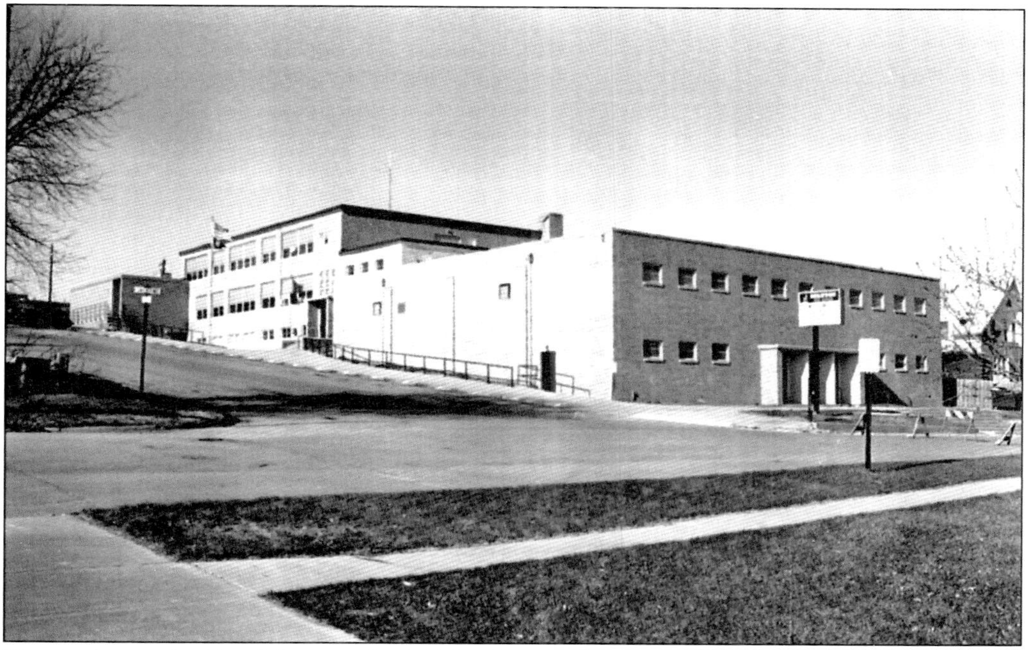

This is the south side of Stanton High School constructed in 1953. The gymnasium is located at the front entrance with classrooms and office areas on the north. Due to an increase in enrollment after affiliation with rural schools took place, this building was expanded on the west side to include a second gymnasium also on the south side and more classrooms to the north. (Courtesy of the Stanton Register.)

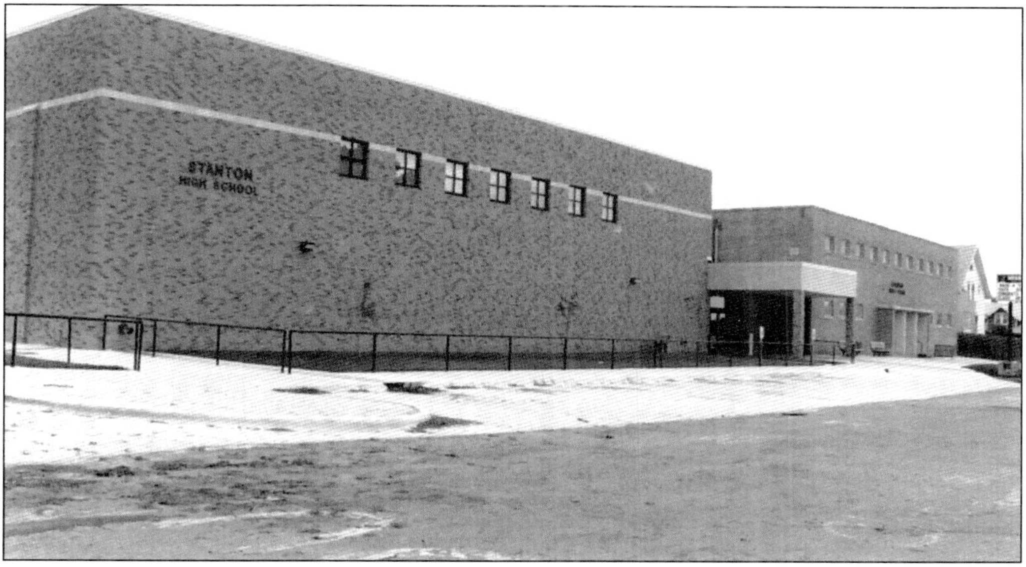

A 1996 photograph shows the addition on the west side of Stanton High School. The gymnasium to the right is for fifth to eighth grades. The $3.8 million bond issue passed by a slight margin of 30 votes with 493 voting in favor and 463 votes against. Any handicapped accessibility issues were solved with installation of a central elevator for access to every floor. (Courtesy of the Stanton Register.)

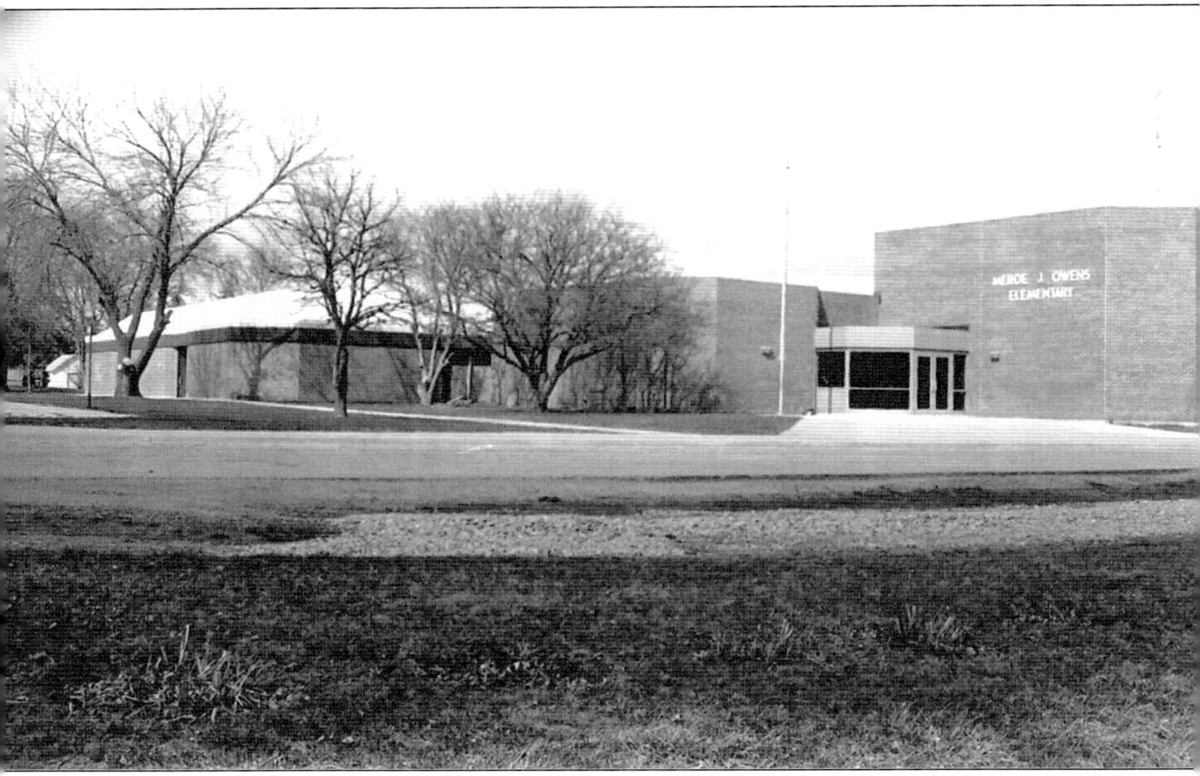

A new elementary school building was built in 1969 at a cost of $332,574. The building incorporated a "pod" design for individual classrooms and had only a few windows installed. The dedication ceremony in September 1969 gave the honor of its name to Meroe J. Outhouse (pronounced *Otis* with a short *o* sound) Owens, a longtime teacher and administrator at Stanton Public Schools. Owens wrote the history of Stanton County for her master's thesis and submitted it to the social studies department at Colorado State Teacher's College, Greeley, Colorado, in 1944. It was subsequently printed and sold in book form. There are not copies readily available, and it is out of print. (Courtesy of the Stanton Register.)

Three

BUILDING A CHURCH
1869

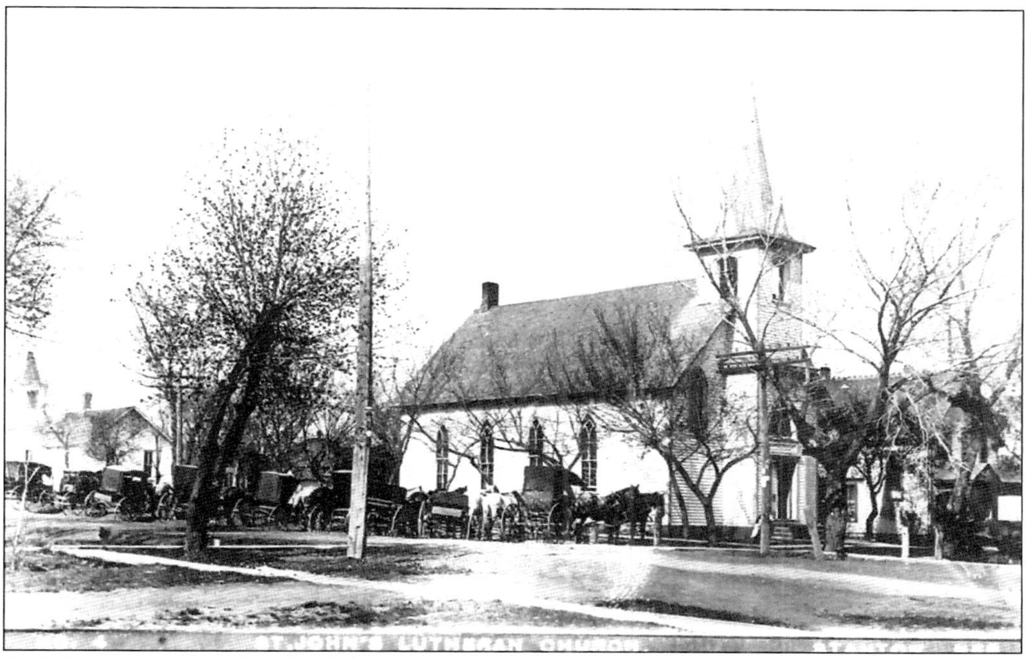

St. John's Lutheran Church of the Wisconsin Synod in Stanton formed like most of the early churches. The first services were held in the home of Carl Schwartz. The first church building was built on a farm east of Stanton in 1872. A fire destroyed the church and most of the records in 1882. The congregation built a new church that was destroyed by lightning in 1890. It was rebuilt and dedicated again in December 1890. (Courtesy of Art Catlin and Mason Moritz.)

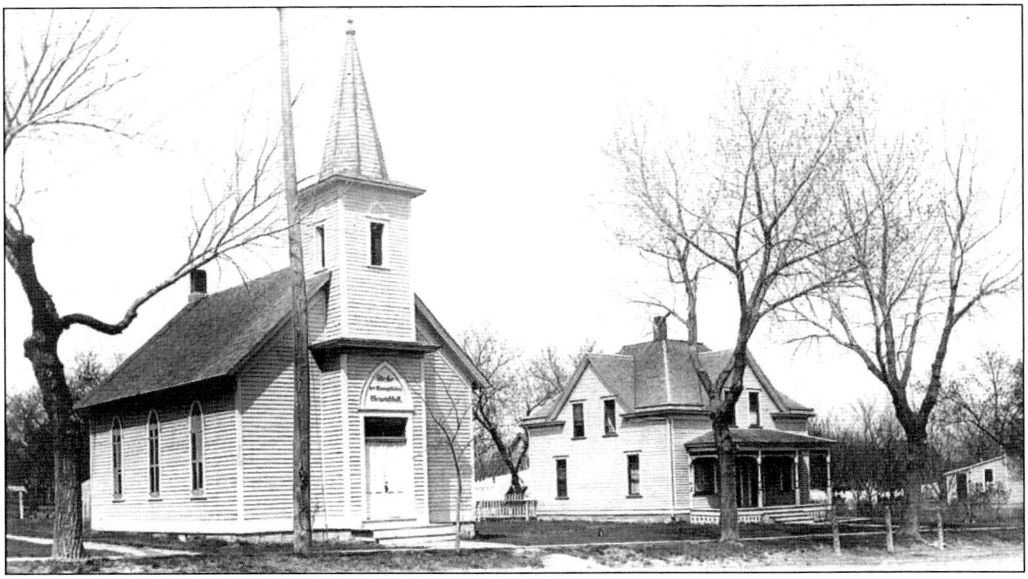

The German Methodist Episcopal Church was the first church to be established in Stanton in 1870. The congregation was known as the Salem Mission of the Evangelical Church. A church, measuring 26 feet by 28 feet, 14 feet high, was built in 1878 at a cost of $1,600. It was used by Methodists, Congregationalists, and United Brethren for services. It was given to the historical society in 1968 for preservation. (Courtesy of Marci Poeschl.)

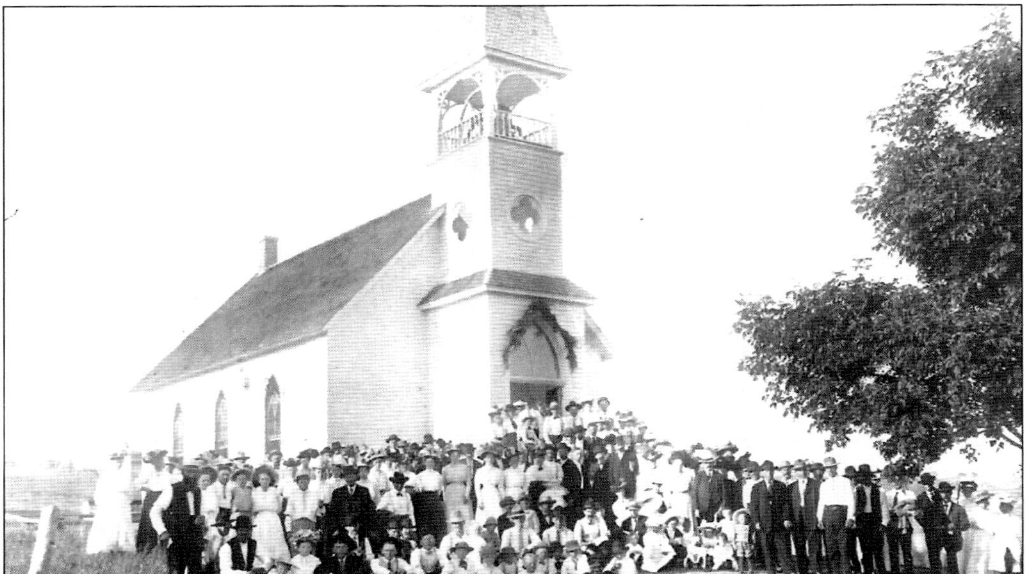

St. Pauli's, or St. Paul's, Lutheran Church was located south of Pilger in Cuming County in the beginning of its existence. Some historical records refer to it as St. Petri's. The Danish and German Lutheran congregations merged and became St. Peter's Evangelical Lutheran Church, of the Evangelical Lutheran Churches of America (ELCA), in Pilger in 1948. A replica of the church, which was destroyed by high winds, is displayed in the Pilger Museum. (Courtesy of Marian Klima.)

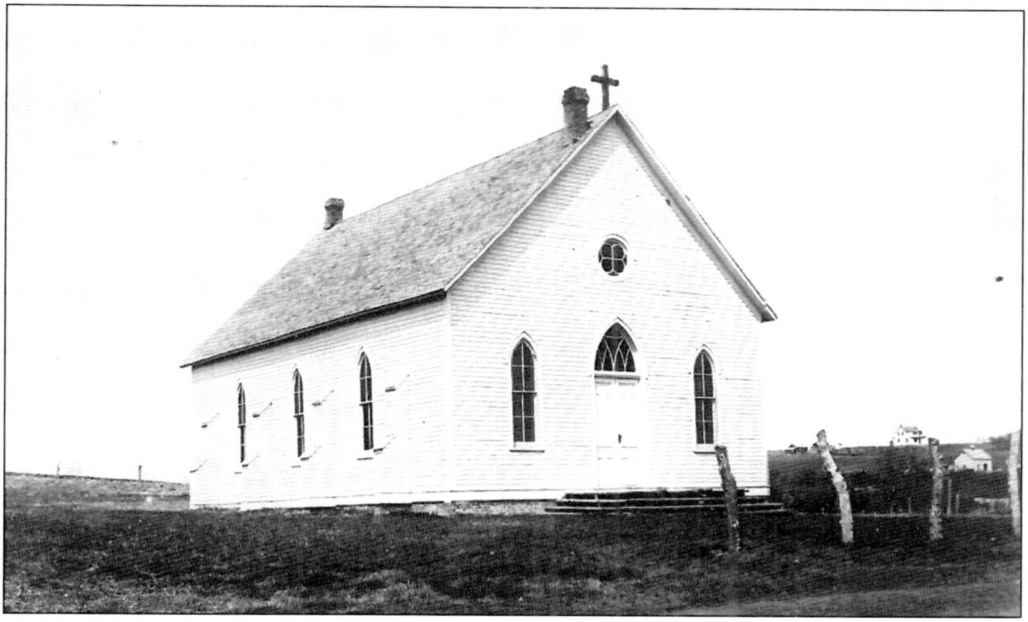

St. Peter's Catholic Church of Stanton held its first services in the home of Joseph Hakl. A church and parsonage were built on a lot north of the Stanton City Park in the west part of Stanton in 1893. The white frame church became inadequate, and a cornerstone was laid for a new brick church building in January 1968. (Courtesy of the Stanton Register.)

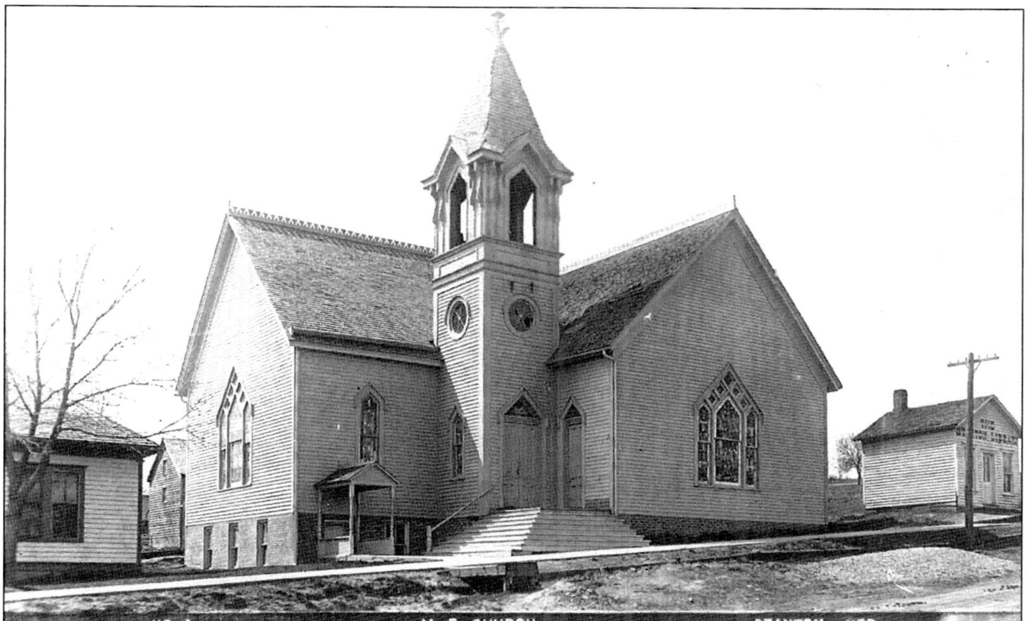

The initial services for Methodist Episcopal Church were held in a private home and schoolhouse in Humbug Precinct in 1866. This church, the largest structure in Stanton at that time, was dedicated November 1884. It burned in 1923 and was rebuilt in brick. The small white building to the right served as the first city library. (Courtesy of Art Catlin.)

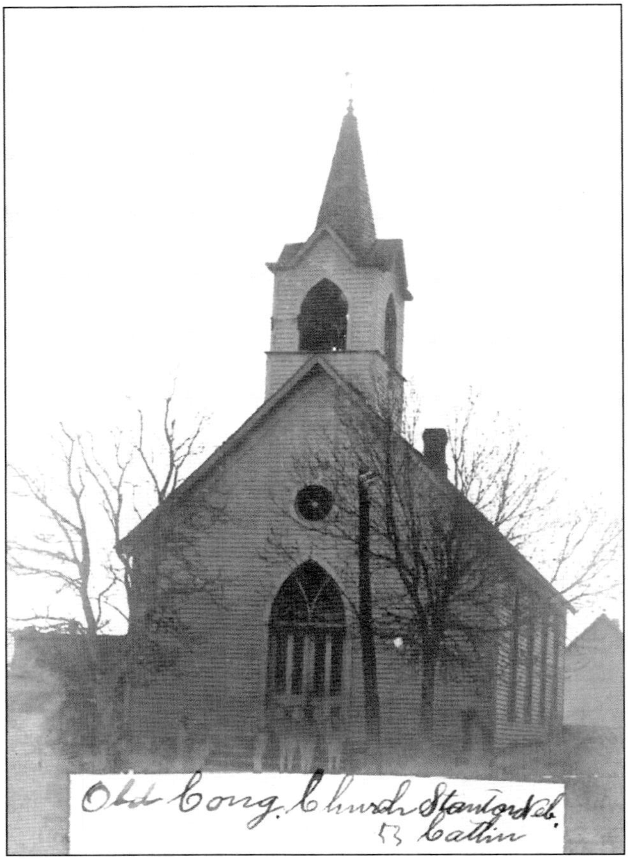

The New England Congregational Church formed on June 9, 1878, and met in the Masonic hall, the schoolhouse, or the Evangelical church. It was the third congregation to build in Stanton and erected a white-framed church one block from downtown. The 28-by-50-foot church was dedicated in April 1883. The ladies society purchased a 500-pound bell and inscribed it with the words "Let him that heareth come." In 1905, this building was moved west from the corner and placed facing north (partially visible to the right, below) to make room for a new brick church. In 1906, one week before dedication, that church was damaged by a Sunday-morning fire. The walls and both towers were saved, the roof was destroyed, and the basement received damage. It was quickly rebuilt the same year. (Courtesy of Art Catlin.)

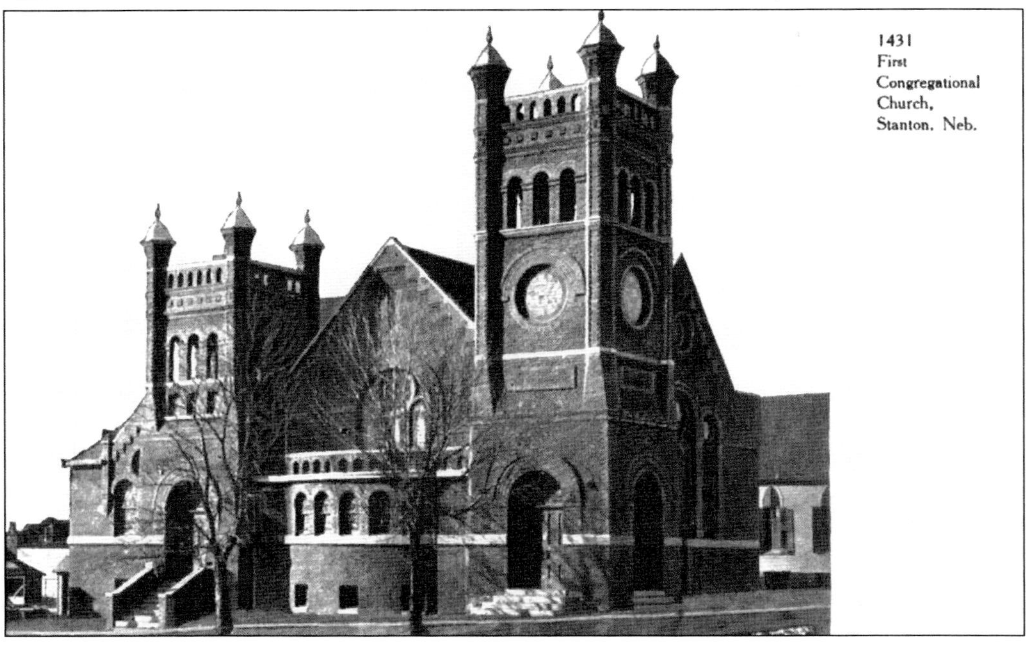

The Pilger Baptist Church members gathered for a 50th anniversary in 1952 with 125 persons in attendance. The sad decision to disband was made in October 1960. The building was given to the Historical Society of Stanton County in 1967 and is the present location of the Pilger Museum and annex. (Courtesy of Marian Klima.)

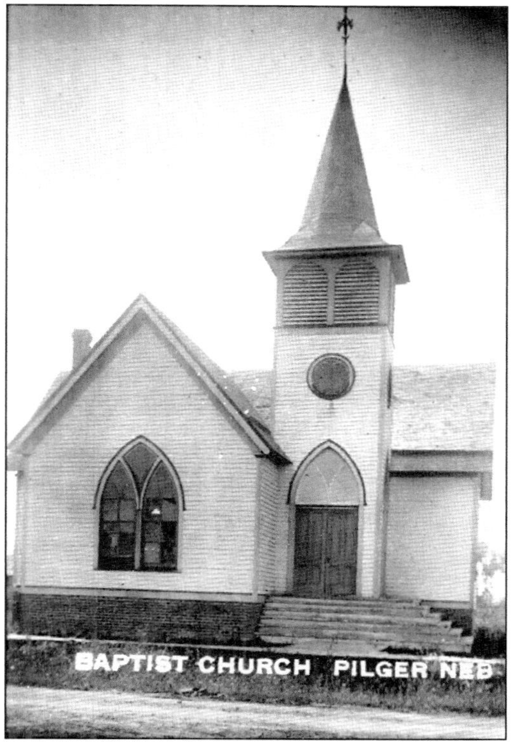

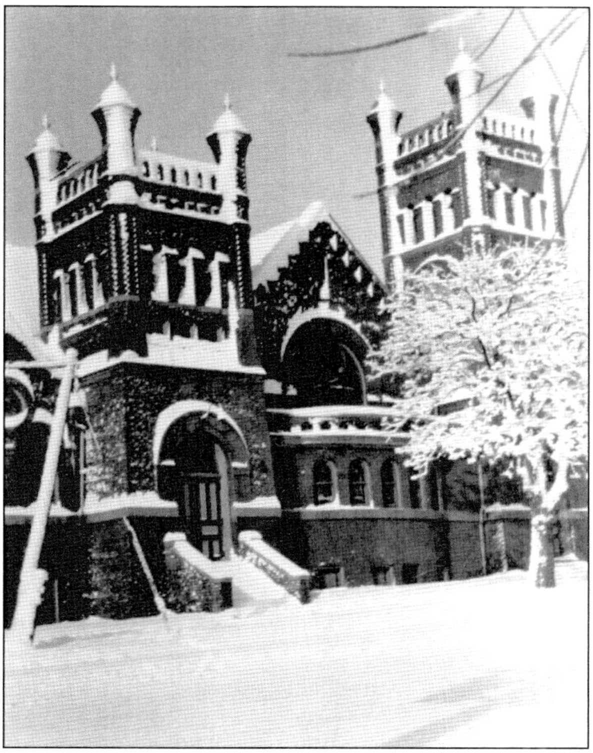

This photograph shows a wintery view of the newly built Congregational church. This was taken shortly before the fire partially destroyed the roof and basement of the brick structure on Sunday, March 11, 1906. This view is from the southeast. A new church complex was built several blocks north and east in 1969, and the old brick building was taken down. (Courtesy of Inez Barth.)

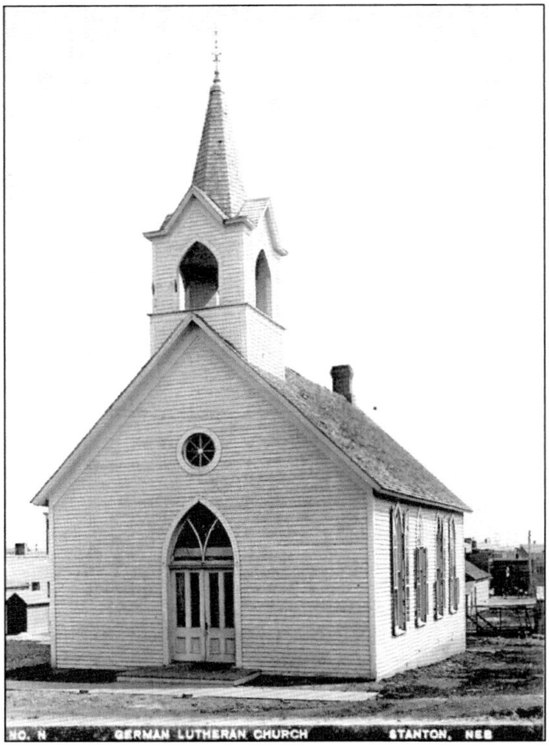

Formerly the home of the Stanton Congregationalists, this church was moved to the west of the newly constructed Congregational church. In 1906, the St. Lucas German Lutheran members purchased the building for $800. The last worship held here was September 1992. The white frame church building was demolished a short time later. (Courtesy of the Stanton Register.)

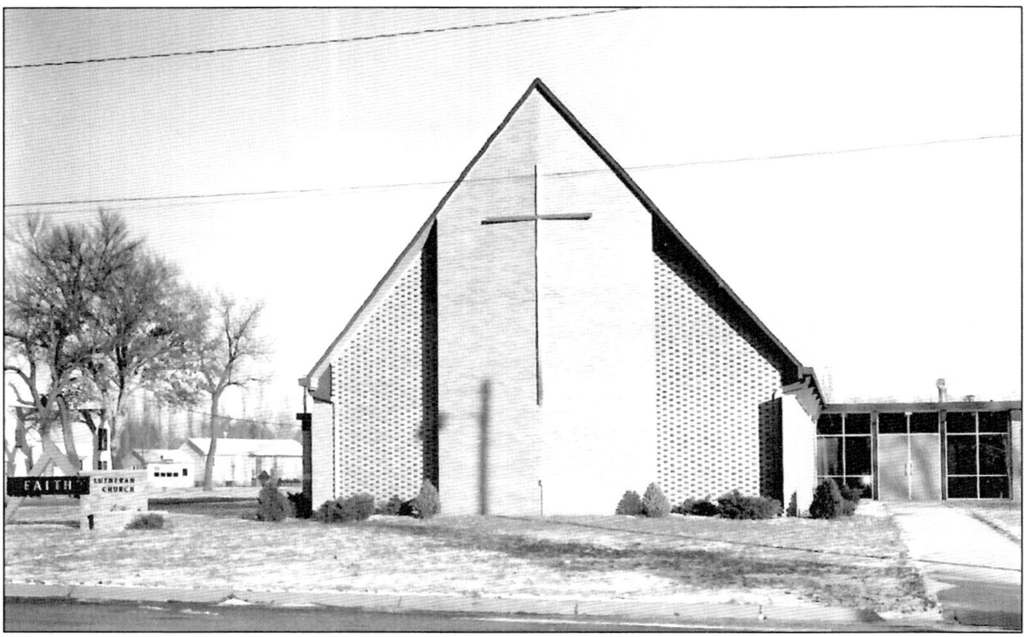

Faith Lutheran Church was a new congregation formed in 1962. The first services were held in the Evangelical United Brethren Church and the Rialto Theater until this new church was finished in 1964. This congregation is the newest to be organized since the Evangelical Free Church organized in 1948 and dedicated its church in 1950. (Courtesy of the Stanton Register.)

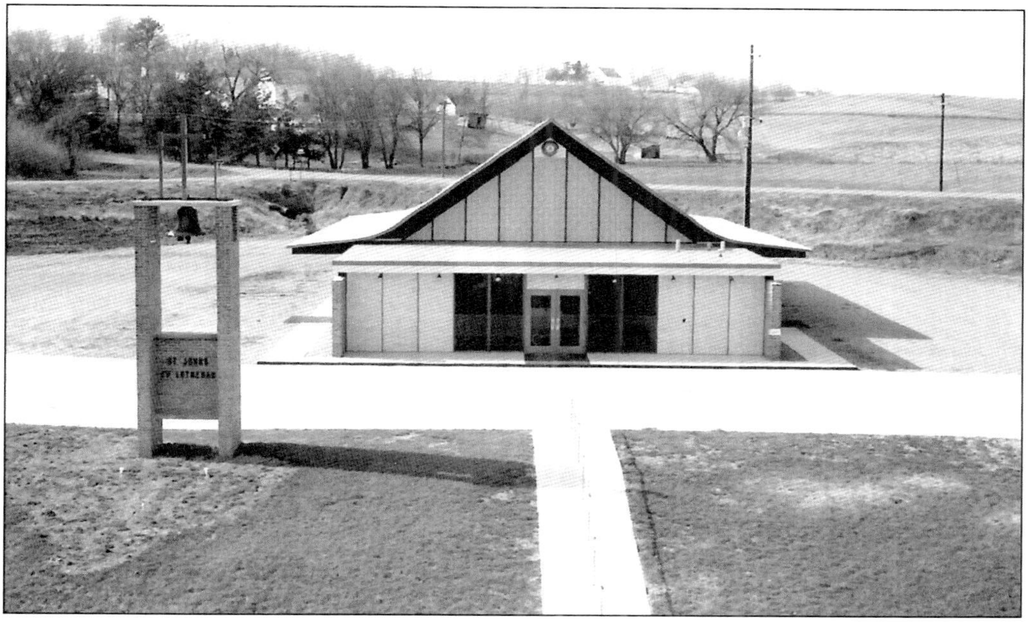

St. John's Lutheran congregation outgrew its wooden frame church built in 1890 and voted to build a brick church northwest of the parochial schoolhouse. The building, measuring 110 feet by 45 feet, provided a welcomed spaciousness at a cost of $124,695.46. The parsonage purchased in 1971 was sold in 2001, and the congregation now provides a monthly housing stipend for its pastor. (Courtesy of the Stanton Register.)

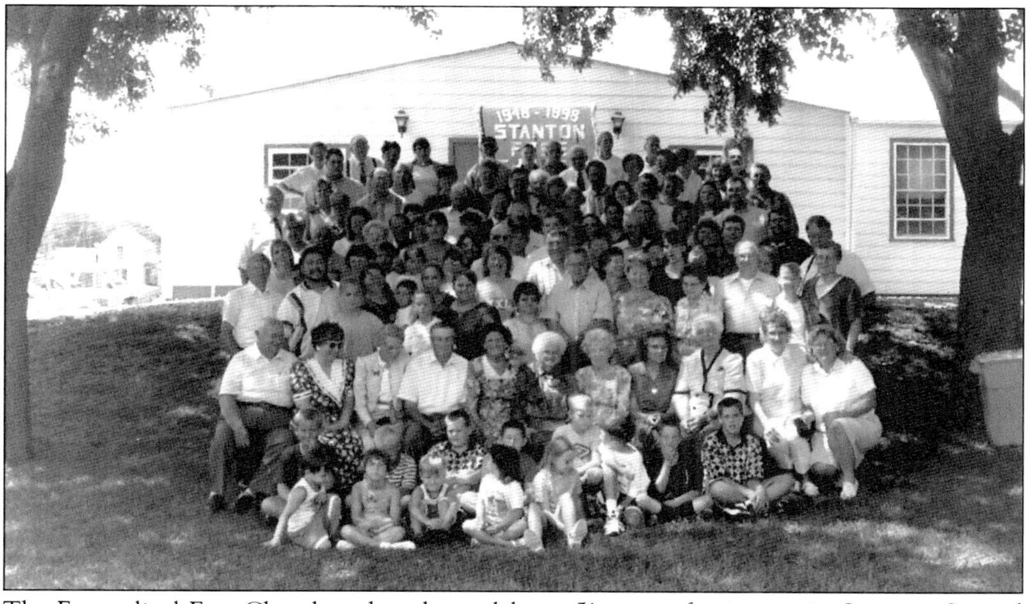

The Evangelical Free Church gathered to celebrate 51 years of existence in Stanton. Several men of the congregation did construction research at the library and said "with prayer and God's guidance" they began to build a church. In 2004, the church underwent extensive renovation to double the seating capacity and modernizing all areas to serve today's congregation and its needs. (Courtesy of the Stanton Register.)

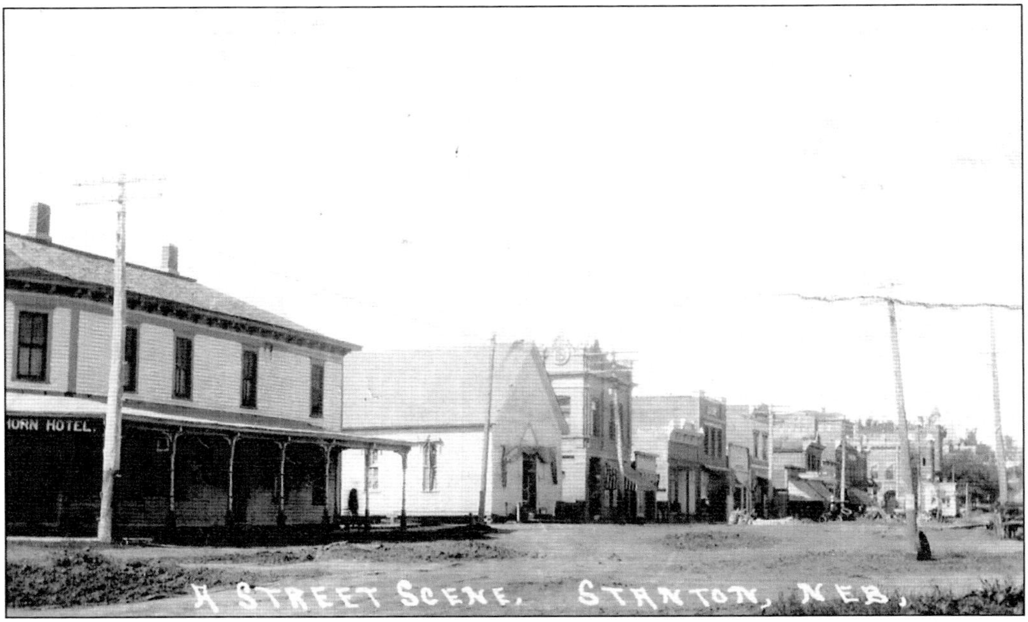

This 1916 photograph shows the Baptist building, which stood formerly on the corner where the library is located. The library board purchased it and the lot for $1,143, then sold the building to Joe Rogers, a general contractor, for $300. He moved it to this lot, shown above, north of the Elkhorn Hotel. The Spangler brothers used it a short time for their grocery business. (Courtesy of Art Catlin.)

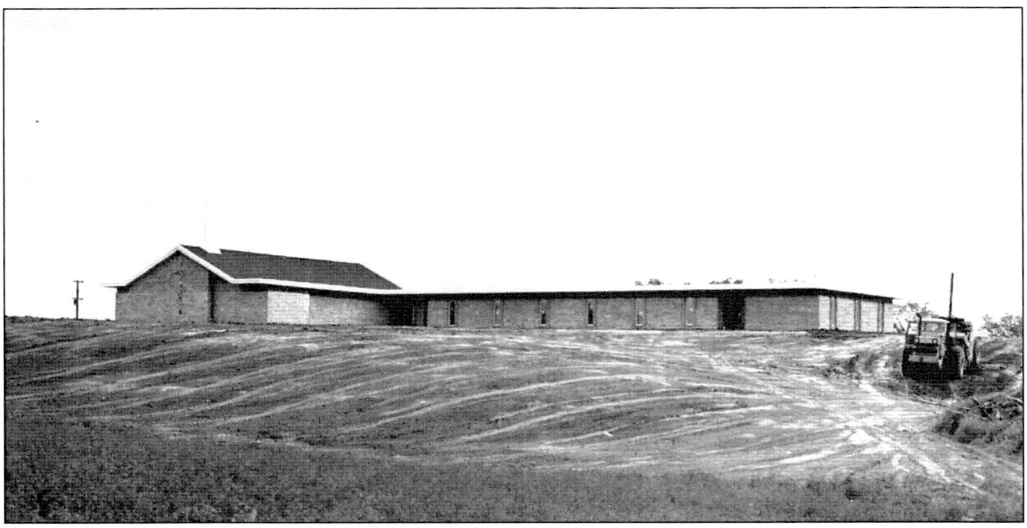

The New England Congregational Church constructed a new church in 1969. Dedication was held on November 30, 1969. The old brick church, several blocks south, was sold and cleared out of the way for a telephone storage building. (Courtesy of the Stanton Register.)

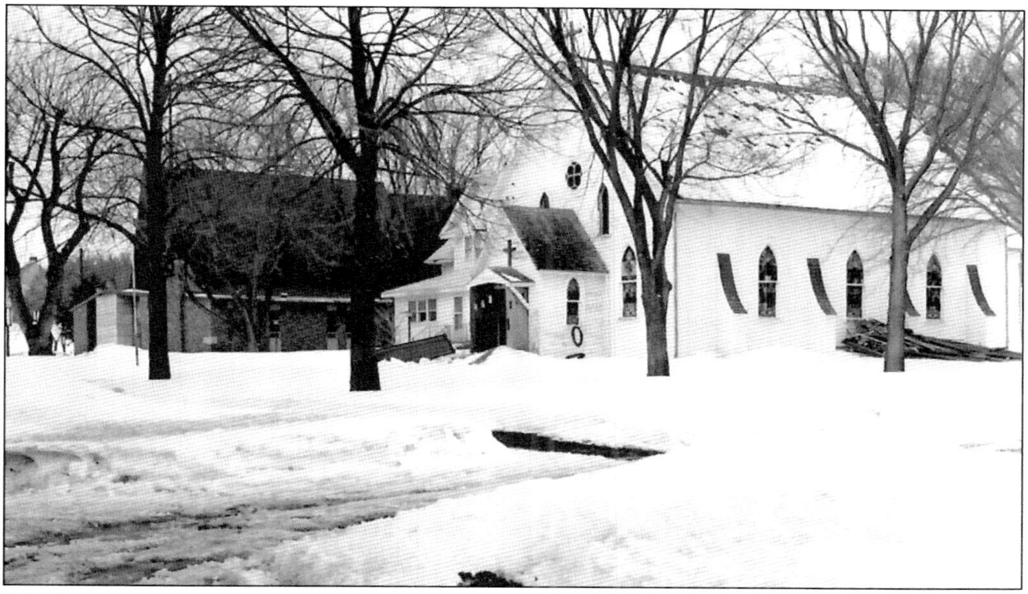

The little Catholic church awaits demolition next to the parsonage on the left and the newly constructed church standing further left. This church, once connected by a tunnel to the rectory basement, had been remodeled in the late 1940s but became too small for the congregation. It was torn down in 1969. The rectory was sold and moved from the site at a later date. (Courtesy of the Stanton Register.)

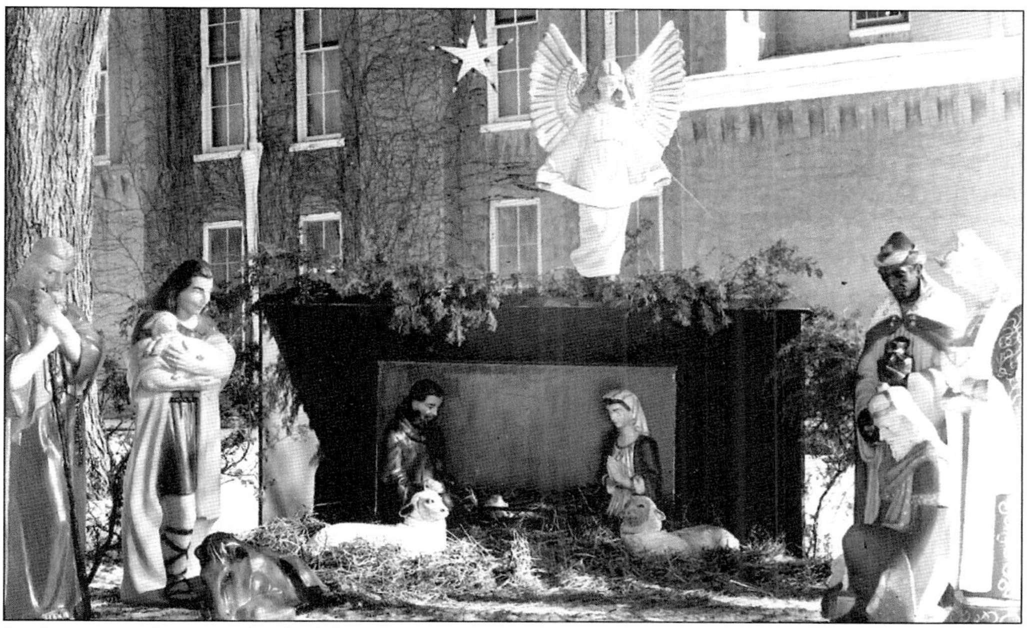

In this 1960s photograph, the life-sized Nativity scene stands on the Stanton County Courthouse's front lawn. It was displayed during the Christmas season for a number of years and was the gathering place for groups of carolers. Several figures deteriorated or were damaged through the years, but those that survived have been displayed near the Masonic lodge on the east end of Ivy Street. (Author's collection.)

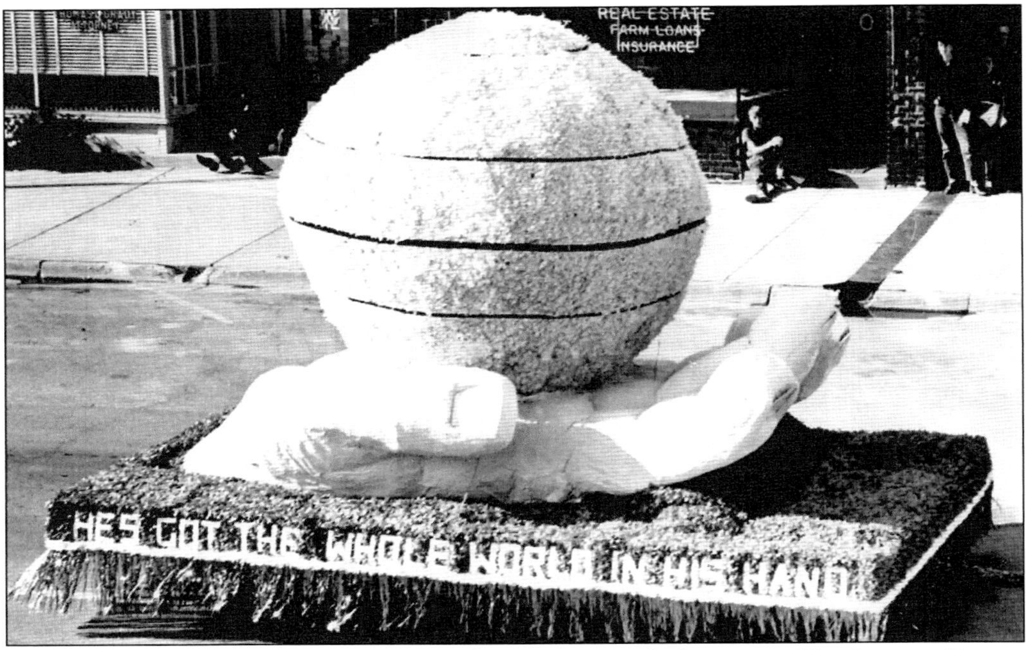

St. Peter's Catholic Church won first place for its 1966 parade float entry. The Stanton County centennial celebration drew entries from 150 groups and area towns surrounding the county. Booster clubs would gather for road trips to announce the celebrations and encourage the public to attend and to participate in all the events. (Author's collection.)

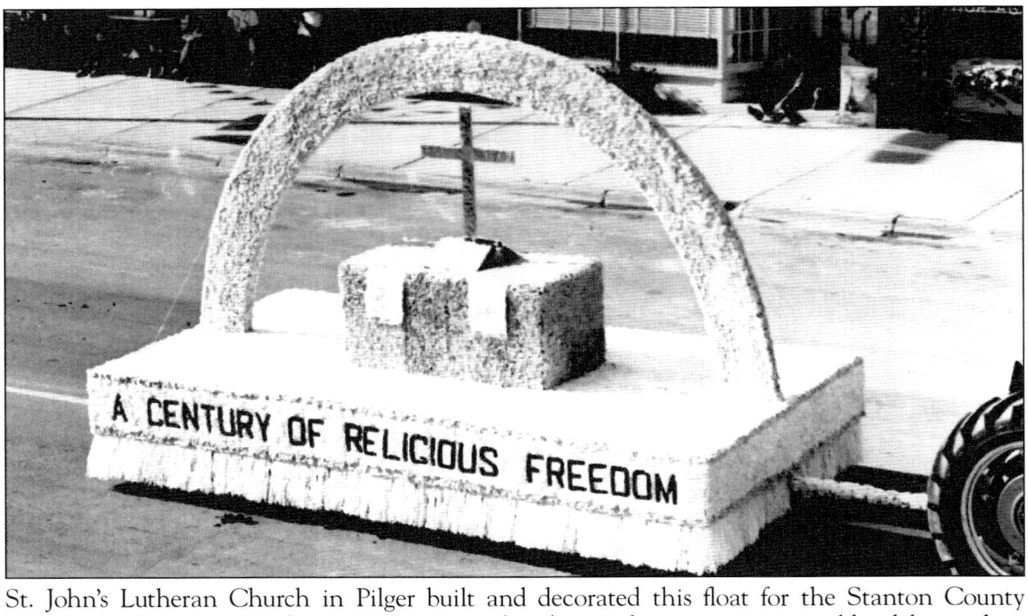

St. John's Lutheran Church in Pilger built and decorated this float for the Stanton County 100-year-anniversary parade in 1966. Many churches and communities would celebrate their centennials during the 1960s, and the Nebraska state centennial year began on March 1, 1967. The Stanton community was active in those parades and celebrations in return. (Author's collection.)

Four

STANTON, GROWING WITH BUSINESS VENTURES 1869

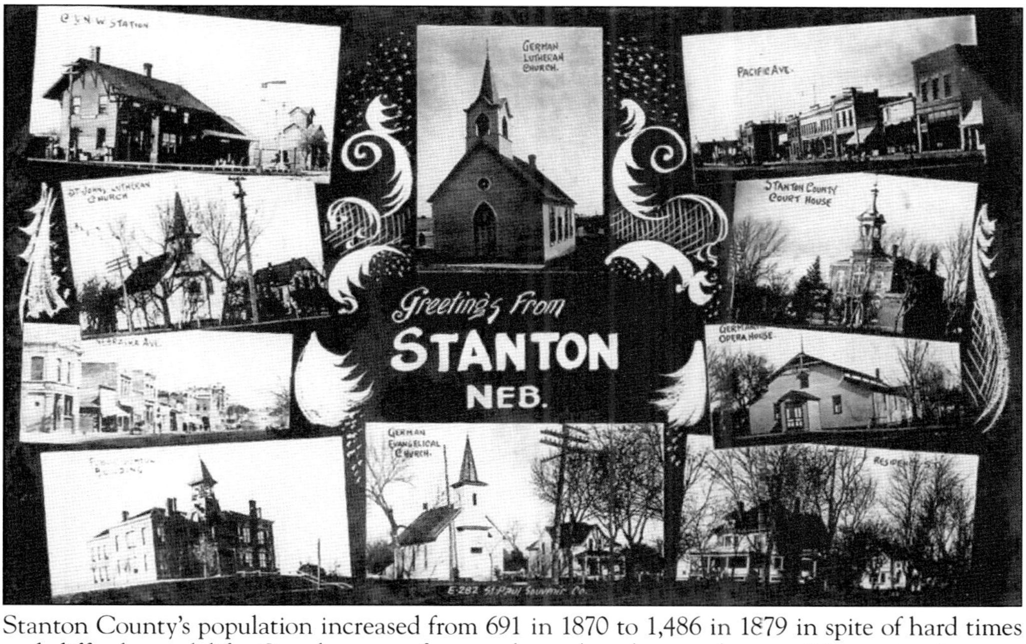

Stanton County's population increased from 691 in 1870 to 1,486 in 1879 in spite of hard times and difficult rural life. Grasshoppers, fires, and weather destroyed crops. The grain that was hand-harvested had to be hauled over difficult trails 30 to 60 miles distance for milling. Penny postcards were used for advertising the growth of the community with photographs of churches, schools, business, and development of the town streets and society. (Courtesy of Marian Klima.)

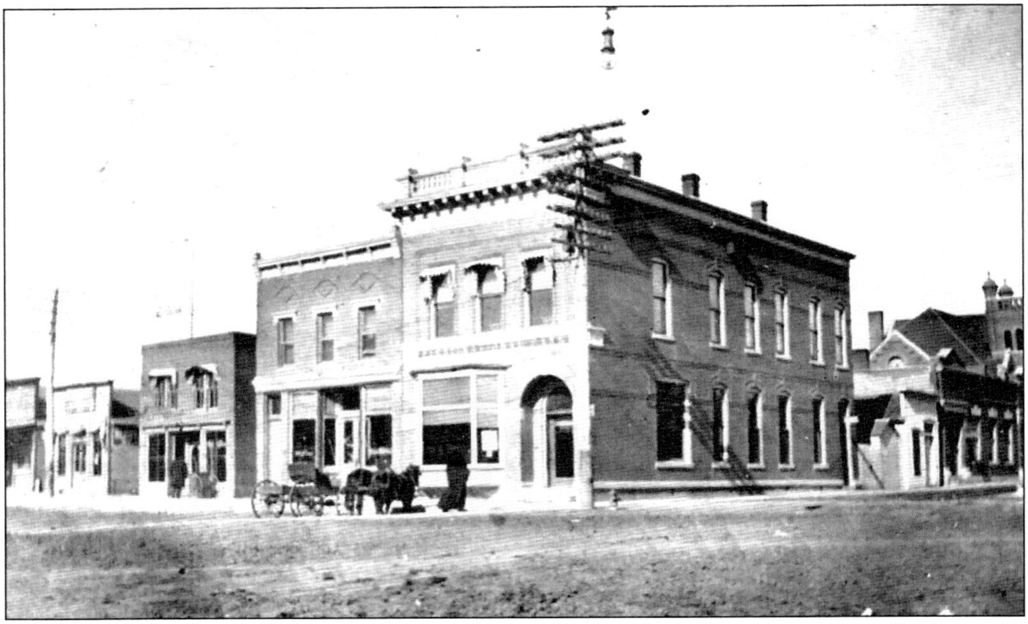

The first years of settlement did not require a public bank, because few settlers had money. Francis McGiverin, in 1879, started his privately owned Stanton County Bank. By 1881, Levi Miller joined him in partnership. Four years later, they filed incorporation papers for the First National Bank. This building is located on the southwest corner of the main intersection, formerly the Elkhorn State Bank. (Courtesy of Art Catlin.)

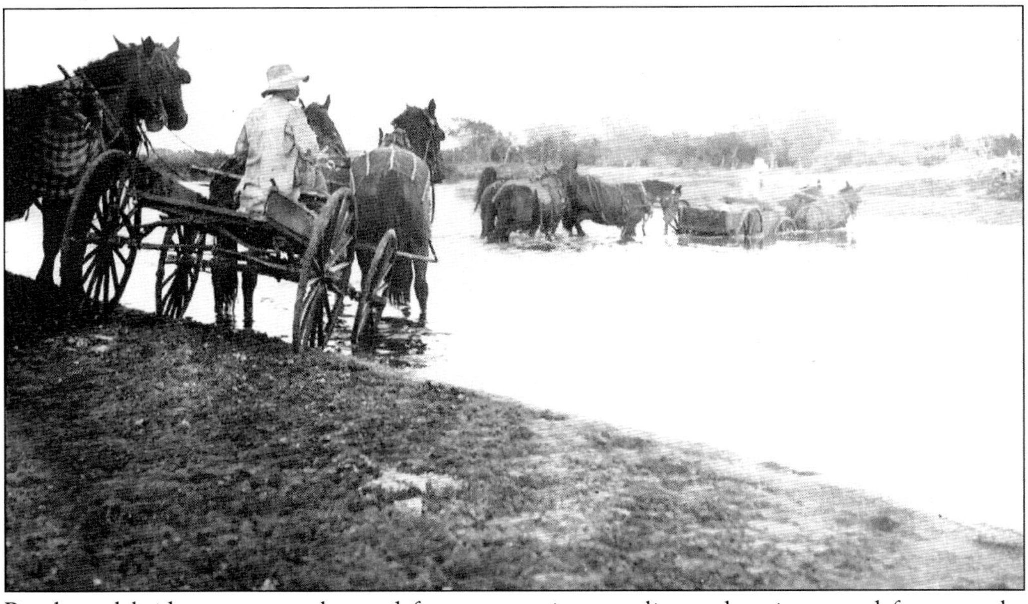

Roads and bridges were sorely need for transporting supplies and grain to and from nearby communities. Before a bridge was built across the Elkhorn River for travel south of the river, this spot, about three miles east of Stanton, was favored for fording through the shallows. Walter A. Schultze is shown following his brother Pat and father, Fritz, across the Elkhorn River. (Courtesy of Milford and Gloria Koch.)

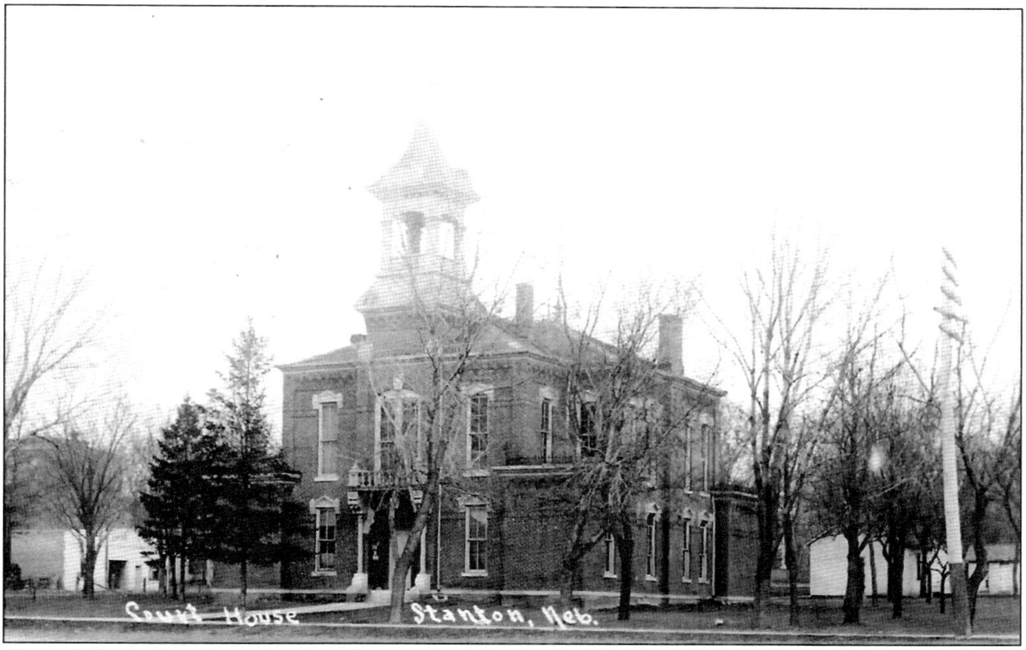

One of the largest businesses in Stanton, as the county seat, was the county government. This courthouse was built at a cost of $10,624. It was used from January 1884, with a number of renovations, additions, and the removal of the steeple, until replaced by a new single-story building in 1976. (Courtesy of Art Catlin.)

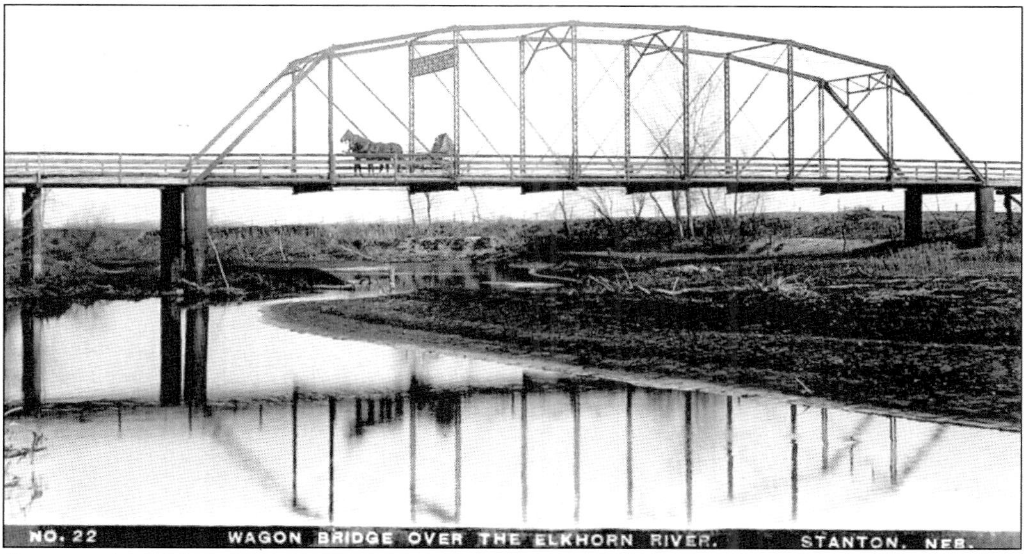

Crossing the Elkhorn River was a necessity for horse and wagons to reach southern parts of the county. Supplies were needed and grains were hauled to mills many miles from harvest. River crossings had to be found in shallow parts of the river or after ice formed thick enough to support the weight. The first wagon bridge was built in 1871, for $4,200, south of Stanton. (Courtesy of Marci Poeschl.)

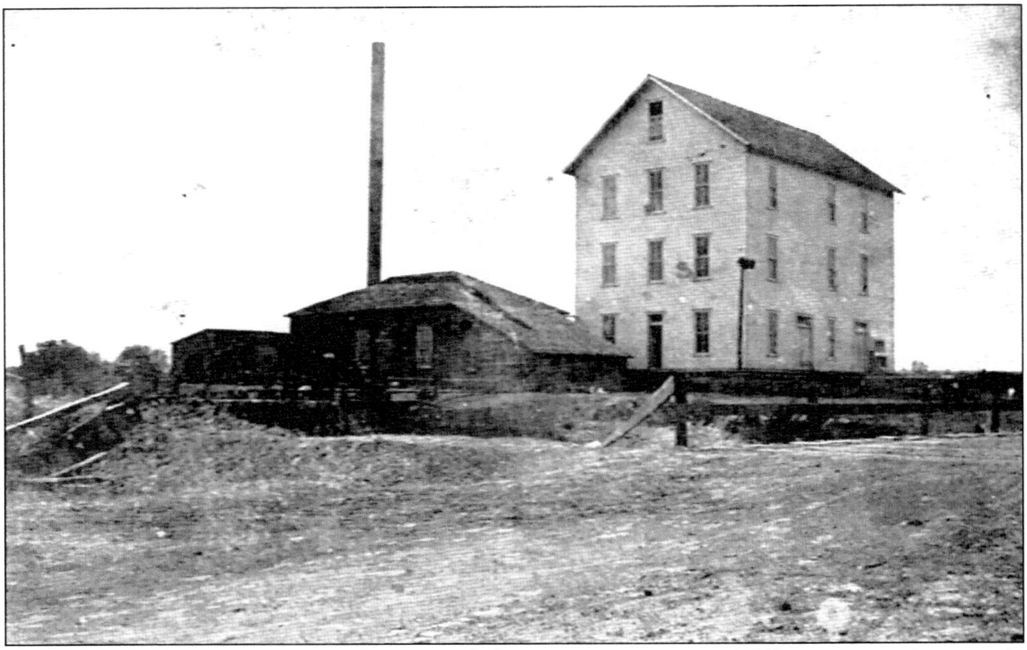

The citizens of Stanton County petitioned the commissioners in 1875 to erect a desperately needed mill. Several feed grinding mills were built and suffered destruction by wind or fire. The first milling of flour was done in 1886, but that mill burned in 1888. The Stanton Roller Mills burned in 1901. The last mill moved into town in 1905 from the Elkhorn River cutoff location. (Courtesy of Art Catlin.)

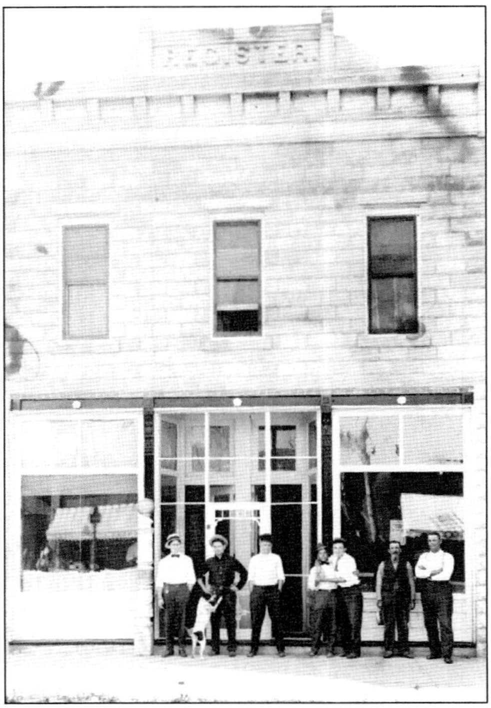

The *Weekly Register* consolidated with the *Stanton Picket* in 1907 under the new ownership of Alfred Pont, pictured to the left. Although there were several other newspapers published since Lewis Ley published the first issue of the *Stanton Bugle* in 1871, the *Stanton Register* is the only one still printed by owner and publisher Laura Forker. It is the official county newspaper for legal notices. (Courtesy of Art Catlin.)

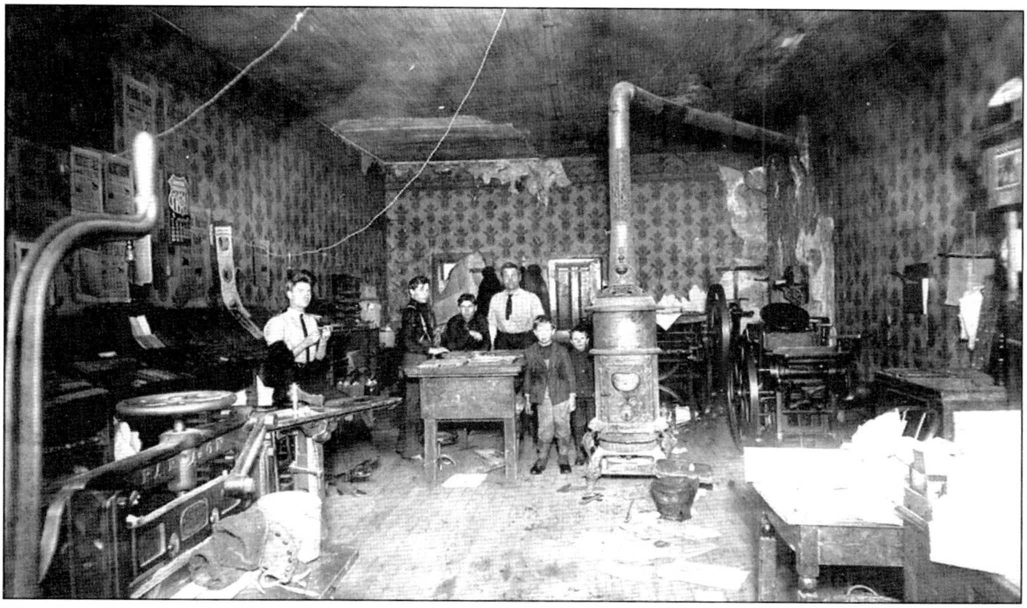

The interior of Alfred Pont's newspaper printing shop in 1907 is shown with him and his staff, who are identified from left to right as Kitty Sharp, Grant McFarland, Ervine Pont, Alfred Pont (owner and editor), Dewey Pont, and Harold Dickinson. The photograph below displays a newer printing office. Staff members are, from left to right, Edith Pont, Alfred Pont, Kitty J. Pont with the telephone at the front desk, Harold Dickinson, and Grant McFarland (back right). The masthead proclaimed the *Stanton Register* to be the "lineal descendent of six newspapers." Those were the *Stanton Bugle*, the *Reporter*, the *Stanton Index*, the *Weekly Register*, the *Stanton Democrat*, and the *Stanton Picket*. Several competitive publications were the *Pilger Picket*, the *Pilger Weekly Herald*, the *Stanton County News*, the *Elkhorn Valley Tribune*, and the *Elkhorn Review*. (Courtesy of the Historical Society of Stanton County.)

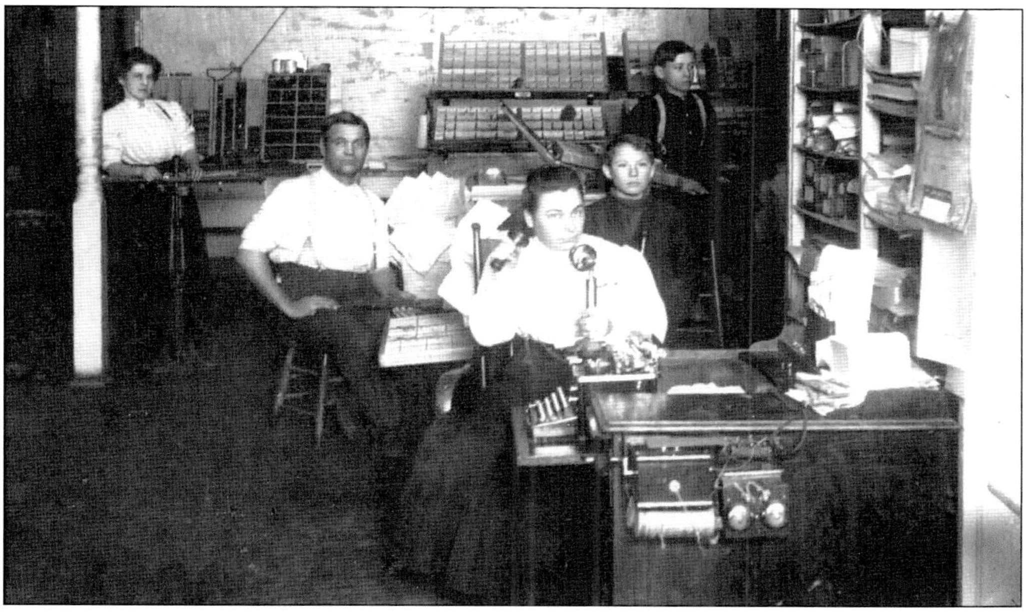

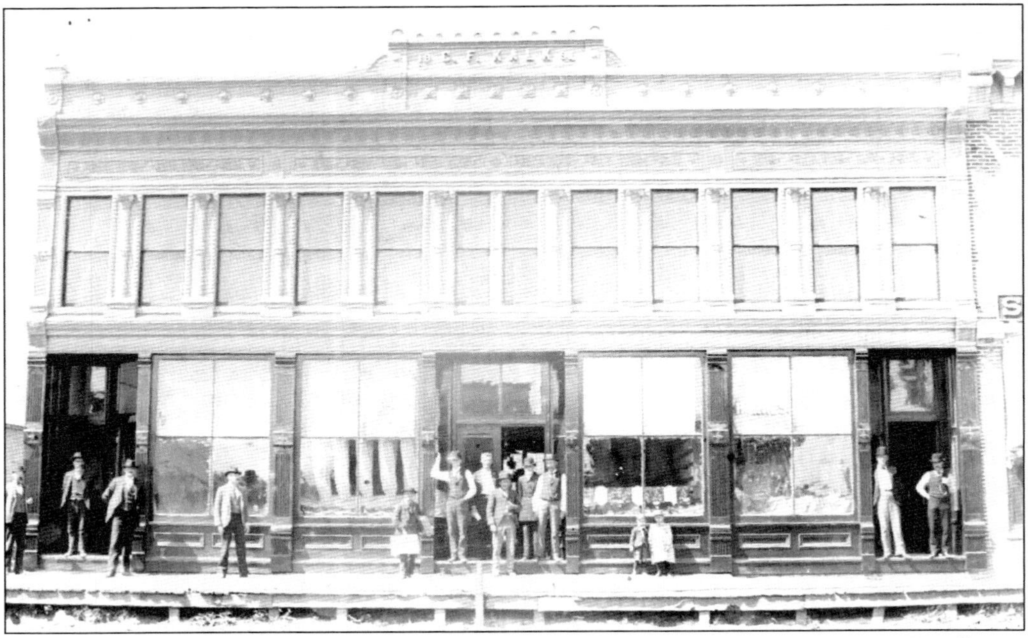

A welcomed business opened in the early 1900s to supply dry goods and groceries. C. F. Kalk Dry Goods is in the center store. Patrons lounge on the sidewalk in front of Young and Eberly's on the left and a harness shop on the right. In the building on the second floor was an opera house. (Courtesy of the Historical Society of Stanton County.)

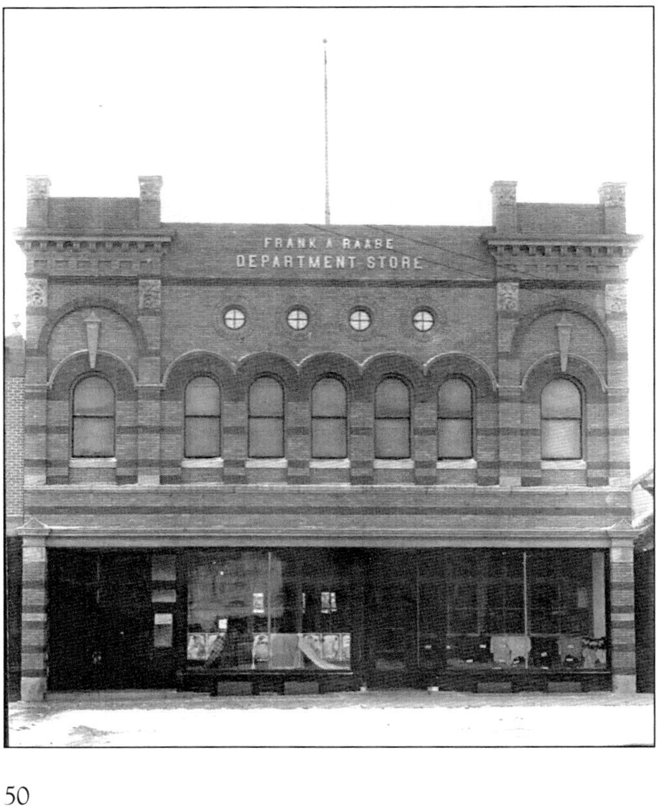

A mercantile business, owned and operated by partners Frank A. Raabe and ? Ruther, occupied a wood frame building on main street. In 1906, Raabe moved into his two-story brick Romanesque-style department store on the south side of Pacific Avenue (now Ivy Street). Frank's daughter, Esther Raabe, continued to run the business after his death in 1924, until she sold it in 1959. (Courtesy of the Historical Society of Stanton County.)

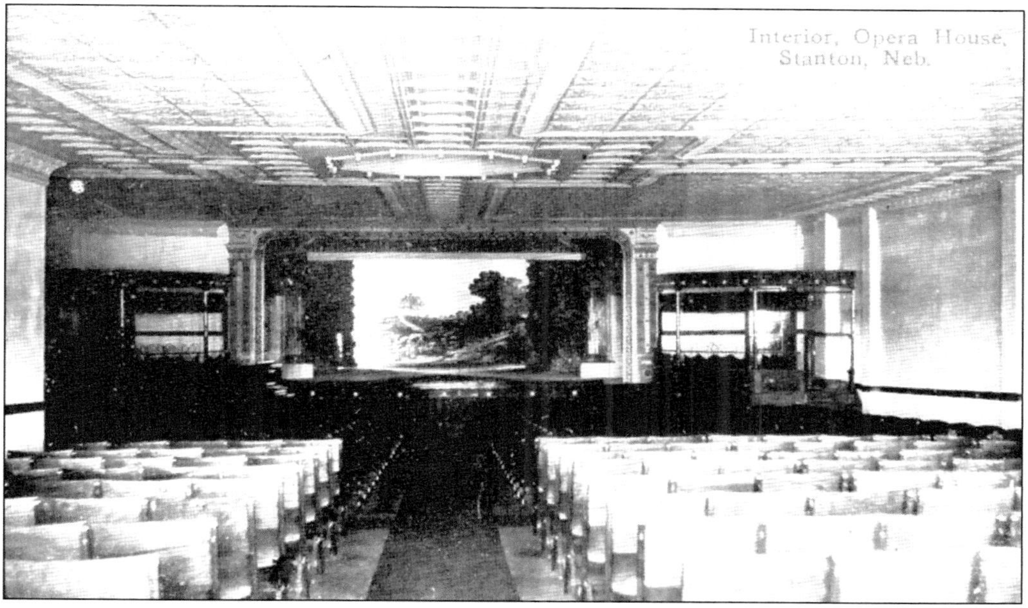

The Raabe Opera House was busy with performances of bands, plays, declamatory contests, vocal concerts, and graduation ceremonies. The floor sloped down to a curtained stage with box seats on each side for honored seating. Father Flanagan's Boys Town Band from Omaha performed here. The building was gutted and destroyed by fire on December 20, 1959, nine months after it was sold to Al and Eldon Johnson. (Courtesy of Art Catlin.)

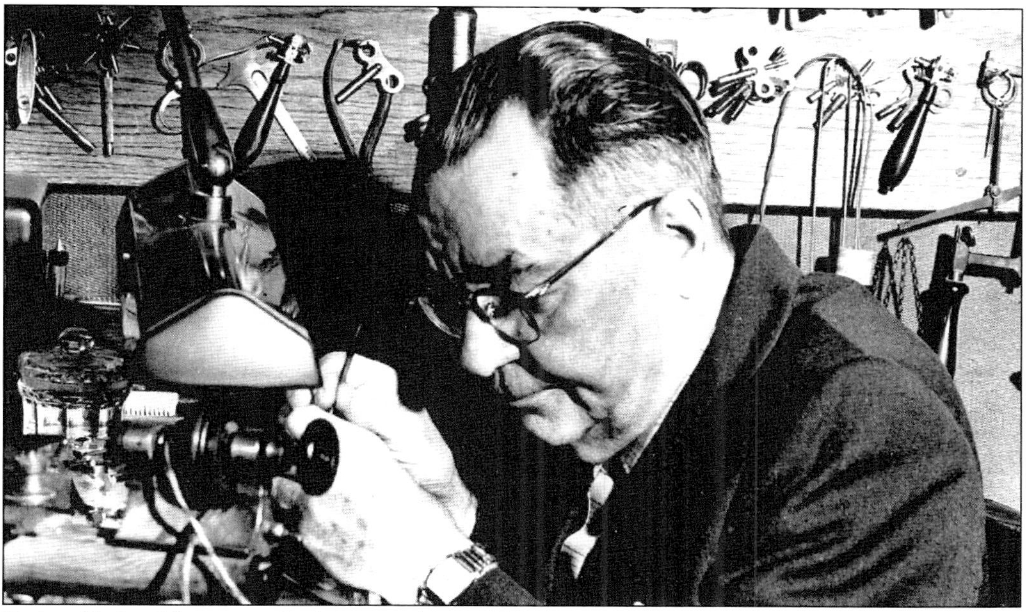

Richard J. Strahle received a degree as doctor of optometry in 1915. He operated a Pilger business two years, served as an army engineer one year, and then purchased the Strahle Jewelry business in 1919. His father, Carl Strahle, established the business in Stanton on February 1, 1889. Strahle retired and closed the family-owned business after 72 years of service to the Stanton community. (Courtesy of the Stanton Register.)

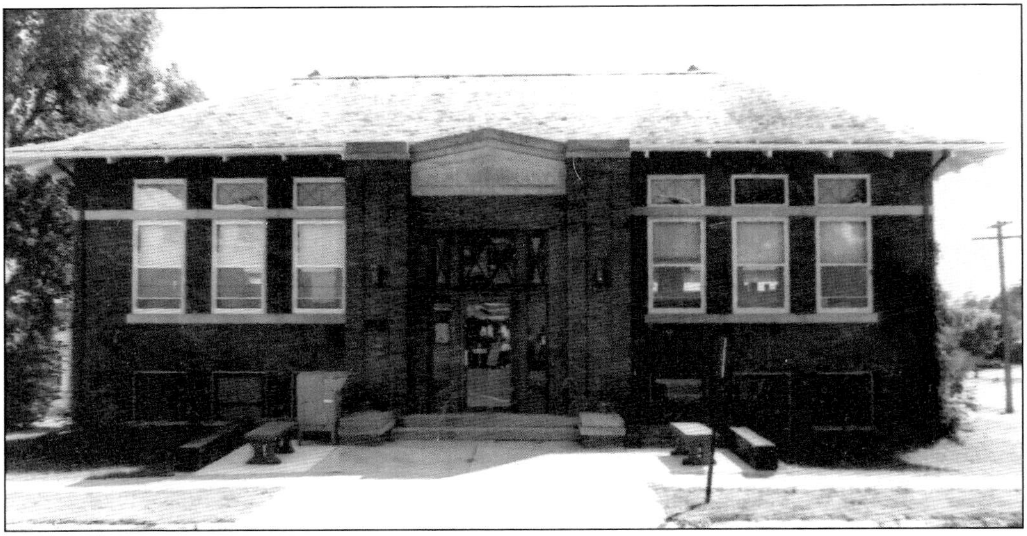

The Stanton Public Library started in 1886 with 300 volumes donated by John Borland of New York, owner of the local Elkhorn Ranch. Housed in a small 14-by-14-foot wood frame building north of the First National Bank, the building was later moved north of the Methodist church. Andrew Carnegie gave $8,000 for this public library, a one-story brick building, in 1914. (Author's collection.)

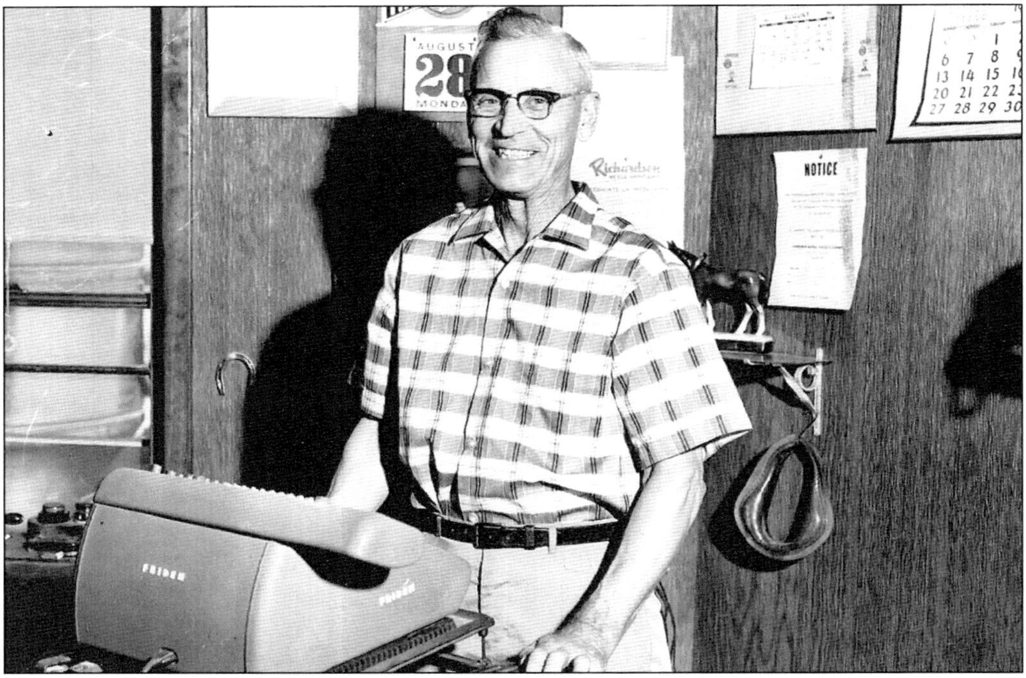

Art Greenslit operated the Greenslit Elevator, built in 1891, and the Greenslit Lumber Company. The elevator, which he purchased from Nye-Jenks Lumber and Grain Company in 1925, was torn down in September 1959. However, one board was preserved, which had all the names of elevator operators who served from 1904. In 1985, Greenslit sold the lumberyard business to Robert Henrickson. (Courtesy of the Stanton Register.)

Louis Smithberger purchased Sanders Elevator from E. A. Marshall in 1946. It had been unused for some time and extensive renovation was needed, including an office building and a 45-foot scale of 50-ton capacity were installed. All grains were bought and sold, but soybeans became one of the major crops for shipping and storage here. In 1965, the elevator was straightened to correct the noticeable tilting, which can be seen in the photograph below. More renovations and storage bins have since been completed, also, with several changes in ownership. The elevator is most recently owned and operated by Farmer's Union Supply. (Author's collection.)

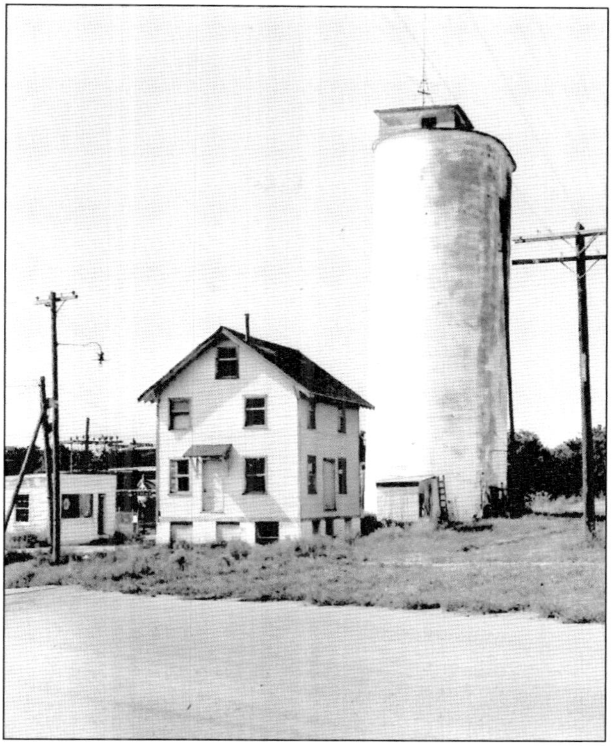

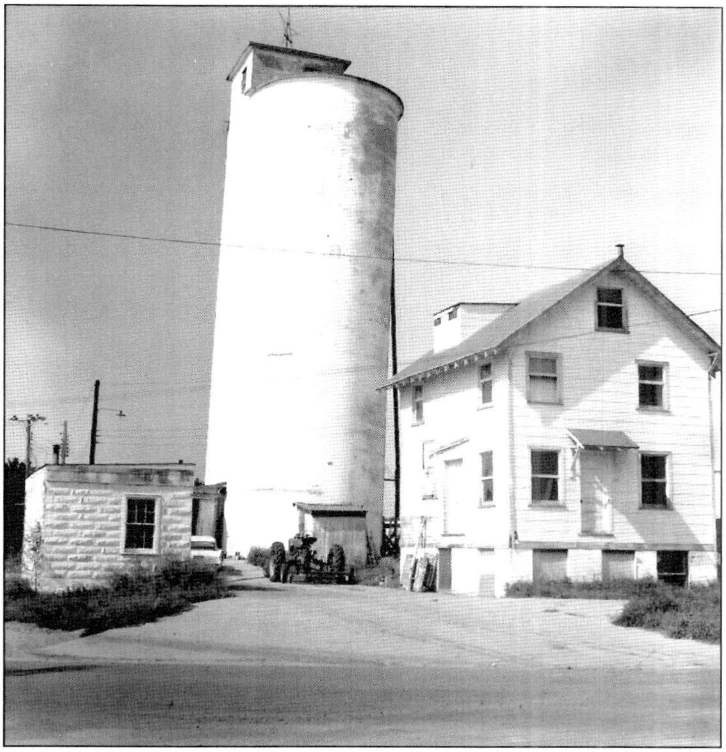

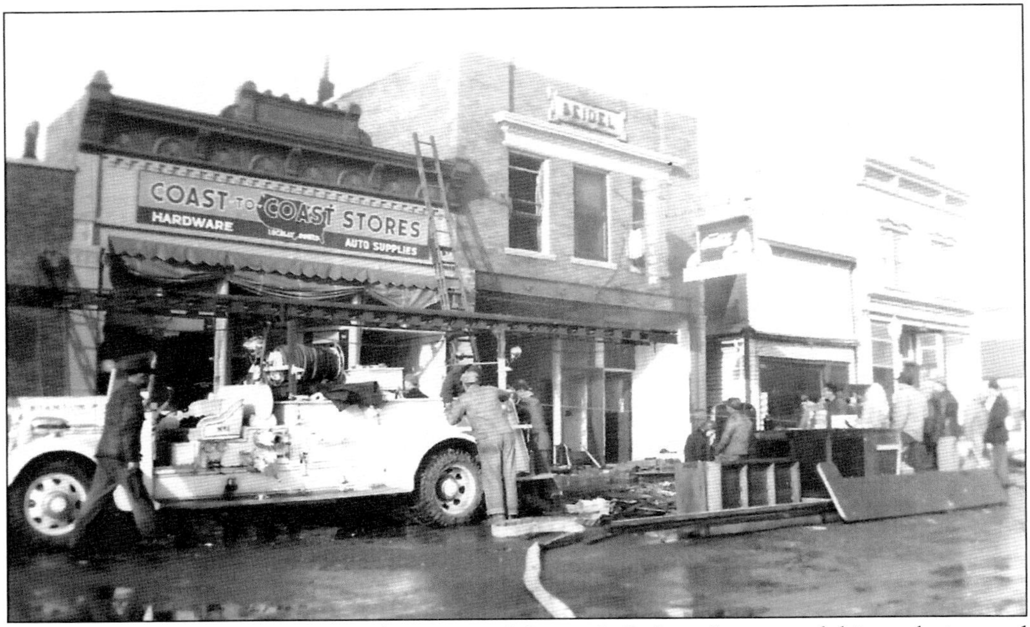

Charles Cooper was the owner and operator of Cooper's Café at the time of this explosion and fire in the 1940s. The café was located in the Seidel building and suffered extensive damage, as is evident in the photograph. The Seidel Millinery store was damaged in the resulting fire and never reopened. No deaths were attributed to the incident. (Courtesy of Larry Belz.)

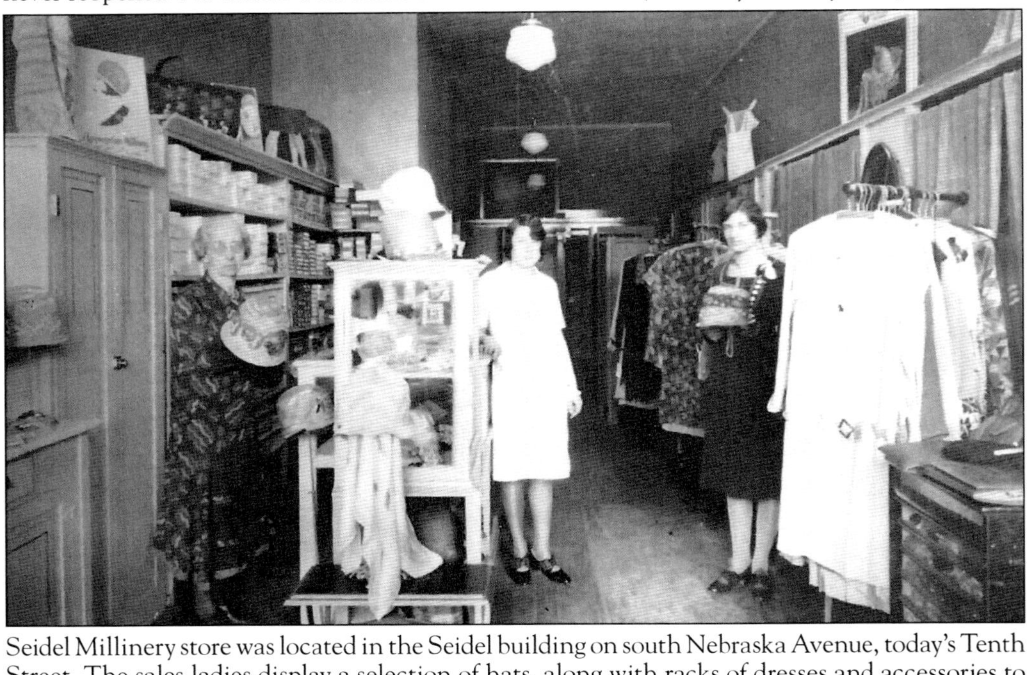

Seidel Millinery store was located in the Seidel building on south Nebraska Avenue, today's Tenth Street. The sales ladies display a selection of hats, along with racks of dresses and accessories to delight the ladies. The business was located in a two-story brick structure on the west side of the main thoroughfare running north and south. This image is from about the 1930s. (Courtesy of Larry Belz.)

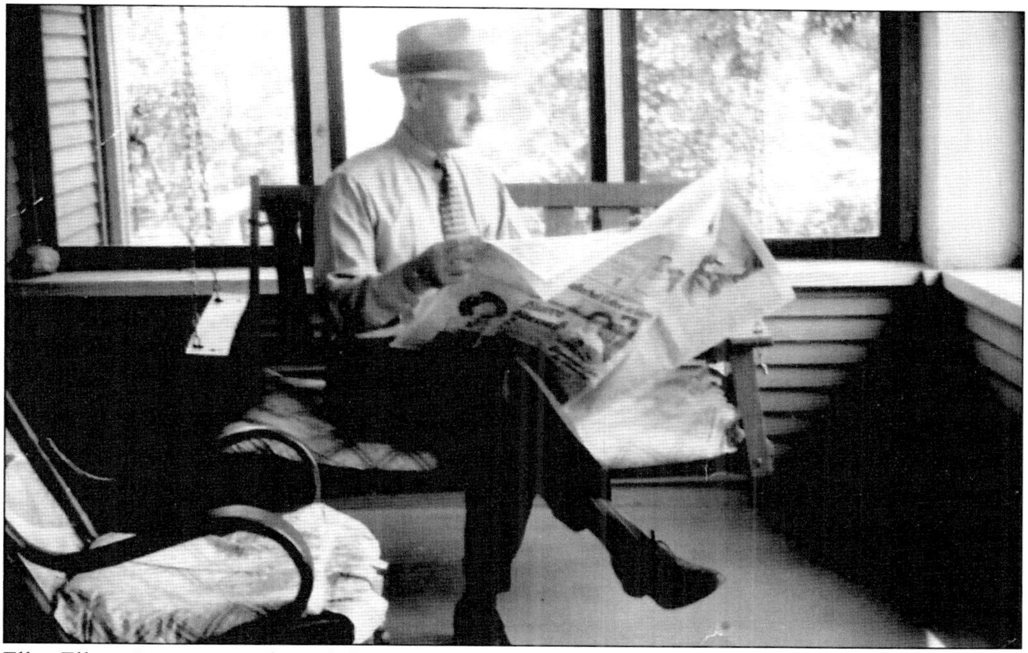

Ellis Ellery Lewton graduated from Highland Park College in 1911. He worked in several drugstores and pharmacies around the state before settling in Stanton in 1929, where he was the owner and a registered pharmacist of the Corner Drugstore in Stanton until his retirement. (Courtesy of Larry Belz.)

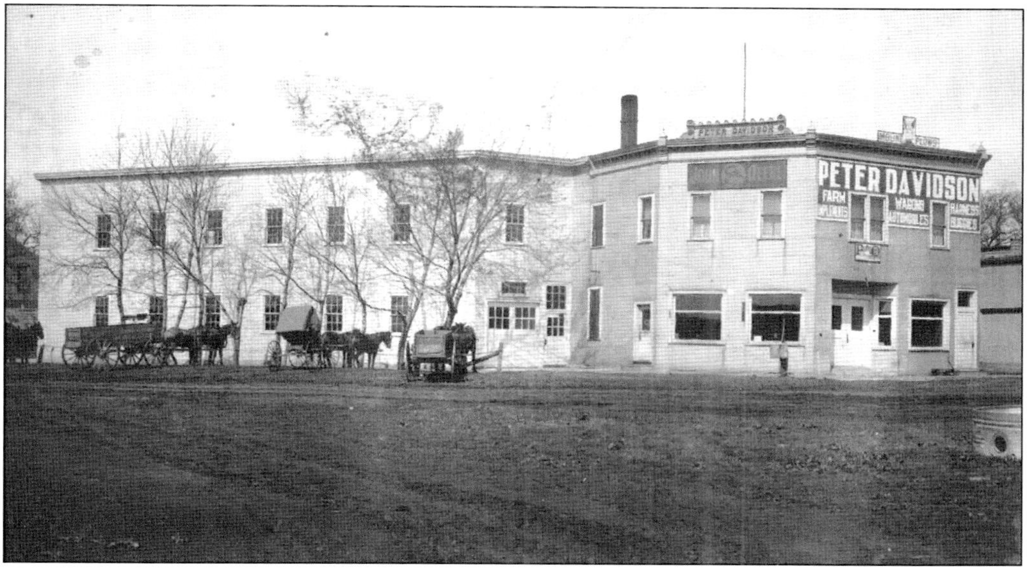

Peter Davidson erected this farm implement building in the early 1900s. He was a John Deere supplies and equipment dealer. Peter's brother Andrew ran the business until it sold to Floyd Mesch in 1937. Charlie Cooper and Mesch held many dances on the upper floor. Mesch's son George took over the dealership from 1946 until his retirement in 1977. In 1975, George demolished and replaced the building. (Courtesy of the Stanton Register.)

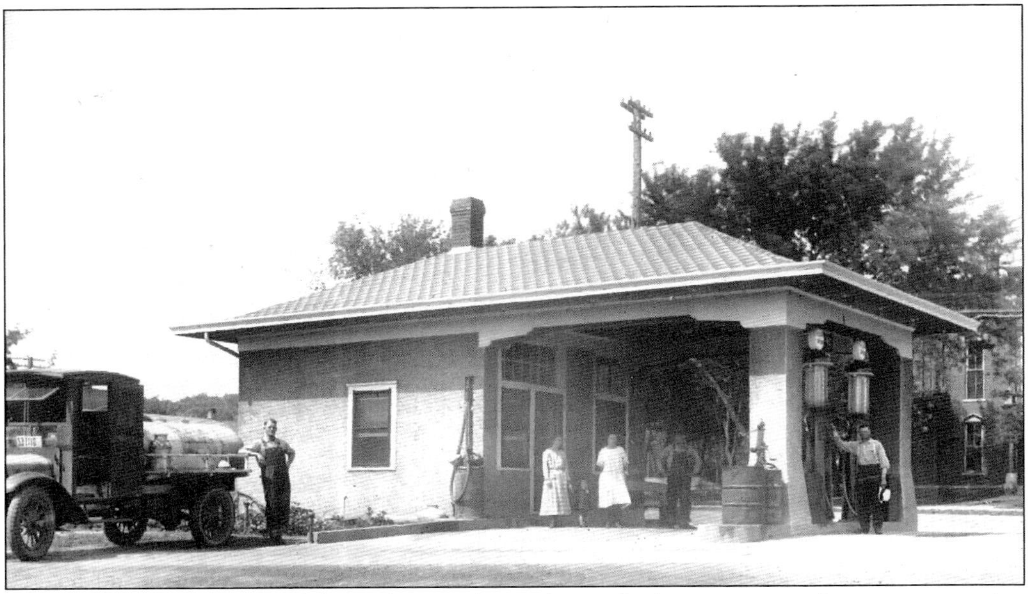

With the coming of automobiles and motor driven farm vehicles, gas stations became a necessity. Charles Luedeke built this filling station across the street from the Stanton County Courthouse in 1921. The business was later handed over to two of Luedeke's sons-in-law, Harold Sanders and Larry Caskey. Then Caskey became the sole manager until his retirement. The Luedeke Oil Company operation is now in the hands of a grandson, Dan Caskey, who manages it in the same location. Services have expanded to include automobile repair, tire sales and repair, a car wash, fuel delivery, and 24-hour gas pumps. Dan received recognition as a business in operation for three generations at Stanton's Q125 celebration in 2007. (Author's collection.)

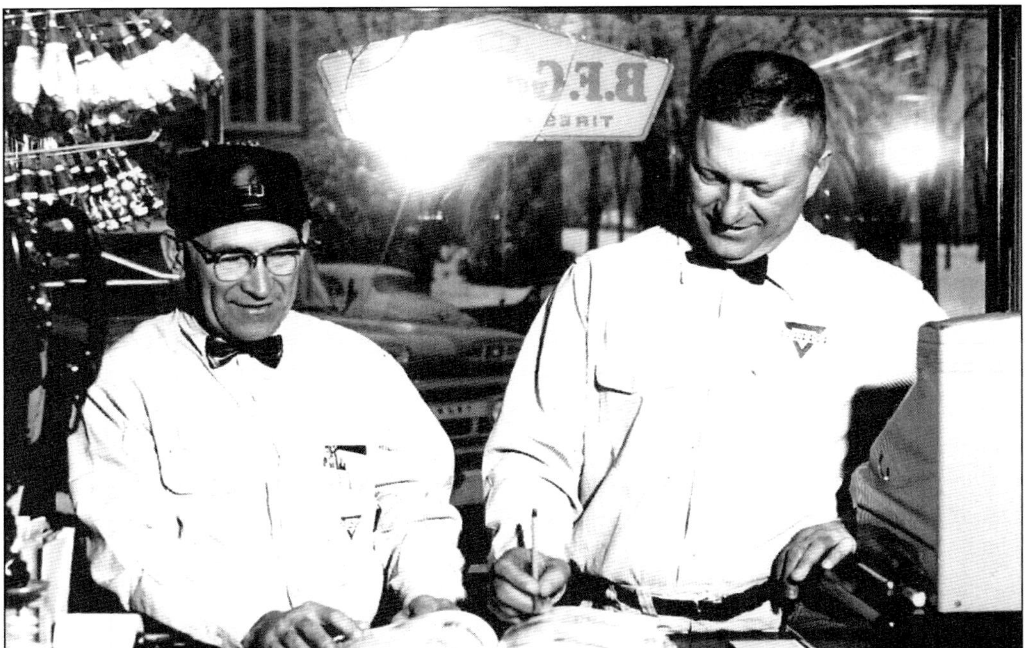

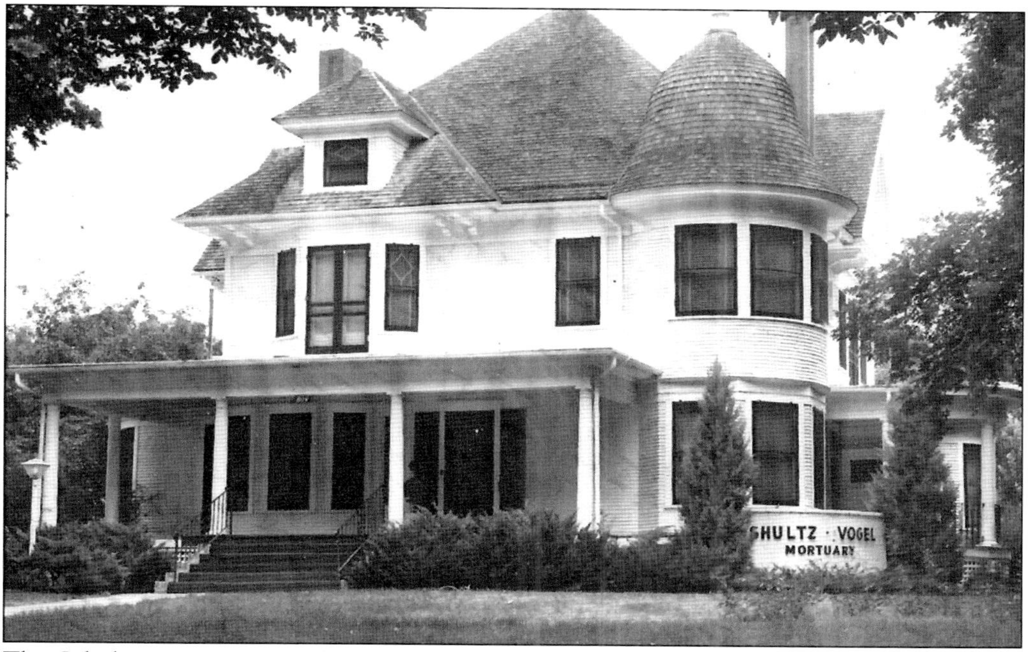

The Schultz Mortuary provided funeral services since 1919. Henry Jacob Schultz, a licensed embalmer and funeral director, started the business in conjunction with his father's furniture store downtown. In 1942, this three-story home was purchased from Charlie Chace to house the funeral business. Morris Vogel joined the partnership in 1959. Brad Johnson purchased the business in 1989 and named it the Schultz Vogel Johnson Mortuary. (Courtesy of the Stanton Register.)

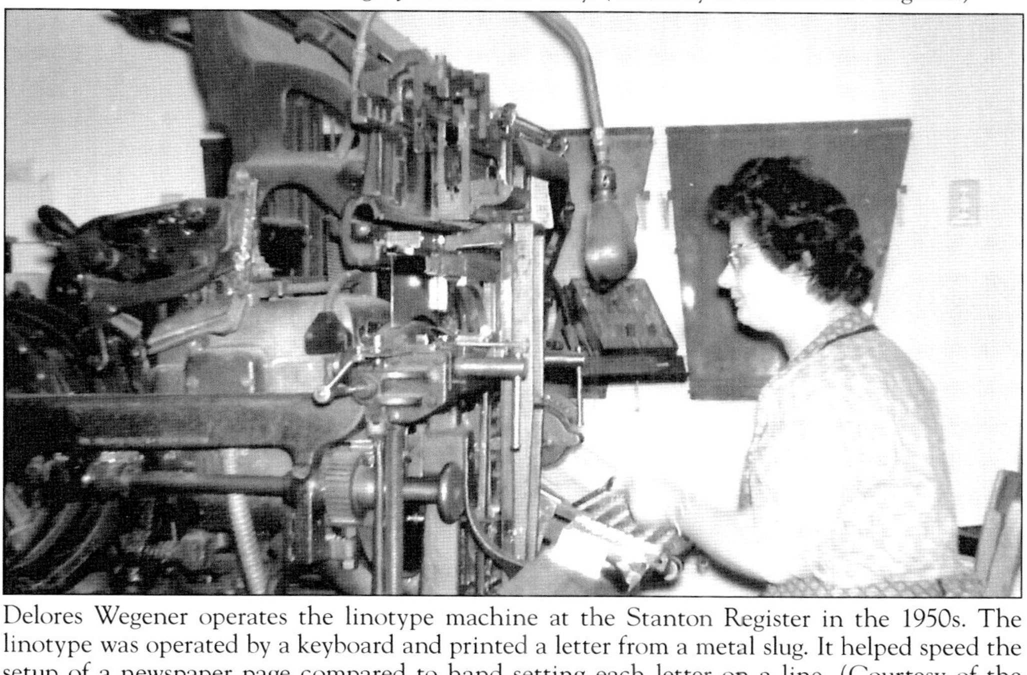

Delores Wegener operates the linotype machine at the Stanton Register in the 1950s. The linotype was operated by a keyboard and printed a letter from a metal slug. It helped speed the setup of a newspaper page compared to hand setting each letter on a line. (Courtesy of the Stanton Register.)

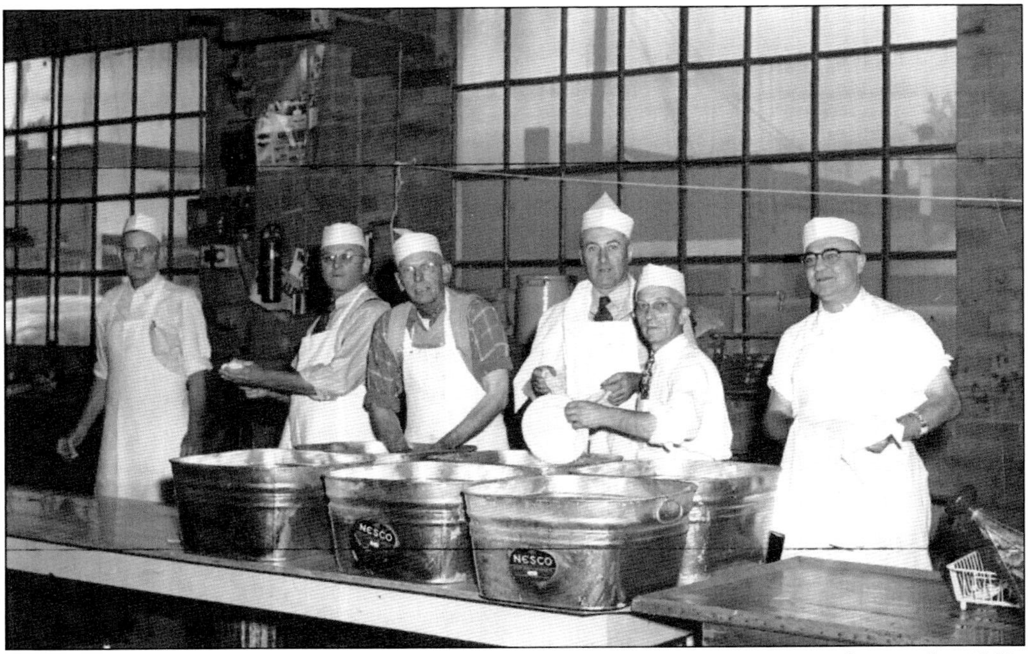

Stanton Businessmen held free pancake feeds annually for their customers during the 1950s and 1960s. Those businessmen in the serving line are, from left to right, William Demaree of Demaree Chevrolet, Rudy Suchan of Suchan's Grocery, Henry Schultz of Schultz Mortuary, James Zoubeka banker, Joe Sazama of Stanton Variety Store, and Howard Hrabak of Hrabak's Grocery. A happy and hungry crowd goes through the line at the free pancake feed while other members of the business community hustle to keep up with the food demands. This feed was held in the downtown farm implement repair shop as the belt and parts on the wall and the view through the large panes of glass attest to. (Courtesy of Larry Belz.)

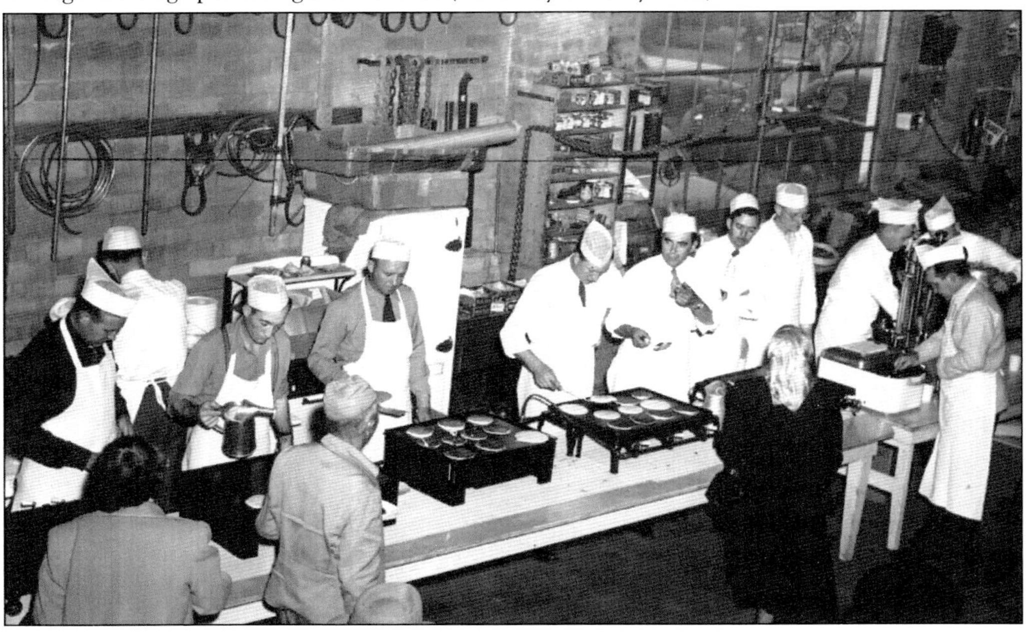

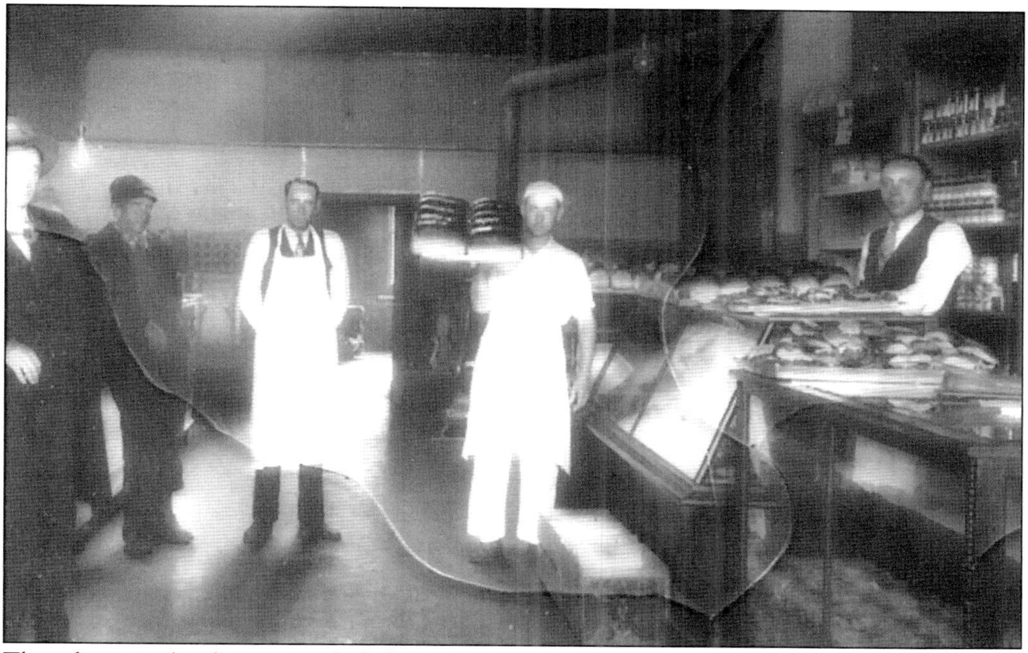

This photograph of a very early bakery shop in Stanton is taken from a glass plate negative. Those identified are, from left to right, Roy Whalen, Dean Whalen, Rink Wright, and the other two are unidentified. (Courtesy of Inez Barth.)

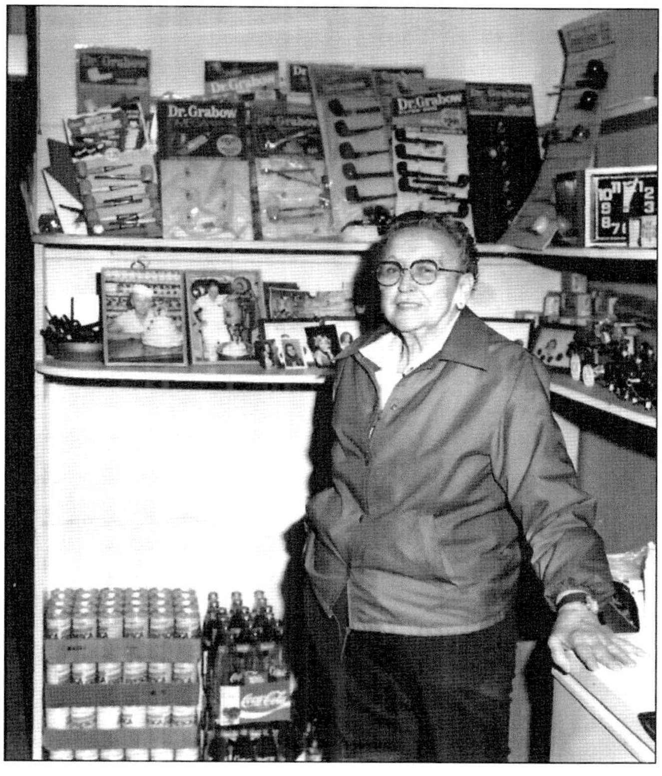

Connie Wagner opened and operated the Stanton Bakery for over 40 years before retiring in the 1980s. She was the proprietor of one of the first convenience stores in the city of Stanton, with a selection of sundries, groceries, cards, snacks, and various household supplies. She was a staunch supporter of all school activities and an enthusiastic sports fan. (Courtesy of the Stanton Register.)

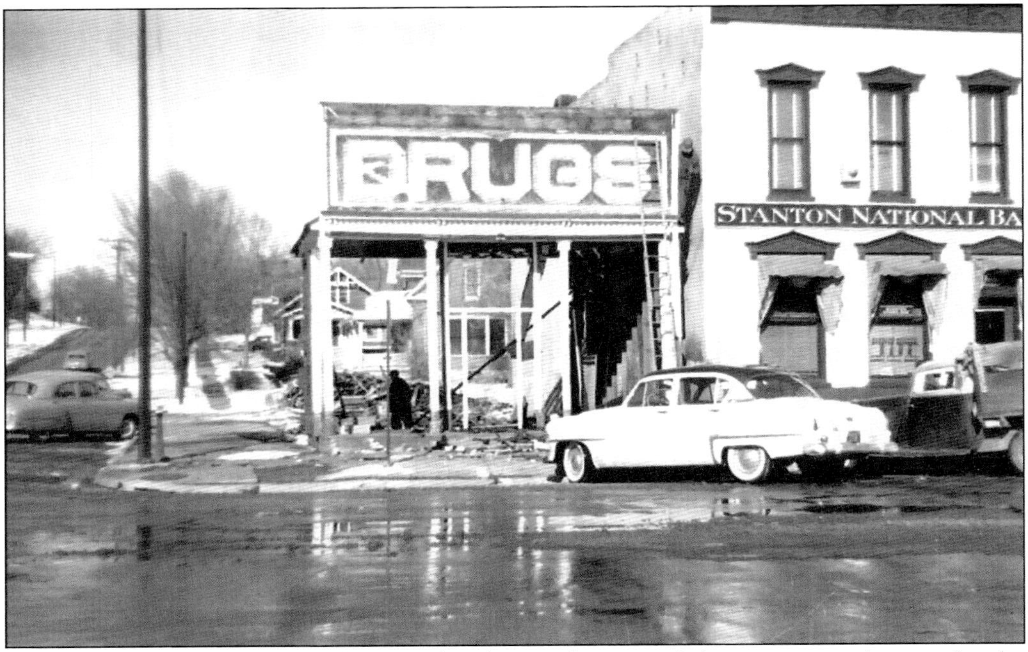

The Corner Drug Store goes down under the wrecking crew's hammer to make way for the expansion of the Stanton National Bank. The old Stanton National Bank, erected in 1898, can be seen to the right side of the demolition site. The new Stanton National Bank is featured below. The Stanton National Bank, established in 1882, began as a partnership of Frank P. Hanlon, John Eberly, and Lewis Ley. It operated as the Citizen's National Bank, a private bank, until 1890. The name changed to Stanton National Bank in 1905, when it became a chartered national bank. George Eberly's sons, John B. Eberly and Don Eberly, are the third generation officers to serve as president and vice president since its beginning. (Courtesy of the Stanton Register.)

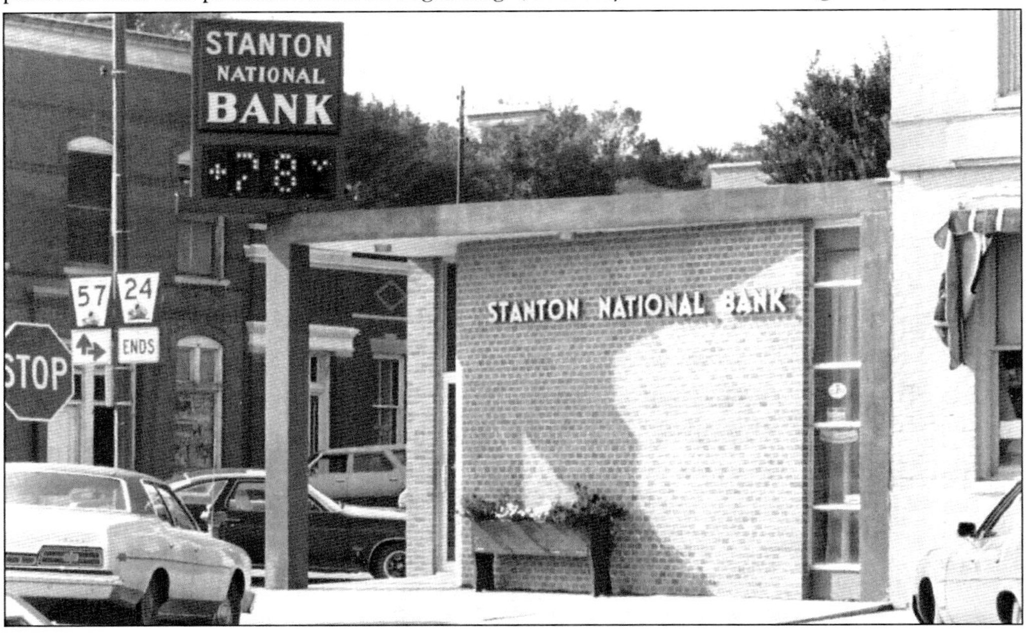

Five

Pilger Grows with Entrepreneurs 1868

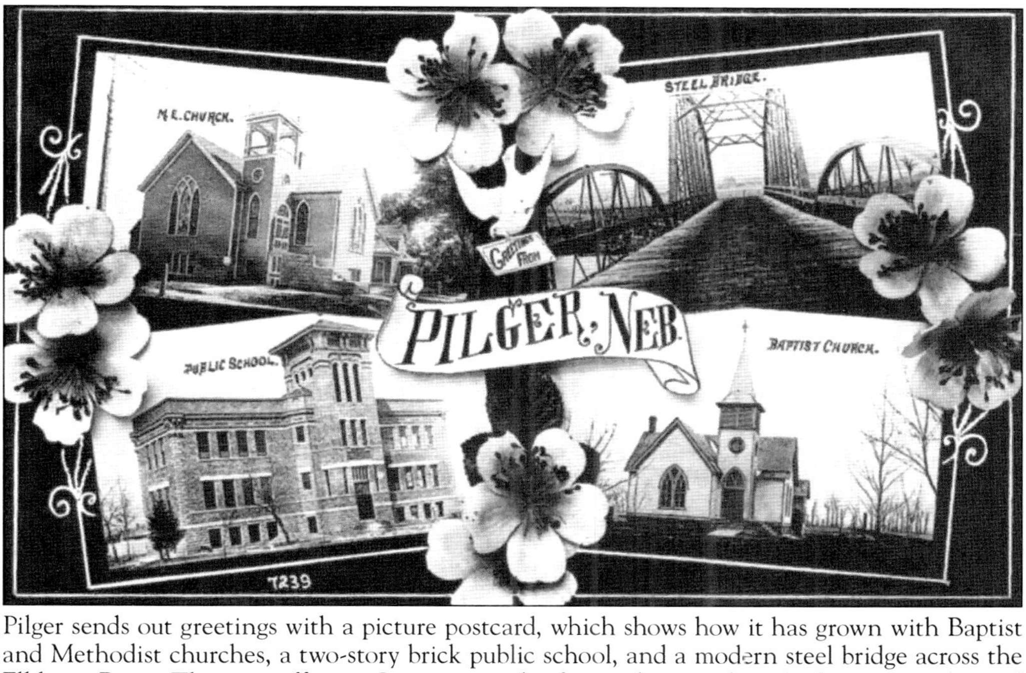

Pilger sends out greetings with a picture postcard, which shows how it has grown with Baptist and Methodist churches, a two-story brick public school, and a modern steel bridge across the Elkhorn River. The post office at Canton was the first gathering place for business and social connections. George Graves opened the first store in the county. Marian Adams opened the first merchandise store in Pilger. The first train passed through Pilger in 1879, quickly drawing much new development. (Courtesy of Marian Klima.)

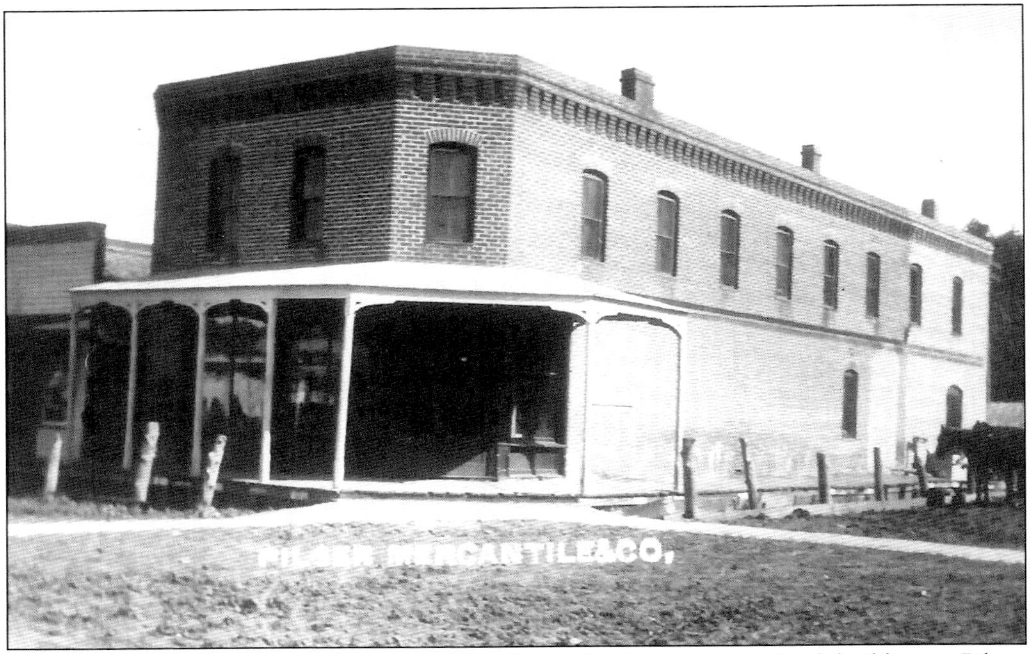

Fred Berger built this mercantile store in 1892. It was the first two-story brick building in Pilger. Berger also built the first blacksmith shop and worked there until 1888. At that time, he moved onto a farmstead in the Kingsburgh area and worked at both the farm and blacksmithing. The Bergers, along with their eight children, left Pilger before 1900. (Courtesy of Marian Klima.)

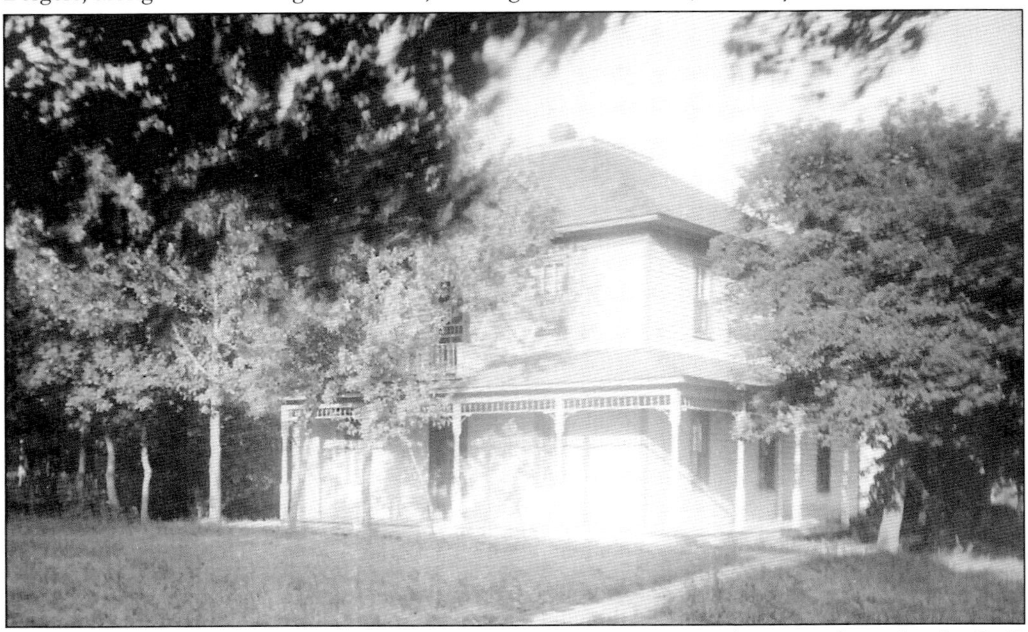

The John Davis Hotel came into being in Pilger in 1897. It was used as a residence by the E. Y. Abbott family. E. Y. Abbott was a pioneer druggist for the Pilger community in 1885 and later. The hotel was also used as a boardinghouse. The Ora Cary family lived there in the 1930s. The building was demolished for the lumber by Allen Tiedtke. (Courtesy of Marian Klima.)

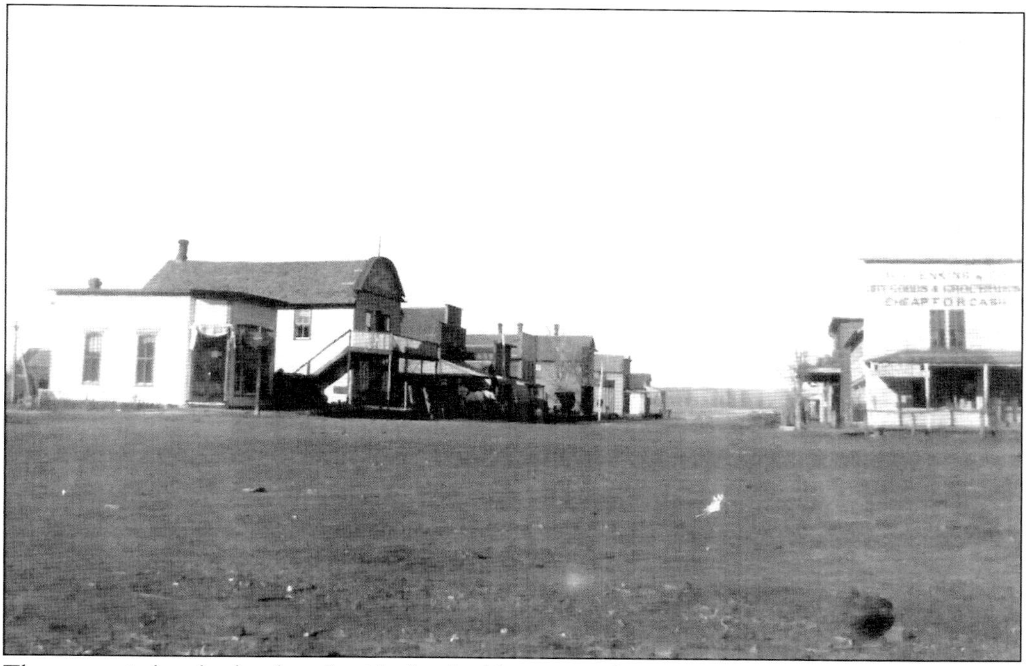

The street is barely developed with few buildings seen here in 1896. The small white frame on the left was a bank and the store facade on the right advertises "H. H. Jenkins & Co. Dry Goods & Groceries Cheap for Cash." (Courtesy of Marian Klima.)

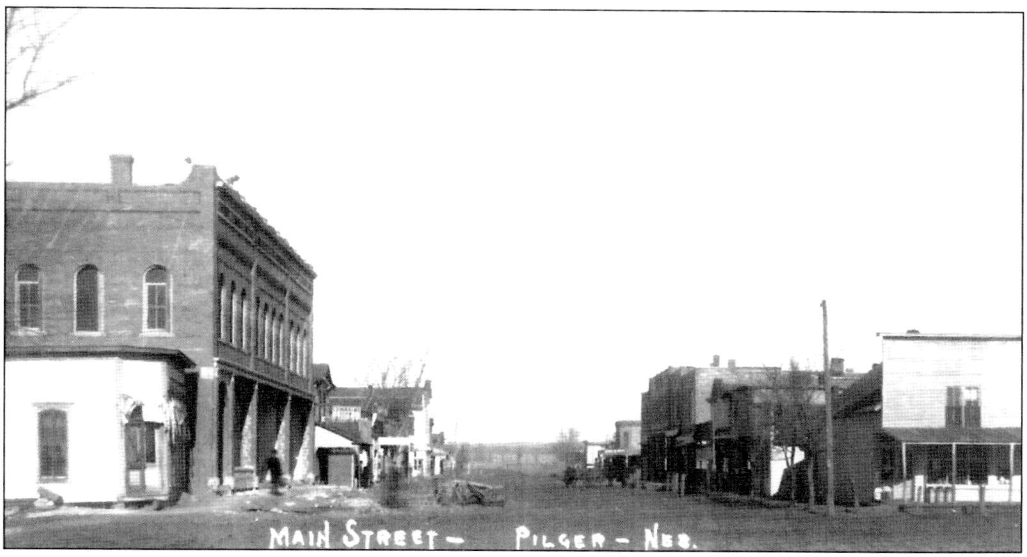

In comparing these two photographs of the same street in downtown Pilger a decade later, 1906, the little white frame building still stands on the corner. Next to it is the new brick two-story bank building, almost completed, to replace it as the First National Bank building. (Courtesy of Marian Klima.)

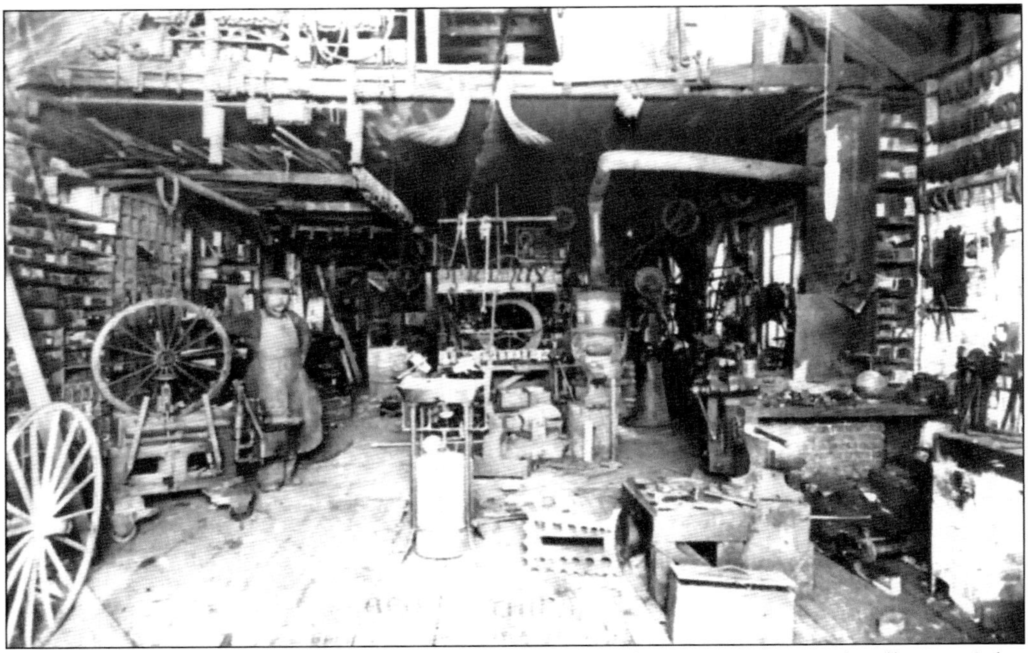

George Theis Blacksmith Shop operated out of the old District No. 1 schoolhouse. John Matheson purchased the building for his implement business after it was not used as the school. This building later housed the Tift Blacksmith Shop and the Hubert Lueck Blacksmith Shop. (Courtesy of Marian Klima.)

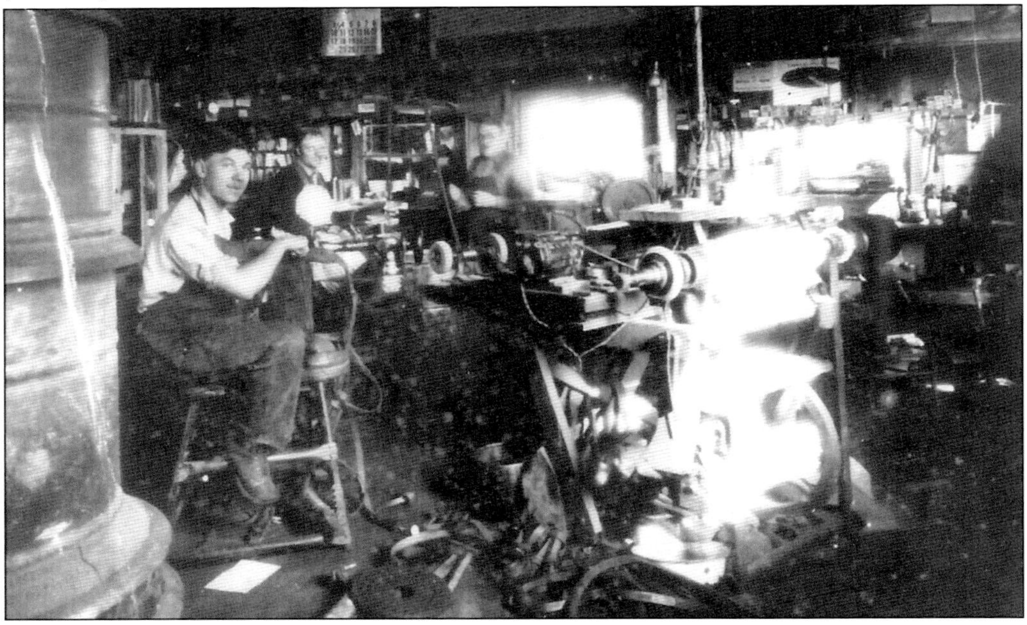

George and Ernest Theis operated a shoe and harness business in a building located just north of the Pilger Opera House on Pilger's main street. Mr. Wax is shown in the front of the picture. The Theis' are the gentlemen in the background. The date cannot be discerned on the calendar hanging from the ceiling in the center. (Courtesy of Marian Klima.)

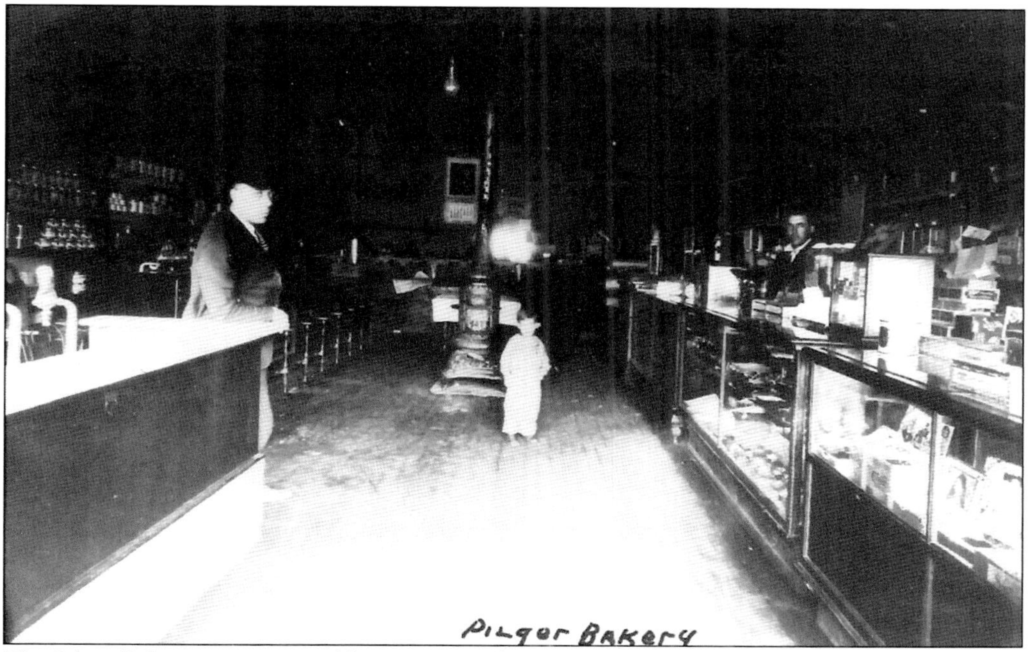

The Pilger Bakery was managed by George and Erma Axen for 10 years or more. August Axen, a brother to George and manager of the Nye-Jenks Elevator and Lumberyard, leans on the counter to the left. The little boy in the center is George's son, Duane. George is the gentleman on the right side behind the glass display cases. (Courtesy of Marian Klima.)

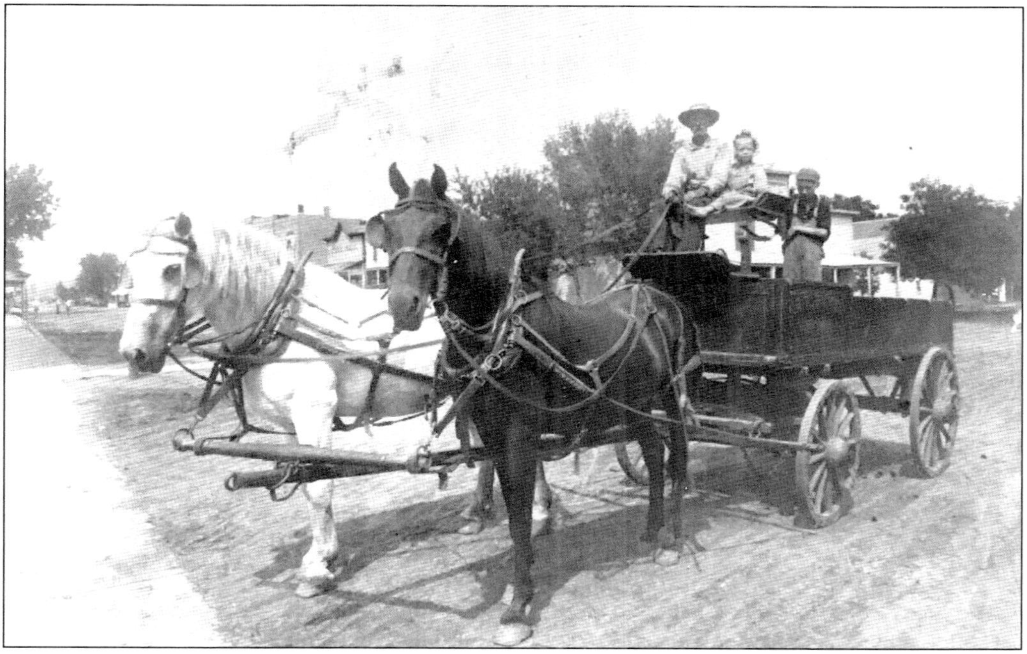

Pilger's pioneer drayman, John Foy, and children sit on top his dray wagon in the early 1900s. Dray wagons were used to haul loads of freight for a fee. Dray wagons could be seen at the railroad depots waiting for freight pickup and delivery. (Courtesy of Marian Klima.)

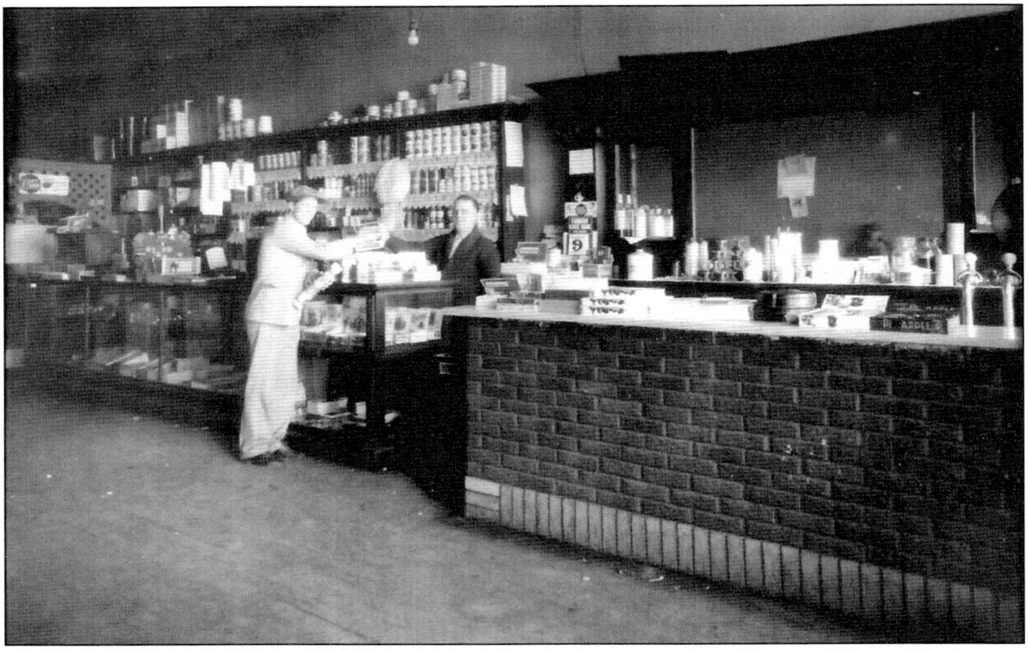

The brick soda fountain was built by Earnest Julke for the Louis "Stub" Foy and Harry Blackstone Confectionery Shop. In July 1919, Foy, shown on the right side behind the counter, returned from World War I to run the business and became the sole proprietor in August. Jack Schaefer is to the left in front of the counter. The shop was on the west side of Main Street. (Courtesy of Marian Klima.)

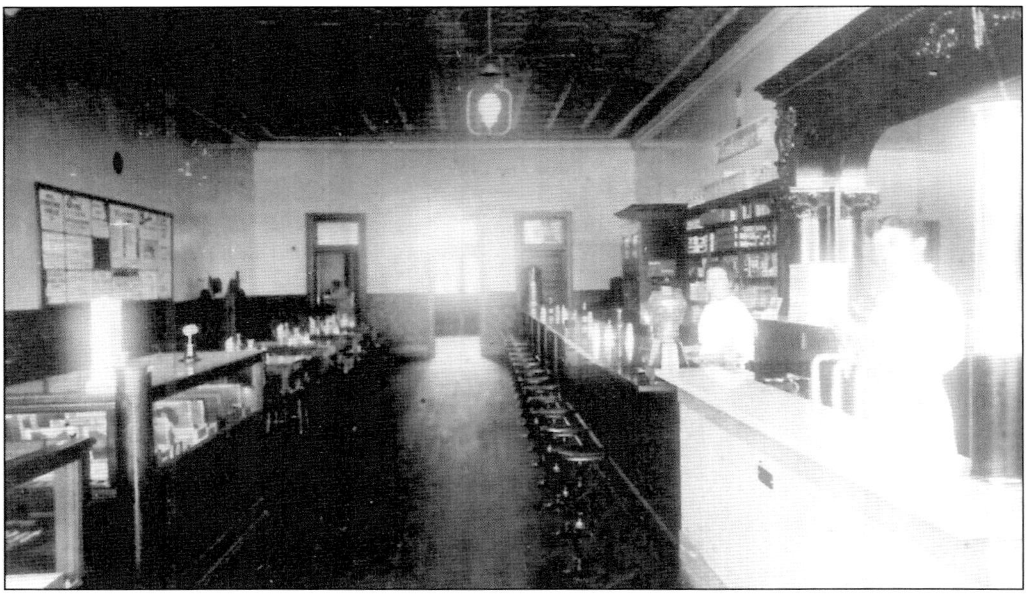

Otto and Anna Tiedtke moved into town from their farmstead in 1914. Prohibition closed their saloon, so they changed their venue to a café in 1915. A soda fountain is in the foreground, with a lunch counter and stools to the back. Tables and chairs are on the left in the rear. Otto became a rural mail carrier in 1921 until 1946. They had 12 children. (Courtesy of Marian Klima.)

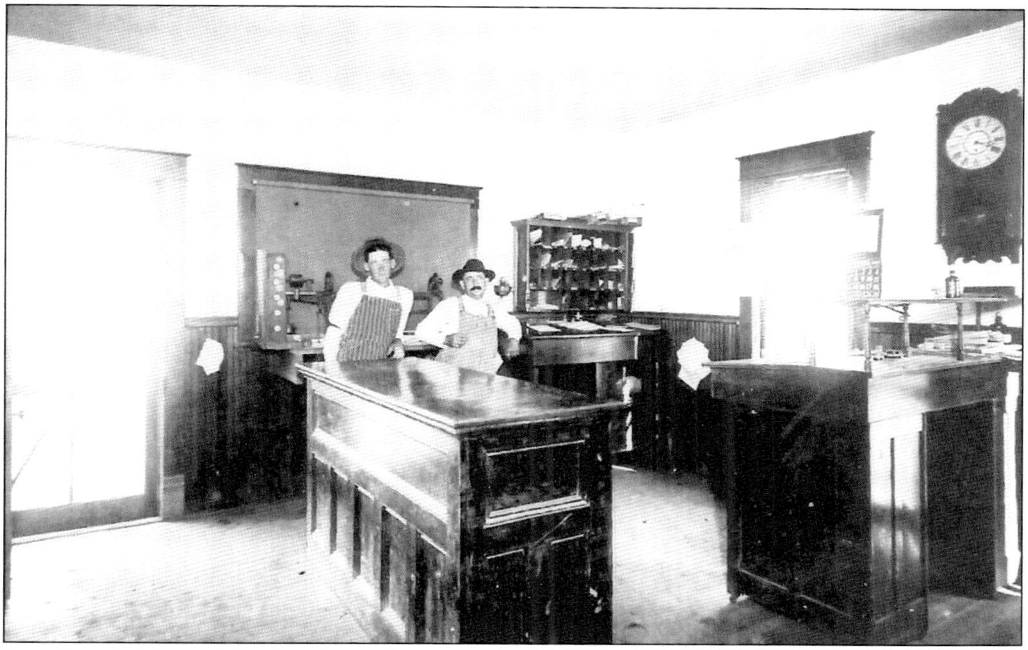

Paul Pestel, left, and his brother-in-law August Grabencamp stand behind the counter in the Munger and Company office. Munger and Company sold grain, lumber, and coal in Pilger. William Munger is noted as a retired lumber dealer in 1899. (Courtesy of Marian Klima.)

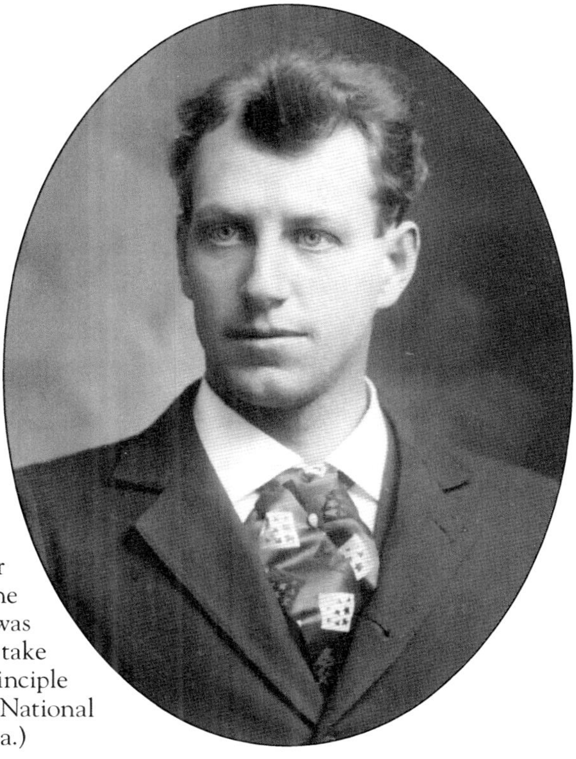

Dr. Walter Key was a physician and surgeon in Pilger in 1894. He had an office on the second floor of the Berger "Brick Store." On January 3, 1903, the young doctor died, and Dr. John D. Reid was implored by two Pilger businessmen to take over Dr. Key's practice. Dr. Key was the principle founder and the first president of Farmers National Bank in Pilger. (Courtesy of Marian Klima.)

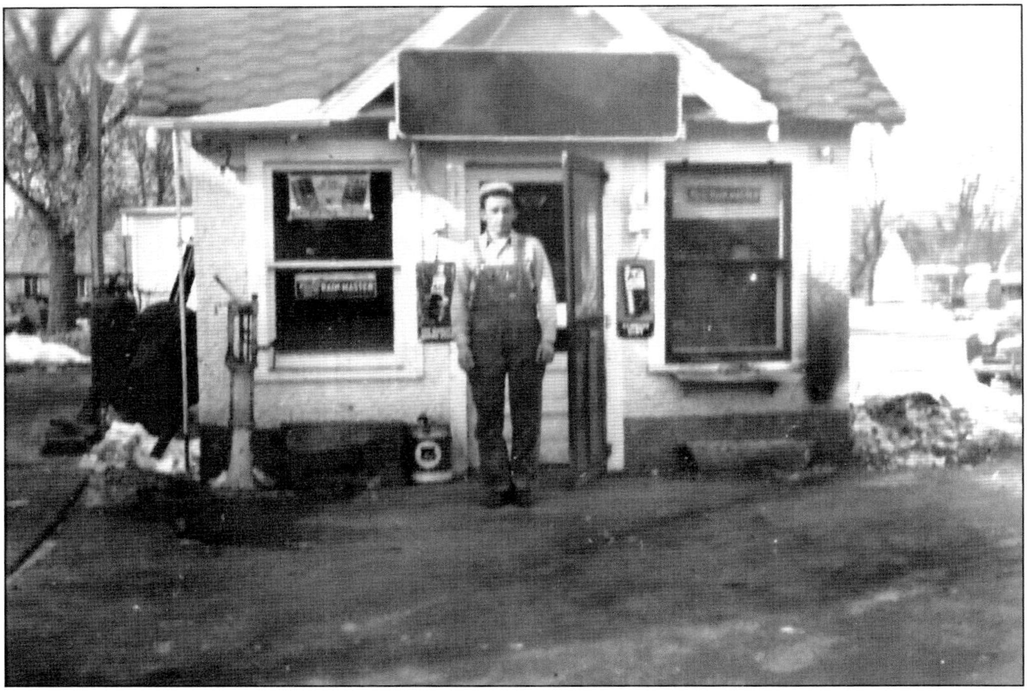

Joseph Klima stands by the front door of the Derby gas station in Pilger. The station was formerly owned by George Kennedy prior to this photograph in 1948. (Courtesy of Marian Klima.)

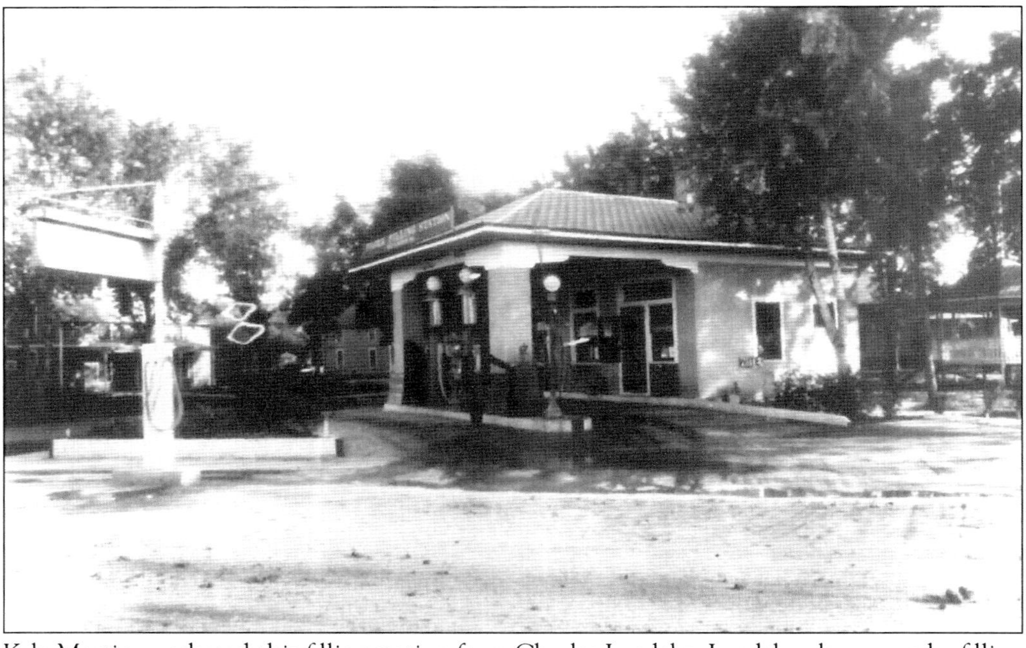

Kyle Martin purchased this filling station from Charles Luedeke. Luedeke also opened a filling station in Stanton in 1921. The marquee on the front above the pumps has the name Pilger Filling Station. The gazebo bandstand, on the right side behind the station, was used for weekly band concerts. (Courtesy of Marian Klima.)

Milton Viersen had a slaughterhouse and handled up to 10 hogs a day. An avid hunter, he would go out on horseback with his hunting dog. All the prairie chickens and grouse he cleaned, packed in barrels, and sent to Chicago. The Viersens are, from left to right, (first row) Lowell Viersen and Obeler Peter Viersen; (second row) Ed Viersen and Milton Viersen. (Courtesy of Marian Klima.)

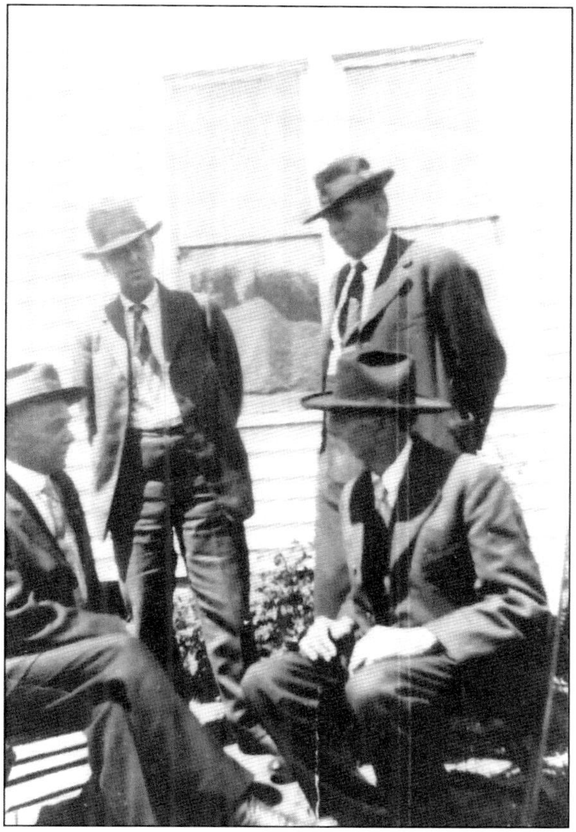

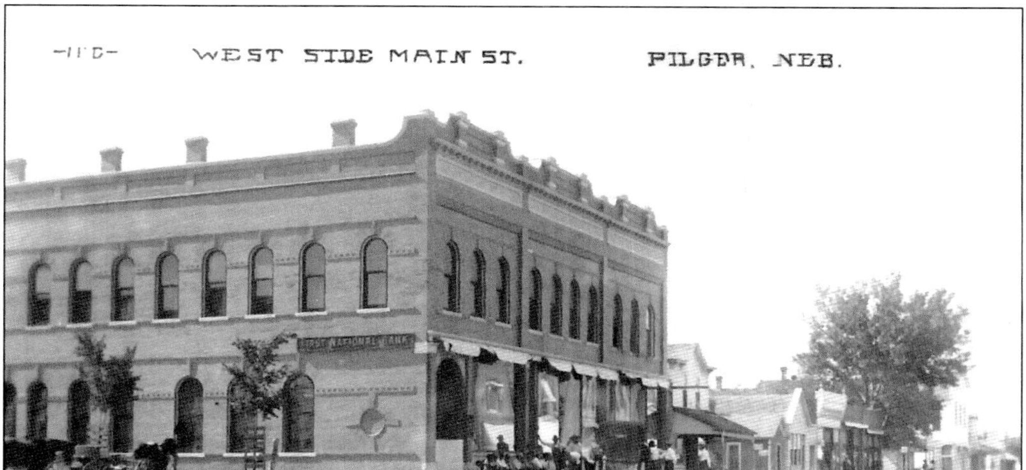

The newly constructed two-story brick First National Bank building prominently stands first in the block on the west side of Pilger's main street looking north. The opera house is several buildings to the north with the tall white facade on the front. This image is from around the early 1900s. (Courtesy of Marian Klima.)

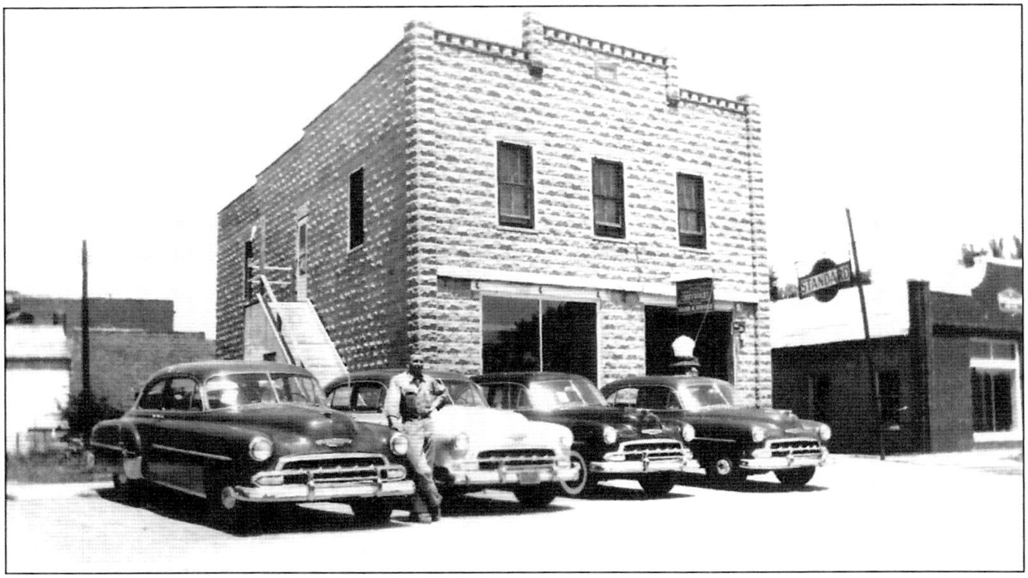

Dave O'Brien went into the garage business in 1922 with his brother William O'Brien and Chris L. Miller. In 1931, it became known as the Miller and O'Brien Company. In 1946, Dave became the sole owner, and it was called the O'Brien Garage. Lester Anderson, seen in this photograph, assisted the O'Briens in the business. The sign says "Chevrolet Sales and Service." Lloyd Bennish built the building. (Courtesy of Marian Klima.)

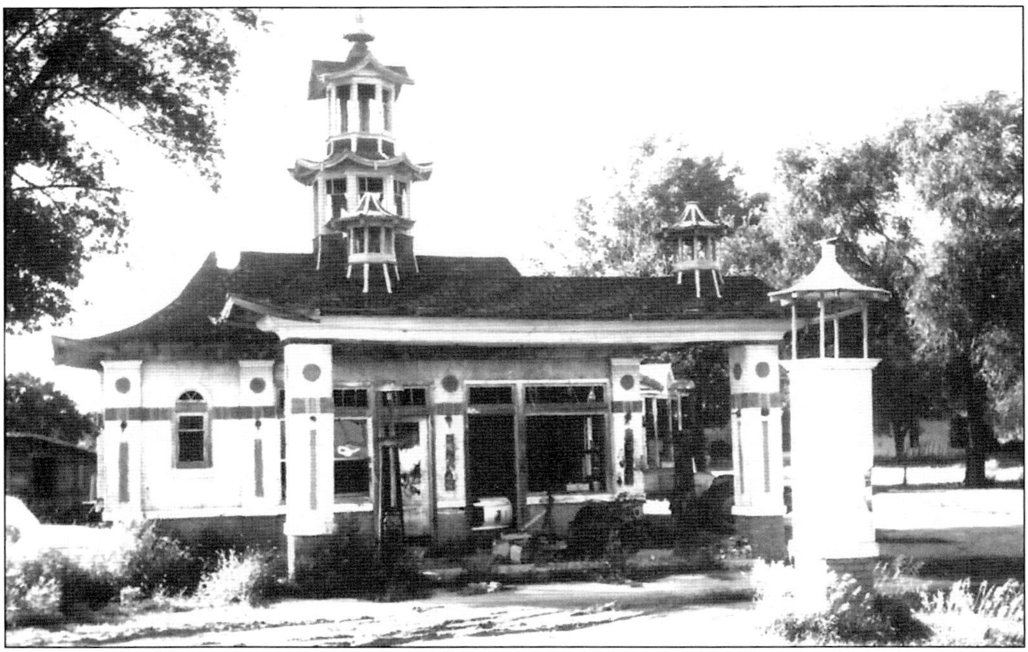

A Chinese pagoda design of architecture was used to build a filling station, in the late 1920s, by Joe Rogers for Kyle Martin of Pilger. It stood on the west side of Highway 15 south of Pilger. It was a well-known and well-remembered landmark in the area. The station no longer exists for people to see and appreciate its contours. (Courtesy of Marian Klima.)

An early automobile is parked in front of Dave O'Brien's garage. The banner placed on the back of the automobile declares it to be "the Nash six." The owner, or year, of this model and automobile is not indicated and the date was not available. (Courtesy of Marian Klima.)

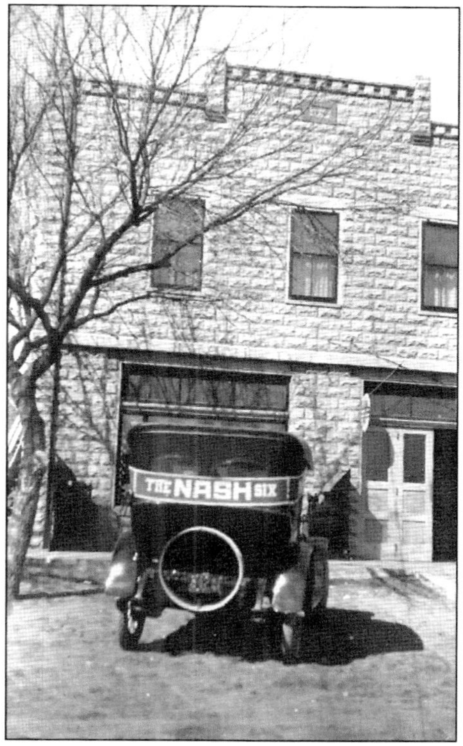

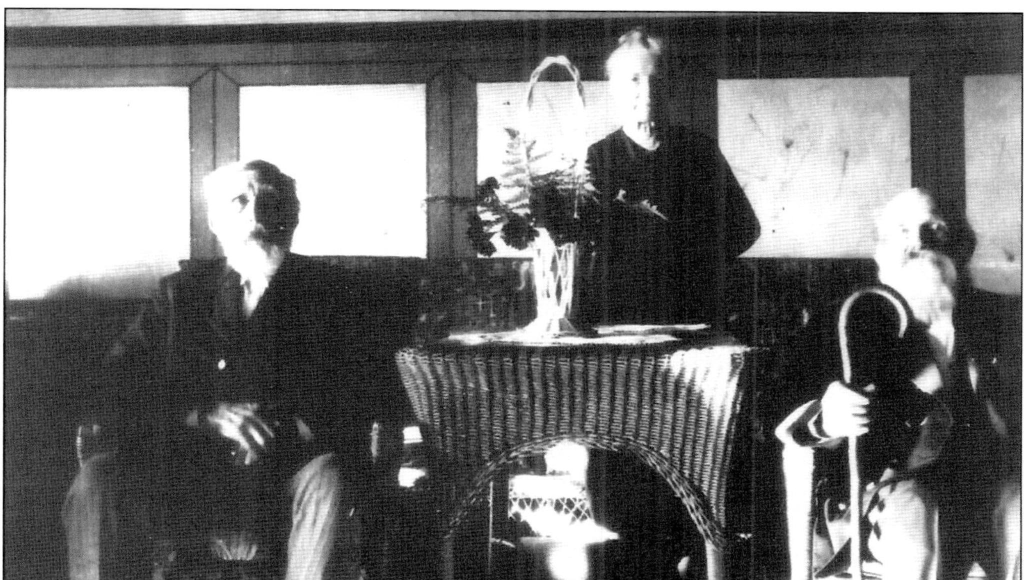

These three pioneers and early settlers in Pilger have names well known in the area. From left to right are John Matheson, who owned and operated the Matheson Implement dealership in 1887 and bought the first schoolhouse to use as his business place; Augusta Sharp, wife of Charles Finney Sharp, the first homesteader in 1865; and Don Matheson, owner of the Matheson Hotel. (Courtesy of Marian Klima.)

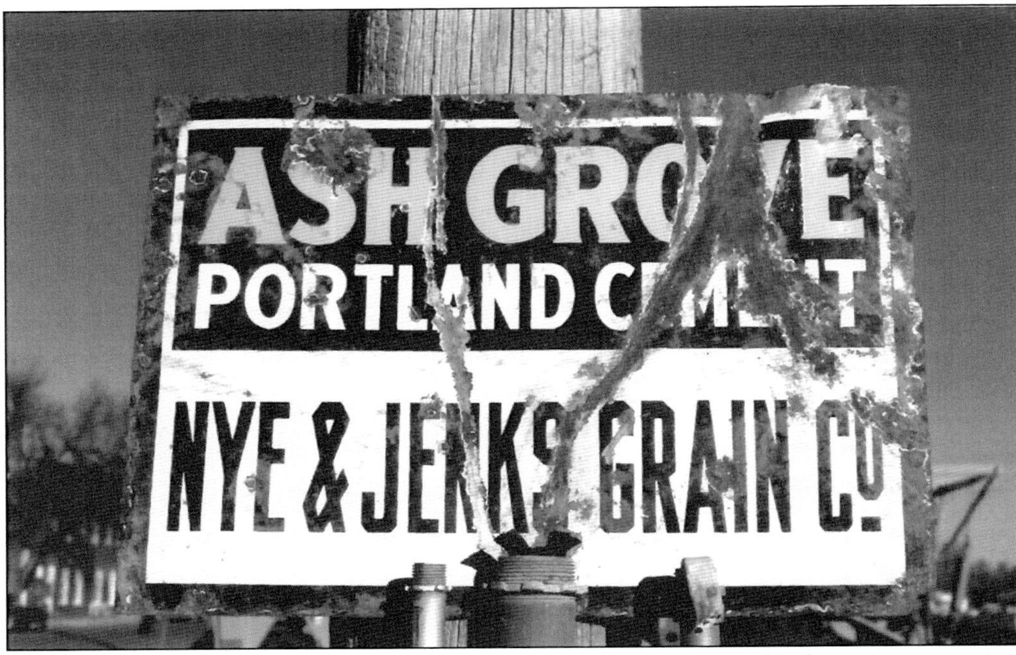

The Nye-Jenks elevator sign was found while digging a utilities trench for the new construction at the Farmers Co-op Storage and Shop buildings. Nye and Jenks were names of the former owners of the east elevator and lumberyard. This sign was unearthed in 1988. (Courtesy of Marian Klima.)

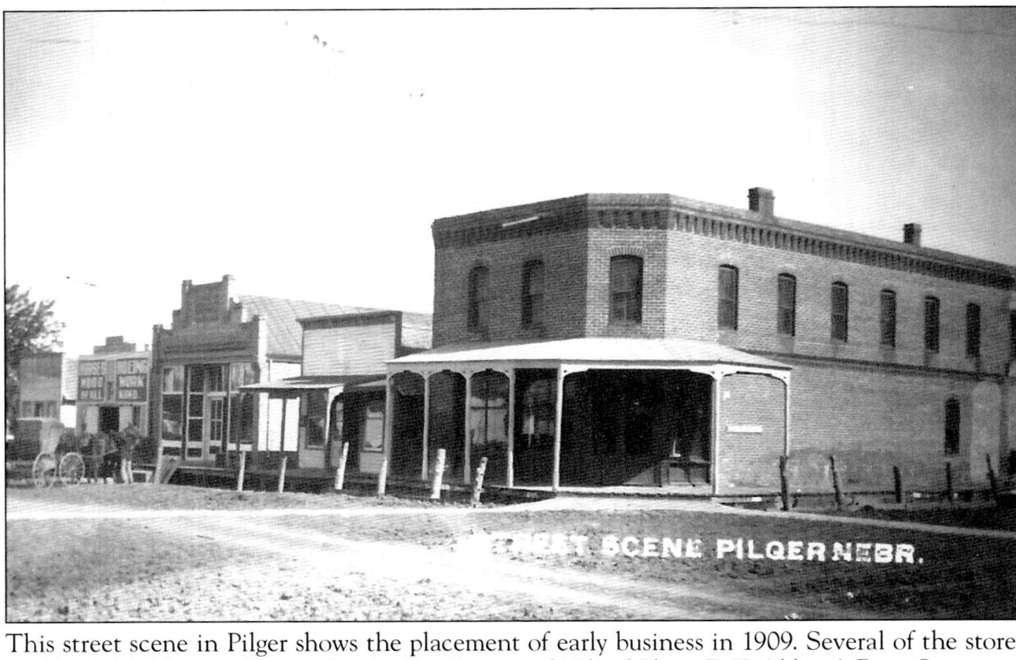

This street scene in Pilger shows the placement of early business in 1909. Several of the stores are Randall's Harness Shop, Theo Olk's Wagon and Wheel Shop, E. Y. Abbott's Drug Store, and the large store on the corner, known as the "Brick Store," was built by Fred Berger in 1892. After a fire in 1908, this was the new replacement. (Courtesy of Marian Klima.)

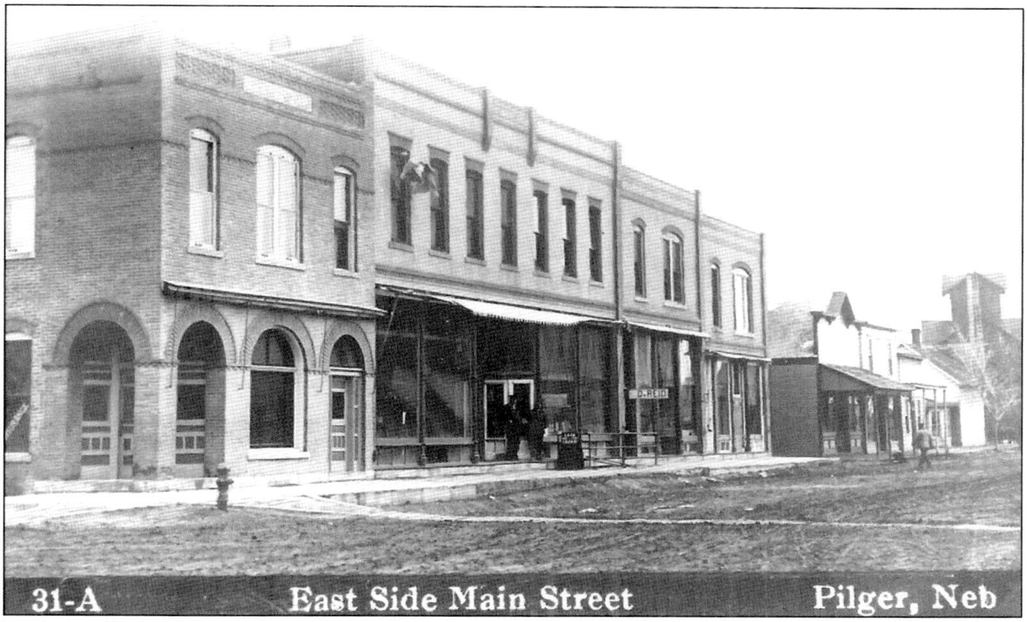

Dr. John D. Reid came to Pilger in 1903, following the death of Dr. Walter Key, and made his office in the second floor of the building on the east side of the main street. The sign on the curb in front of two gentlemen says, "Cash for your Cream," and the 1909 photograph shows a wooden elevator that stands to the far right. (Courtesy of Marian Klima.)

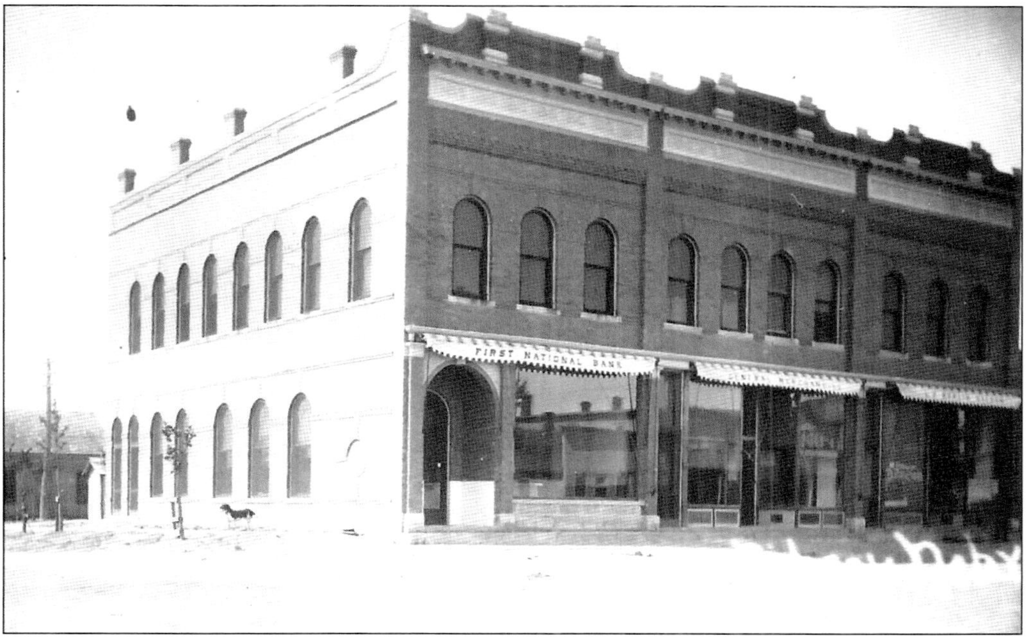

The First National Bank closed its doors in 1914, and the Pilger State Bank was established in the building seen on the left. Karel's General Merchandise store is in the middle, and the Olk Hardware building is in the right portion of the brick buildings. This scene may have been photographed in the 1920s. (Courtesy of Marian Klima.)

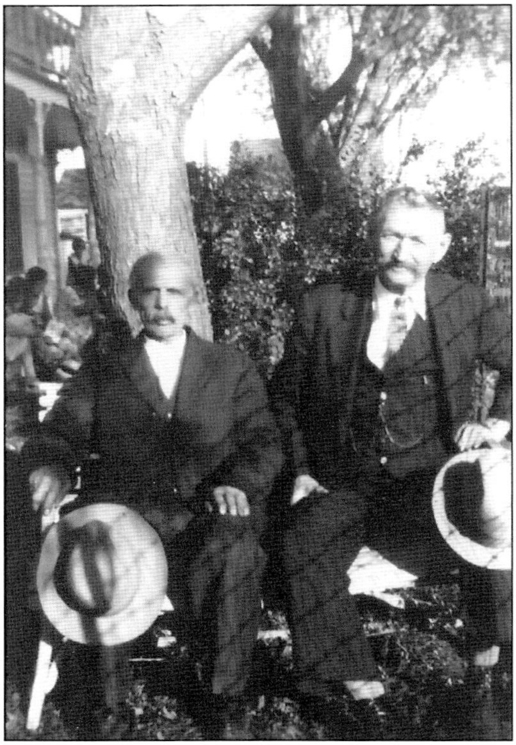

Jacob Olk is pictured on the left with an unidentified gentleman in 1858. He arrived, emigrating from Germany, at Pilger in the 1880s and started the Pioneer Blacksmith and Repair Shop. His brother, Theodore Olk, followed from Germany and operated an implement shop in Pilger. A son, Otto Olk, purchased a building and hardware stock from Henry W. Asch in 1923. (Courtesy of Marian Klima.)

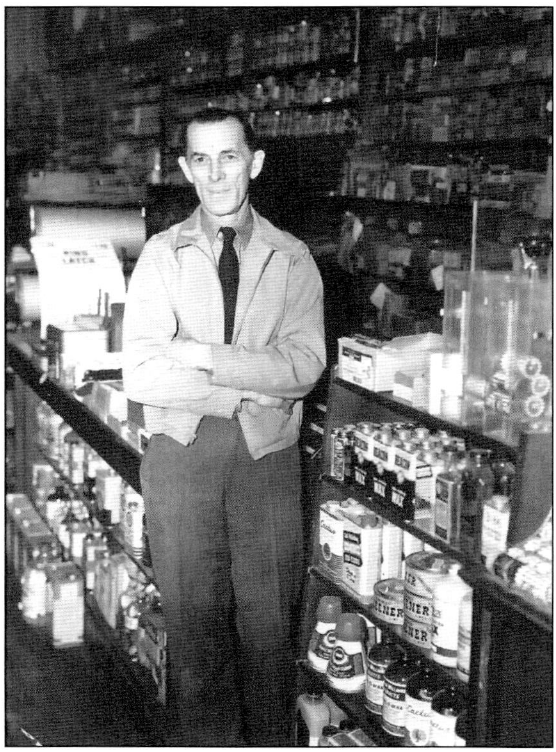

Otto, son of pioneer Jacob, stands in the Olk Hardware store in Pilger. He and his wife, Ceil, operated the hardware store for 50 years, from 1923 to 1973. They had their living quarters above the store during that time. The business expanded to include an appliance store constructed a few doors to the north in 1947. (Courtesy of Marian Klima.)

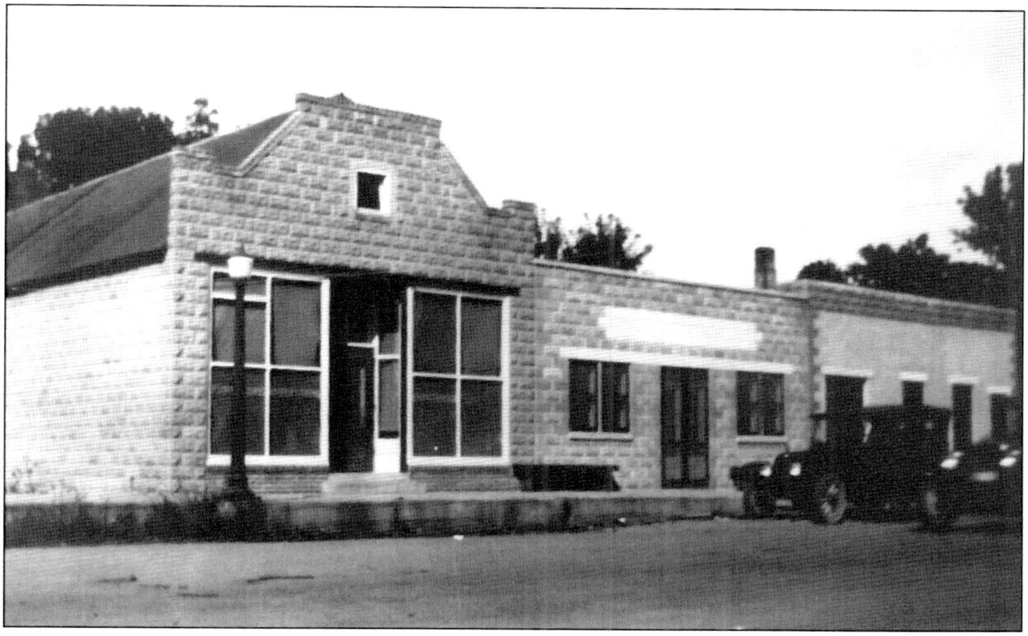

Carl Axen arrived in Pilger in 1900 to start a hardware and furniture enterprise. He built the first cement block building to house his furniture business, after divesting of the hardware line. Carl and William Tapken partnered in a creamery venture in 1927 and built the second block building then produced Cornhusker Brand sweet butter. Dr. Hansen had a dentistry office on the far right. (Courtesy of Marian Klima.)

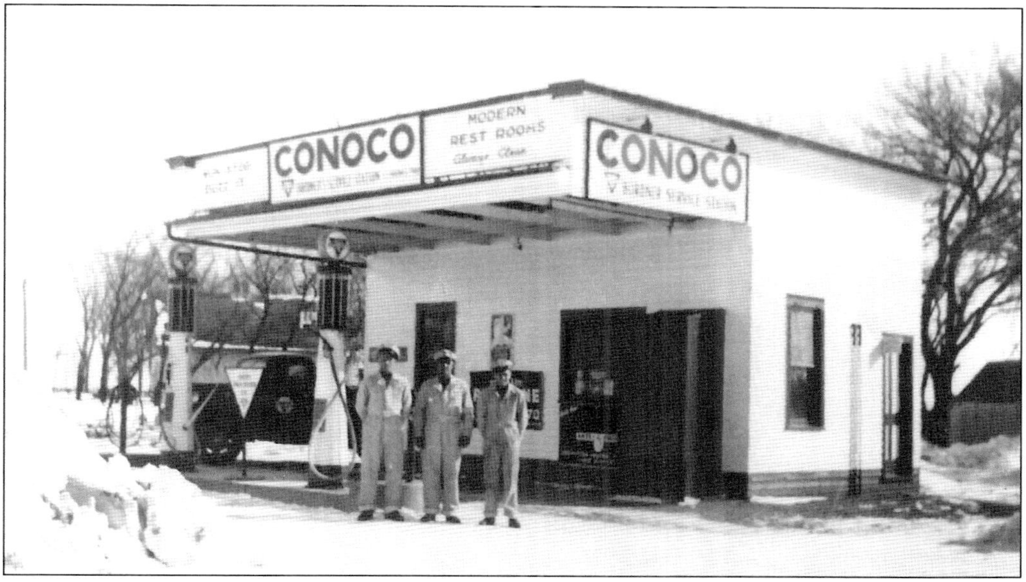

Leland Bordner Sr. opened Bordie's Service Station at the intersection of Highways 15 and 275, north of Pilger. From 1935, he and his son, Leland Jr., ran the station until 1950. The gentlemen in the photograph from left to right are Ray Armbrust, Leland Bordner Jr., and Leland "Bordie" Bordner Sr. The name was changed to the Corner Service Station later. (Courtesy of Marian Klima.)

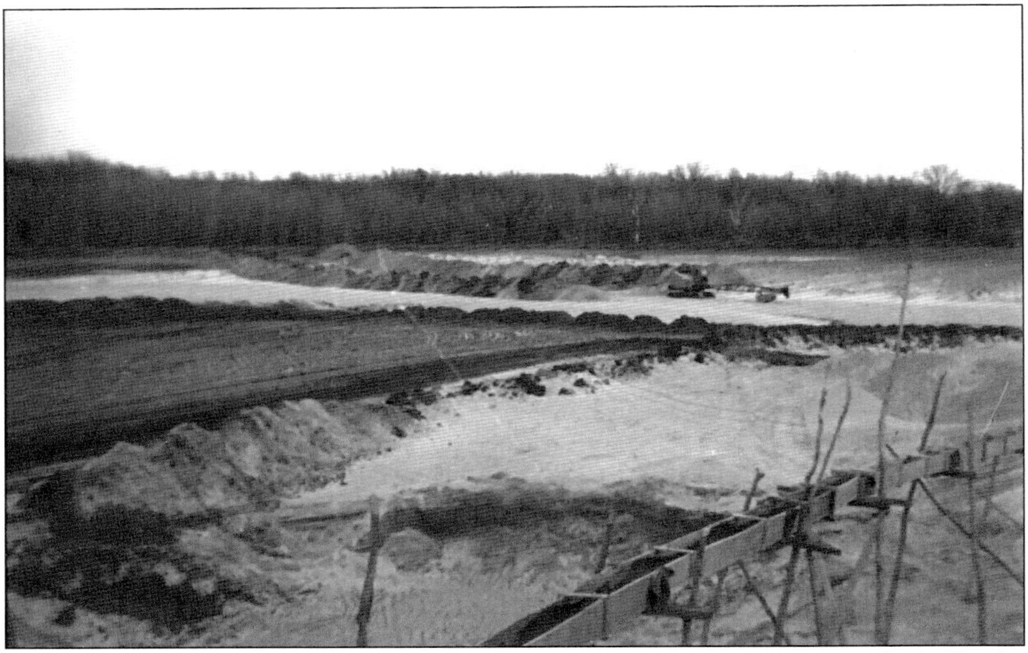

Harold O'Brien located the H. A. O'Brien Sand and Gravel Pit business one and a half miles south of Pilger on the east side of Highway 15 and began pumping in 1951. The pit was in full operation until December 1966. The trough in the foreground carried waste sand from the screening sieves. The business operated year-round, with three to eight employees. In the photograph below, Laverne Raabe loads gravel with a loader built from a truck chassis. The lake was stocked by Nebraska Game and Parks for fishing. A sandy beach provided a place for picnics and sunbathing. Many boats used the lake for recreational and fishing activities. (Courtesy of Marian Klima.)

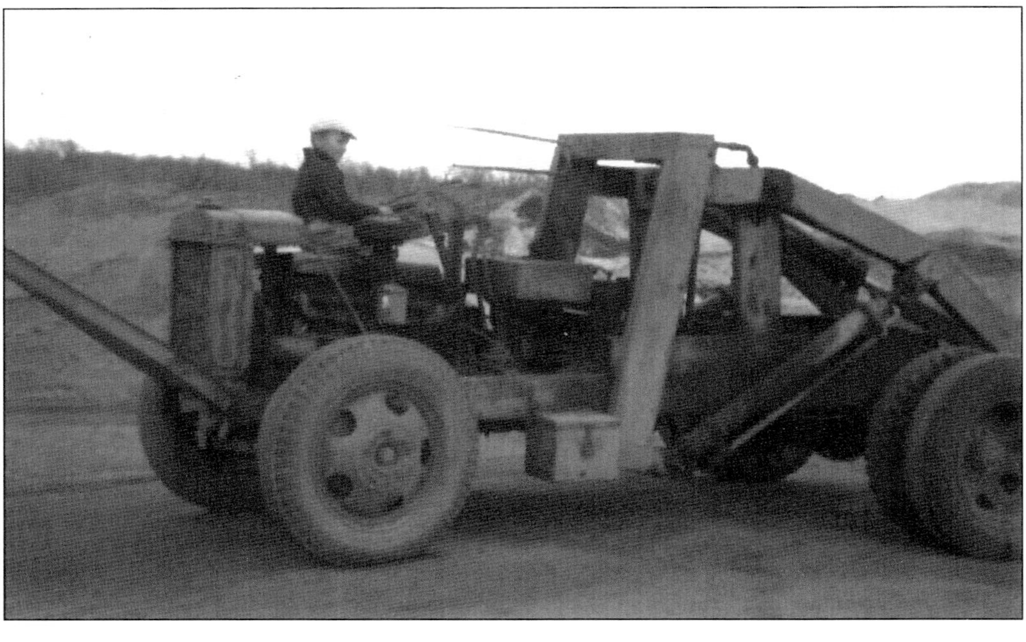

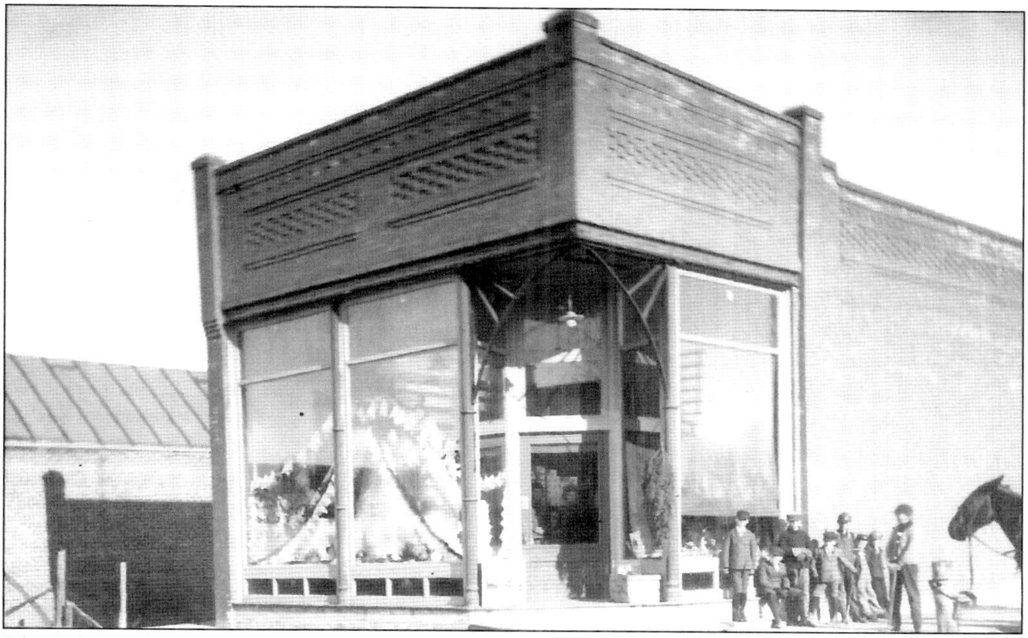

The Pilger Mercantile Store was sold to Adam Pilger in 1896. After a fire in 1908, the building was rebuilt and looked like this. It remained so for 100 years. His sons Albert and Louis Pilger both entered the grocery business. Albert ran the Pilger store until his nephews Russell and Robert Miller took the business over in 1948. The store closed its doors with an auction in 1991. (Courtesy of Marian Klima.)

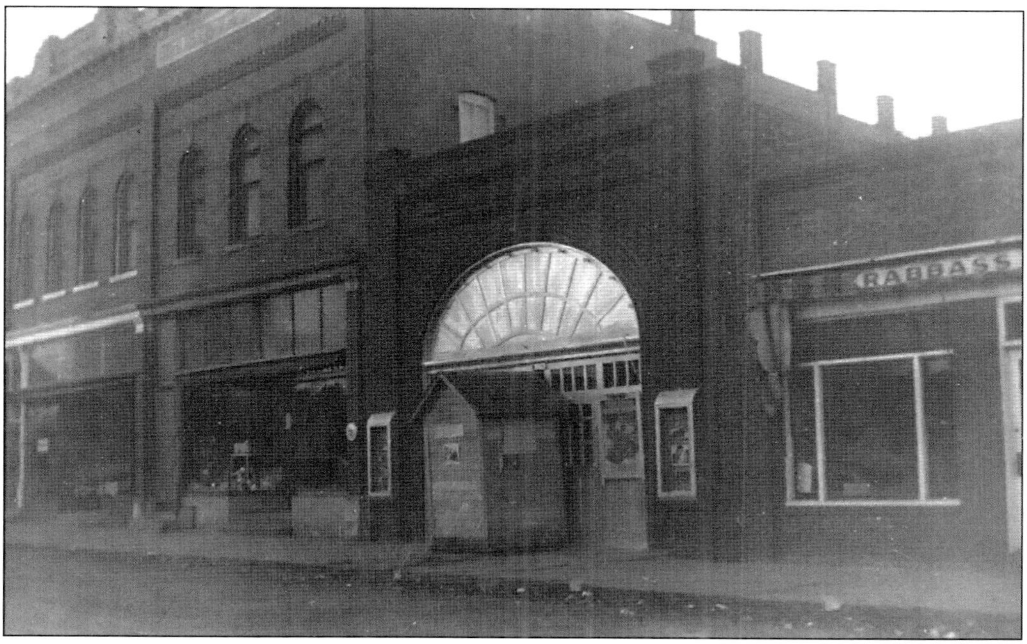

Pilger celebrated its Diamond Jubilee in 1962 with fun and fanfare. This photograph was taken at that time of the Harvey Rabbass Grocery Store. The theater next door was advertising a "Ma and Pa Kettle" show. Wendy Hill was the owner operator of the theater. (Courtesy of Marian Klima.)

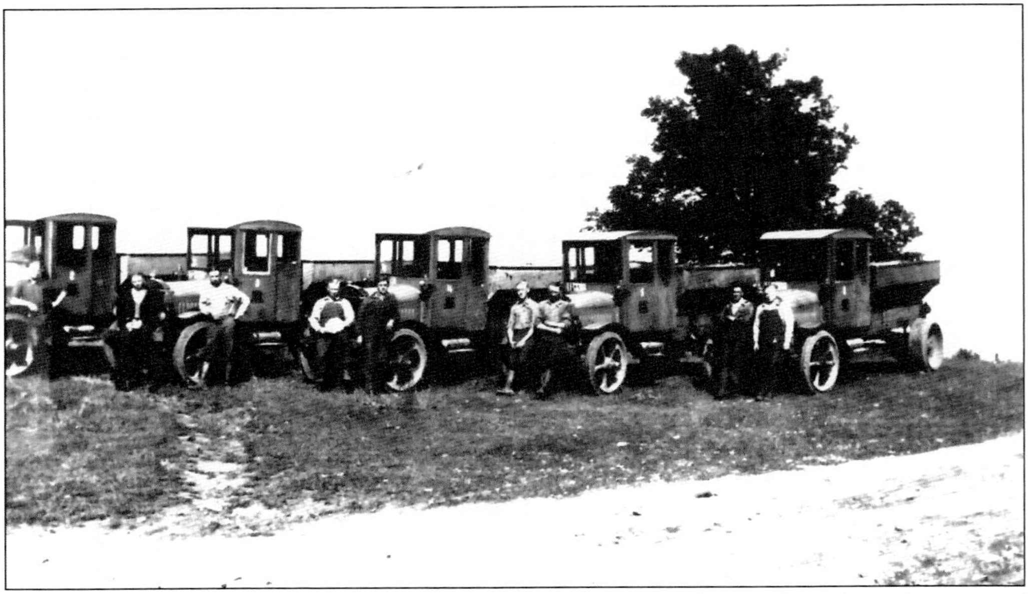

John M. Einung started a sand and gravel company in 1928 at the Gus Lueschen place east of Pilger. This is his fleet of gravel trucks, with solid rubber wheels, at one of his five gravel pit enterprises. The Luverne trucks were manufactured in Luverne, Minnesota. He started a block plant in the 1930s, using sand and gravel from the Pilger pit. He sold it to Husker Concrete Company. (Courtesy of Marian Klima.)

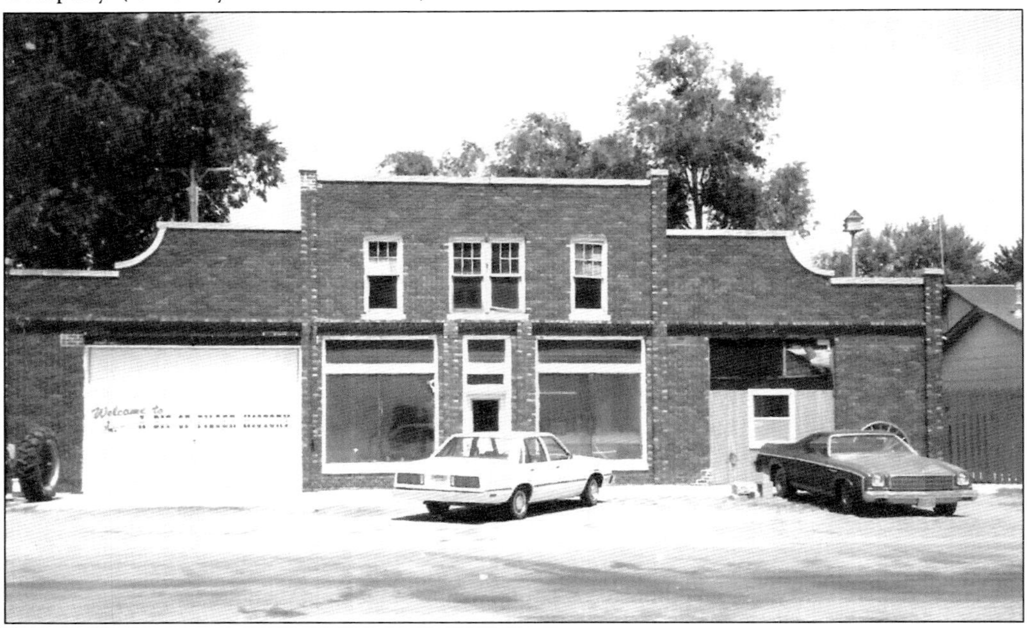

After returning from army service in 1953, Lige Klima Jr. set up L&K Repair Shop for farm implement and tractor repair in the Matheson building. In 1982, the business moved to the former George Rasmussen Ford Garage, built in 1919 on the site of one of Pilger's livery barns. He married Marian Marlatt in 1951. His lifelong collection of postcards is shared in this book. (Courtesy of Marian Klima.)

Six

Woodland Park Development 1964

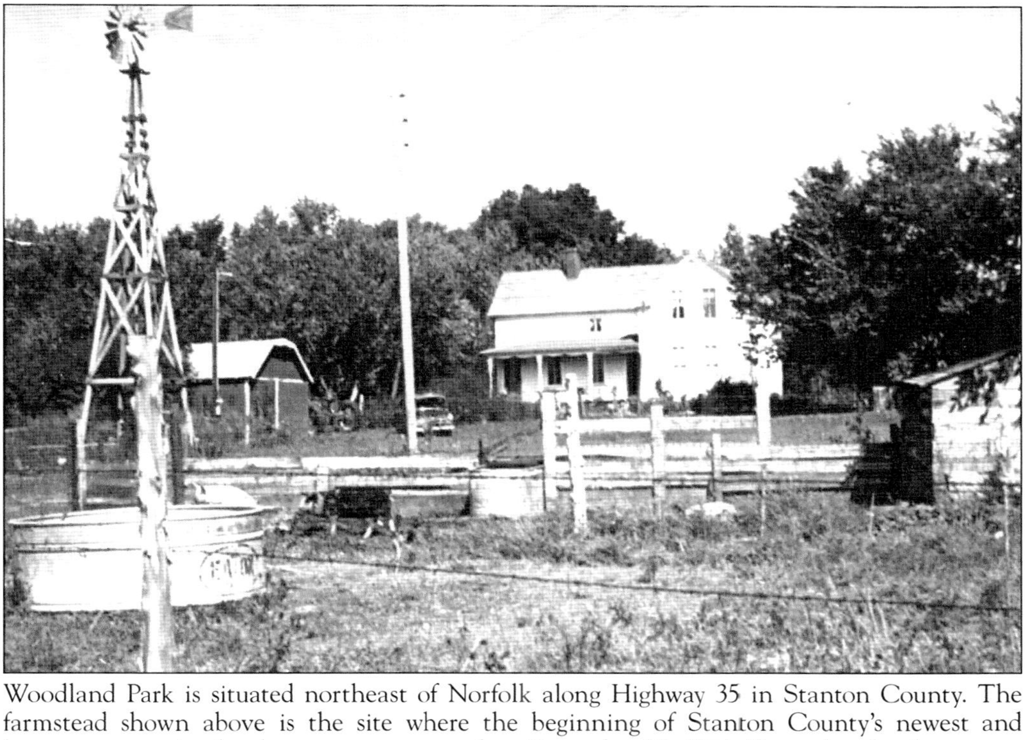

Woodland Park is situated northeast of Norfolk along Highway 35 in Stanton County. The farmstead shown above is the site where the beginning of Stanton County's newest and largest community development commenced on December 10, 1964. Since that first house was constructed, there have been more than 425 homes built, and the Woodland Park population has ballooned to more than 1,950 residents. Woodland Park is a sanitary improvement district and is not incorporated as a municipality. (Courtesy of Roland Jensen.)

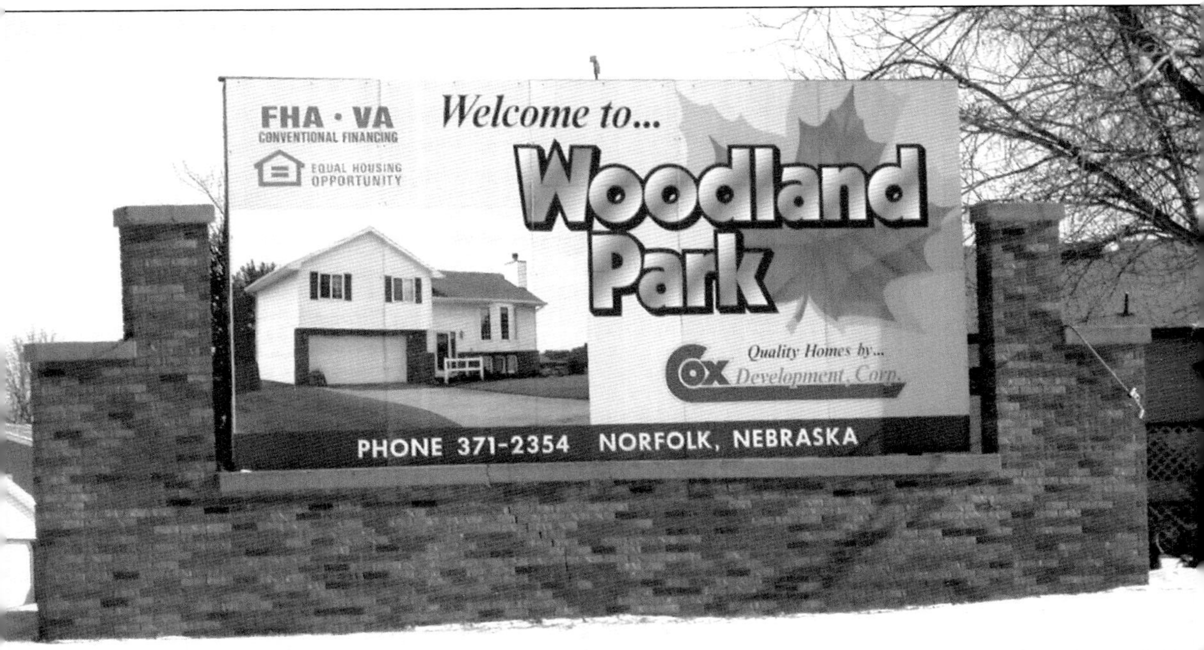

The original entrance sign to Woodland Park welcomes visitors and residents. It gives the phone number for the developer, Cox Development Corporation, which maintains an office in a commercial building located in the development. Cox Development Corporation is looking forward to further expansion in both homes and businesses in the community. The nearby city of Norfolk, with many industries, businesses, a two-year college, and job opportunities is a draw for those looking for a home that would be close to their education and employment. The school is attractive and well updated for families with children, and the community is small enough to be close knit and friendly. (Courtesy of Roland Jensen.)

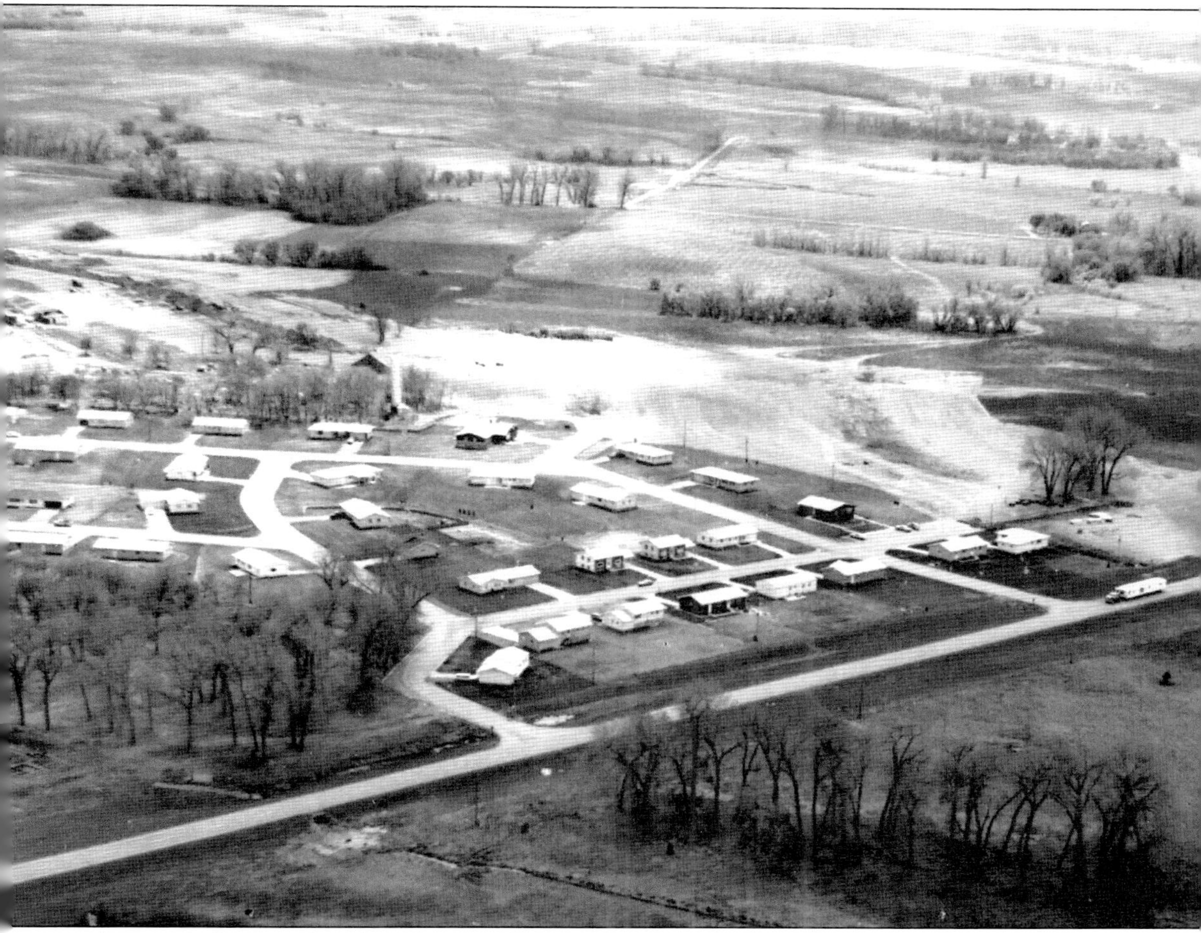

An aerial photograph, taken in 1968, shows 50 homes that were already established in the new development. The truck is traveling Highway 35 past the entrance of Woodland Park. By 1975, there were about 100 homes built in the complex, and the additions concentrated mainly in the lighter shaded area seen to the upper center and right on the photograph. This community had been well planned, and the expansion invited more commercial interests to build close by and in the future. The nearby access to a highway helped bring more commuters to build here or to buy established homes. The Cox Development Corporation had a vision for the community to be progressive and continues to work toward its betterment for all the residents. (Courtesy of Roland Jensen.)

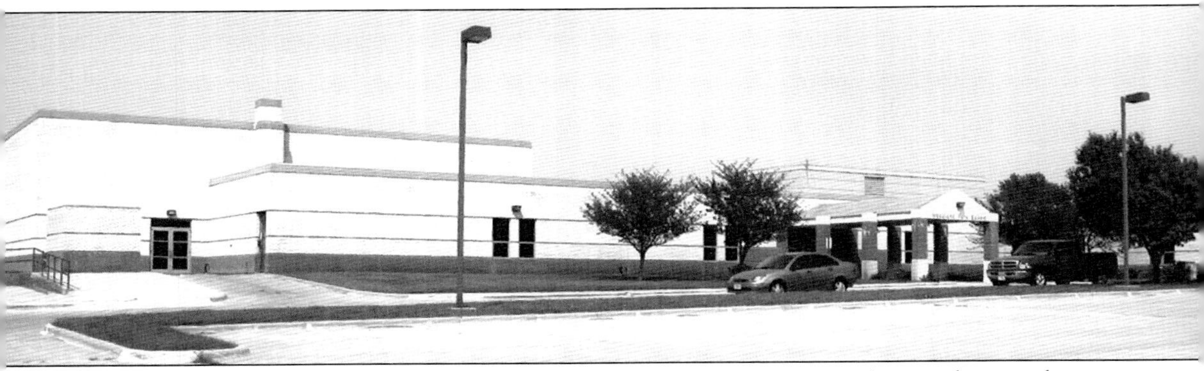

Woodland Park Elementary School contains a double-track system, with two classes splitting each grade level, from kindergarten through the sixth grade. The first year that the school opened, in 1989, the enrollment was near 250 students with many more attending from the community since. It has a gymnasium, library, computer lab, and offices in addition to the regular classrooms. There are separate classrooms in the facility for art and music instruction, a special education room, and storage. It was designed for a capacity of 350 students. The original cost of the building was $1.9 million with extensive renovation for security and additional room completed in the recent years. (Courtesy of Roland Jensen.)

Seven

Agriculture and Progress 1865

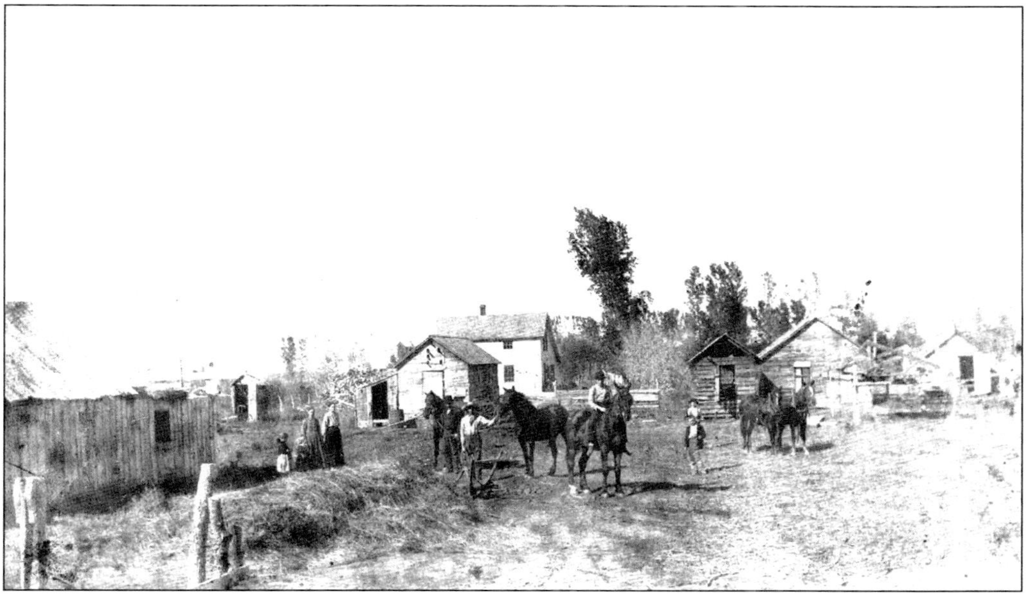

Stanton County is a rural agricultural community and has been since the first settlers came to stake their claims for homesteads. They planted gardens of potatoes, corn, and beans. Chickens, ducks, and geese were raised for eggs and earned small amounts of cash if sold. Planting crops was done by sowing the seed by hand after breaking the sod with a walking plow and horses. This is the Herman Wagner farm around 1900. (Courtesy of Richard Kuehn.)

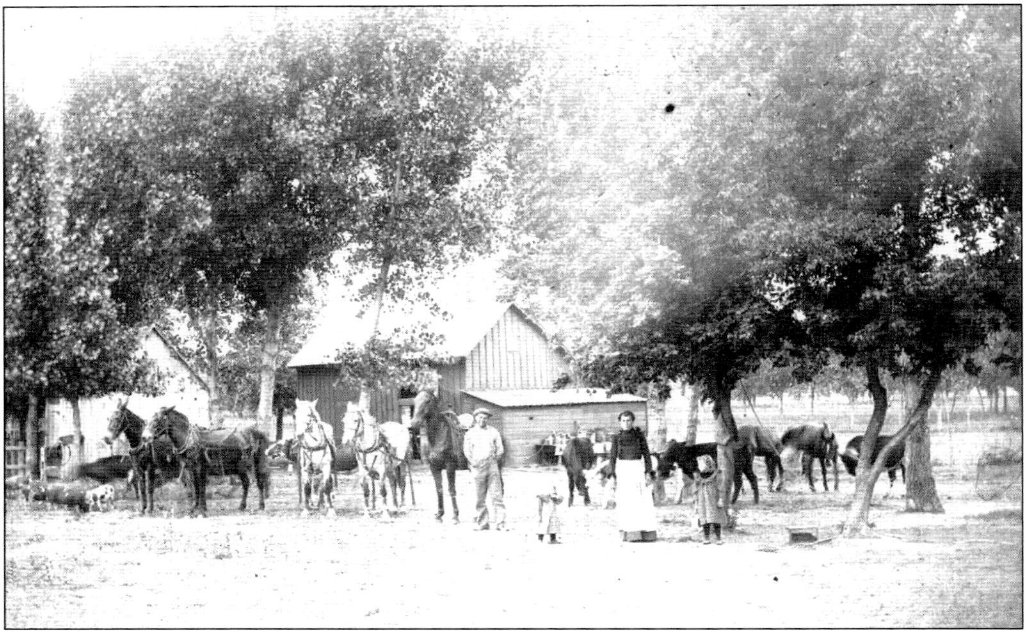

Another photograph shows the progress of the Herman Wagner family farmstead. This photograph was taken at a later date and is a good picture of working horse teams in harnesses, a saddled riding horse, cows and calves, colts, and the pet dog. (Courtesy of Richard Kuehn.)

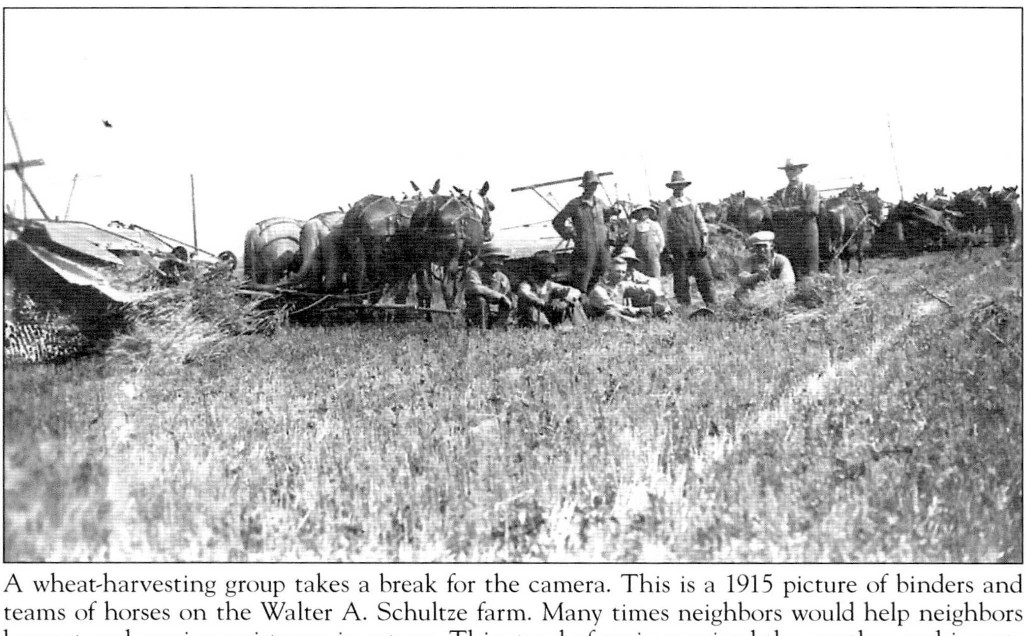

A wheat-harvesting group takes a break for the camera. This is a 1915 picture of binders and teams of horses on the Walter A. Schultze farm. Many times neighbors would help neighbors harvest and receive assistance in return. This stand of grain survived the weather and insects until harvest. (Courtesy of Milford and Gloria Koch.)

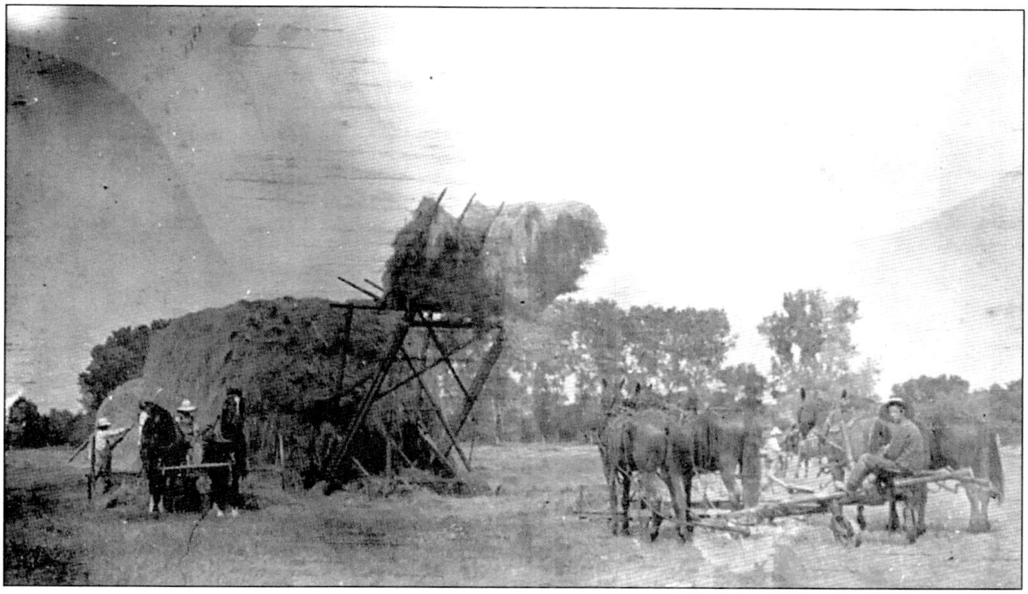

This is a hay day at the farm with horses and crews about 1916. Walter A. Schultze is in the back on the stack to the left, and Pat is running the sweep on the right side. The hay was spread evenly by hand and pitchforked over the top of the stack. The other two men are not identified. (Courtesy of Milford and Gloria Koch.)

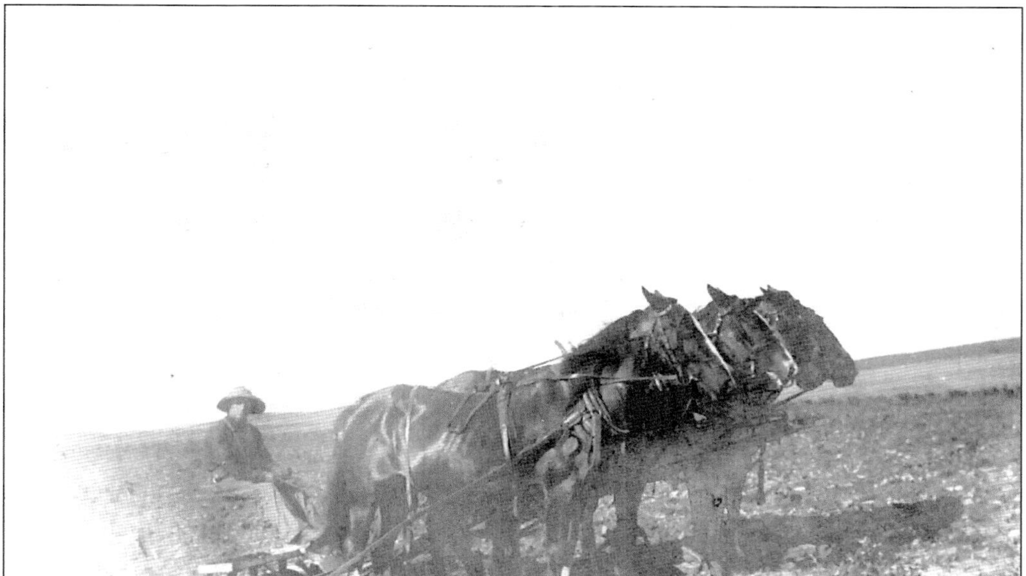

Clarence Anderson does his fieldwork with a three-horse team. This photograph, although somewhat faded, shows how early farmers would break up clods and stubble with disks. It was slow, hard work for both man and the horses. The harder the task, the more horsepower that was needed to do the job. (Courtesy of Art Catlin.)

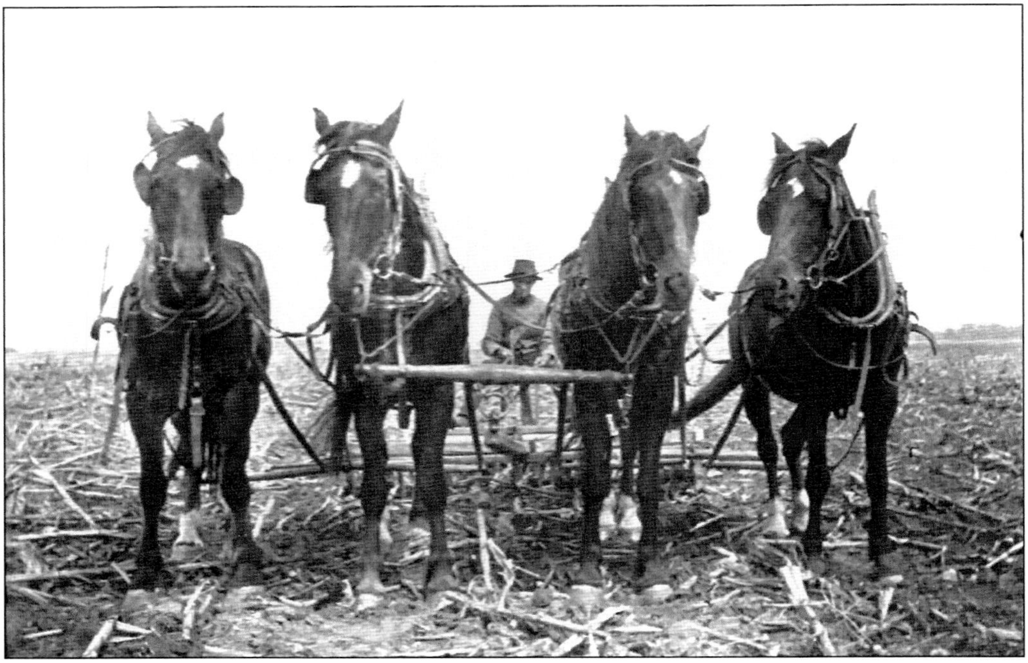

This time the fieldwork required four horses to pull the equipment and the man holding the reins. The horses had to be well trained to work together for the fieldwork. This farmer is seen preparing the field for the next crop. (Courtesy of Art Catlin.)

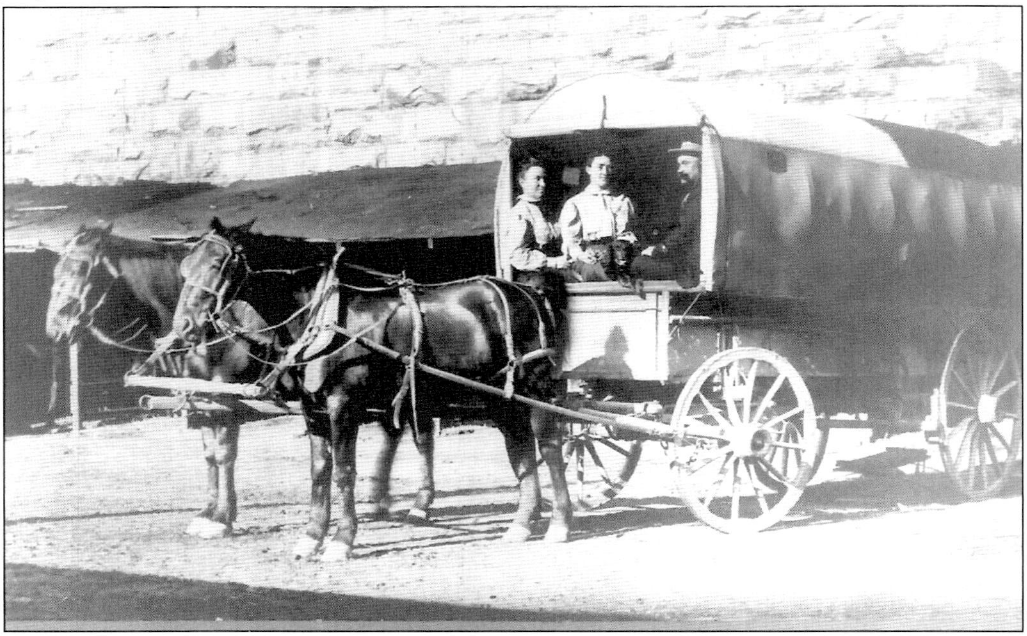

Some of the early settlers decided not to put down their roots in Stanton County. Anson Bennett and his family stayed only a short time on the Bordner farm, before deciding that the greener pastures were further west. They pulled up stakes, packed their wagon, and headed for Idaho. (Courtesy of Marian Klima.)

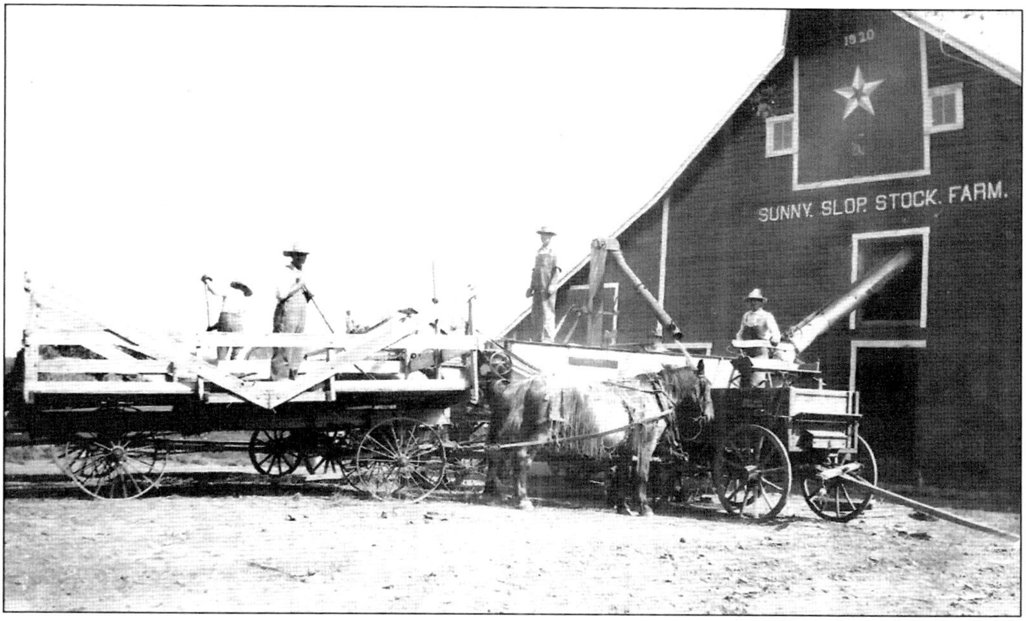

Barns were as important on the farm as a house and were usually built much bigger. Here four men are unloading hay racks and sending the hay up into the haymow on the Herman Ritze farm, five miles northwest of Pilger. This photograph was taken in 1918; later the barn was destroyed by a tornado. The name painted on the barn is the Sunny Slop Stock Farm. The names of the men who are operating the Woods Brothers thresher are unknown. (Courtesy of Marian Klima.)

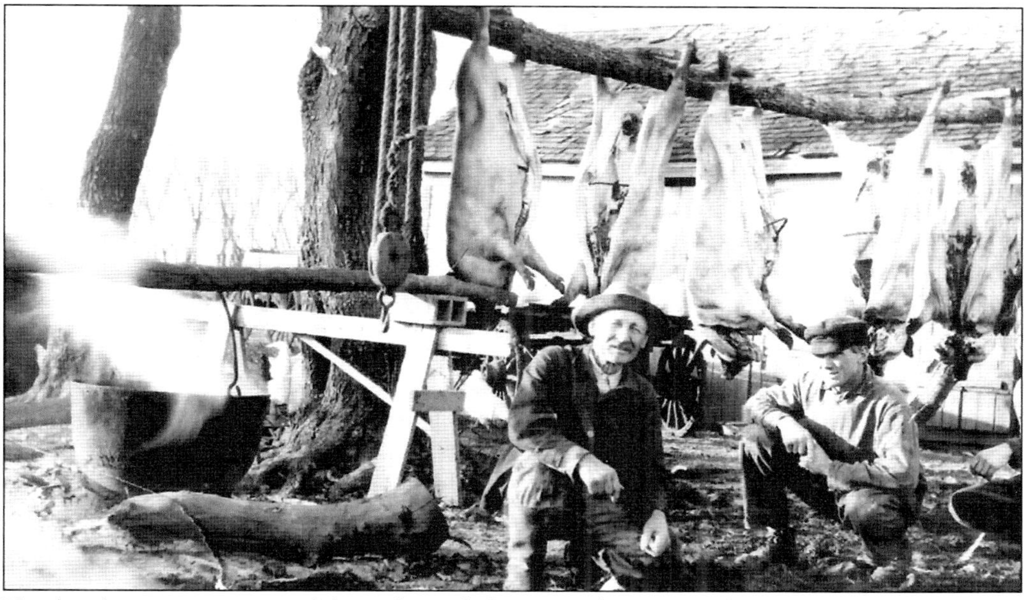

Hog butchering is just one of the tasks to do between plantings and harvesting. Here are, from left to right, Otto Koehler Sr., Charles Roe, and Grover Koehler, who have killed and gutted the hogs. The hog-scalding kettle is boiling hot and is used to help remove hair from the hide. The metal bars are braced to hold the carcass open to cool. (Courtesy of Marian Klima.)

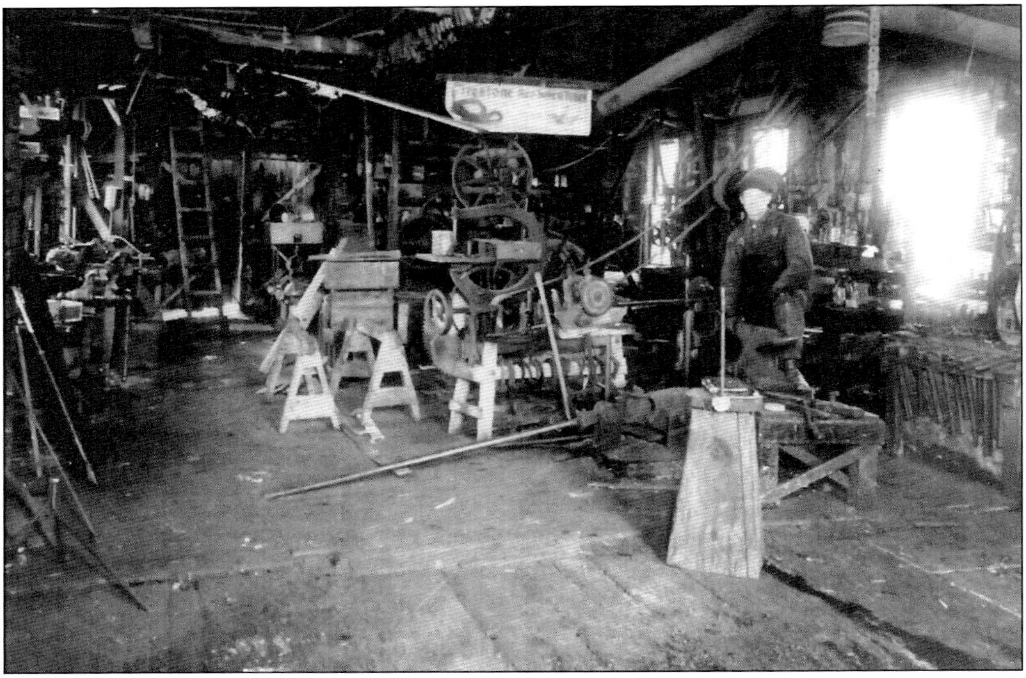

A blacksmith shop was needed for repairs of equipment. George Theis had one of the early blacksmith shops in Pilger. The building housing his shop was the original Pilger District No. 1 schoolhouse, which had been replaced and the building sold to J. G. Matheson for a sum of $105 in 1890. (Courtesy of Marian Klima.)

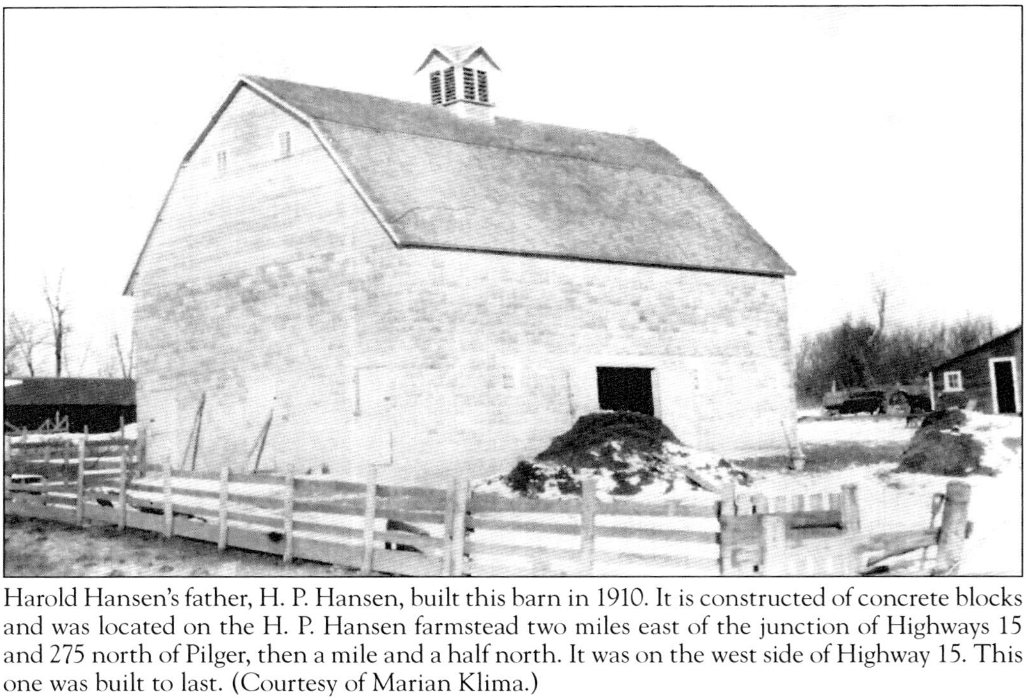

Harold Hansen's father, H. P. Hansen, built this barn in 1910. It is constructed of concrete blocks and was located on the H. P. Hansen farmstead two miles east of the junction of Highways 15 and 275 north of Pilger, then a mile and a half north. It was on the west side of Highway 15. This one was built to last. (Courtesy of Marian Klima.)

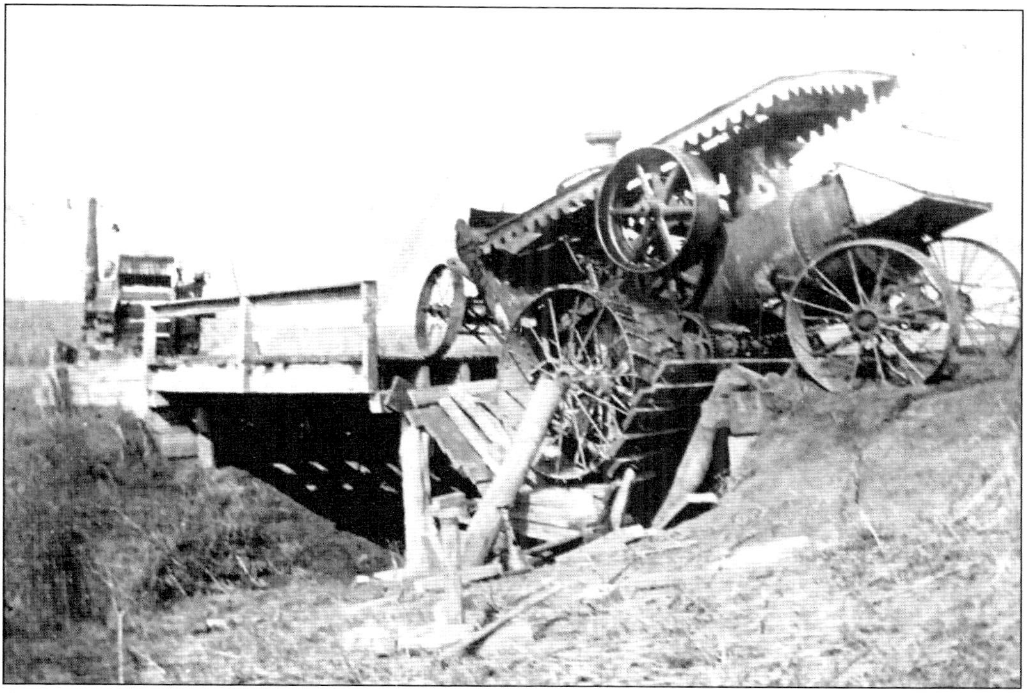

Operating a thresh machine was not without its dangers. The Saase and Schulz threshing machine obviously was too heavy for this wooden planked bridge. It fell through and lodged against the bank in November 1904. Fortunately the creek bed was dry, and the machine did not roll off the bridge. (Courtesy of Marian Klima.)

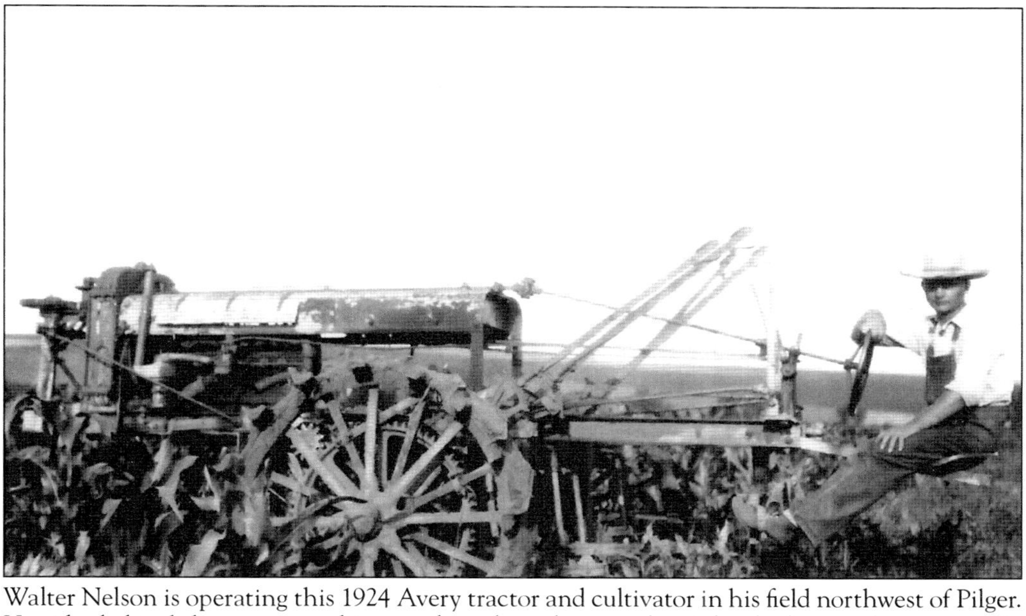

Walter Nelson is operating this 1924 Avery tractor and cultivator in his field northwest of Pilger. He rides behind the tractor and is seated on the cultivator that is hooked up to the tractor. He used the hand levers to control the adjustments on the cultivator. (Courtesy of Marian Klima.)

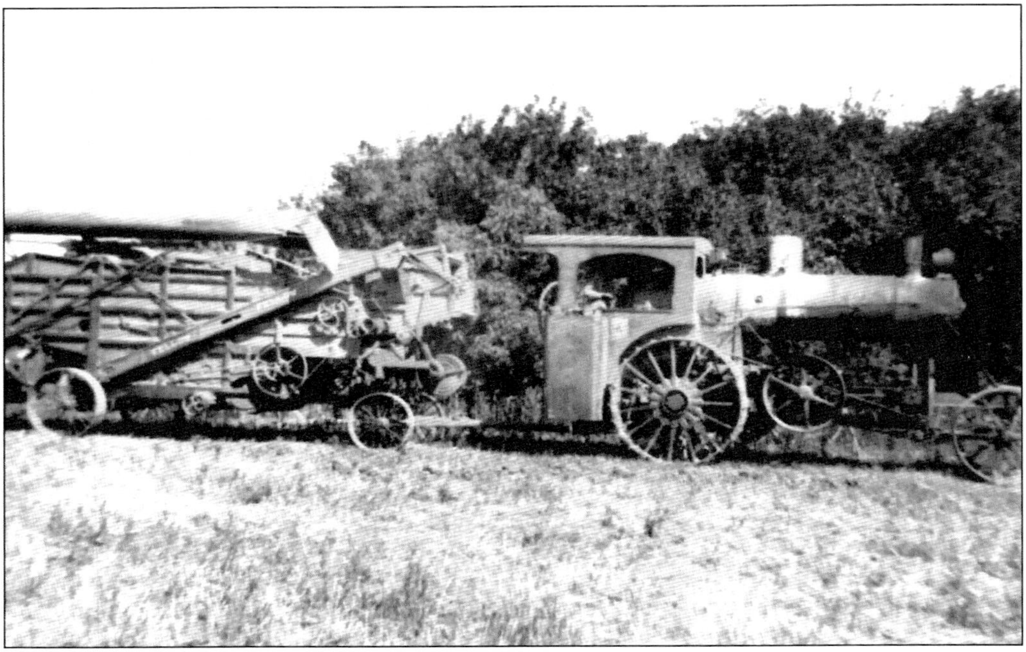

In 1913, this Avery tractor and thresher were made by the Avery Company in Peoria, Illinois. It had a 40-horsepower two-cylinder engine. It has a locomotive-style, under mounted, yellow Willow Threshing Machine behind. This belonged to Heller, and threshers were hired out to farmers, as most did not buy one of their own. (Courtesy of Marian Klima.)

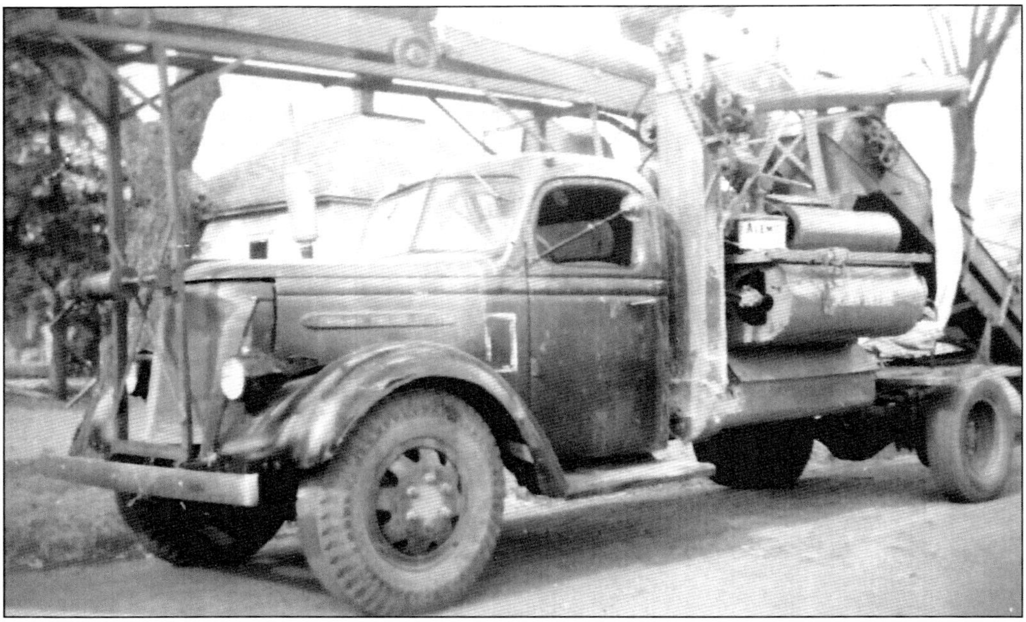

Pat Brockman of Pilger owned and operated this No. 6 John Deere 1950 Sheller. He had it mounted on a 1940 GMC truck bed. Shellers were hired by most farmers to shell corn from the ear out of the corn crib. Brockman's house is in the background of this photograph. (Courtesy of Marian Klima.)

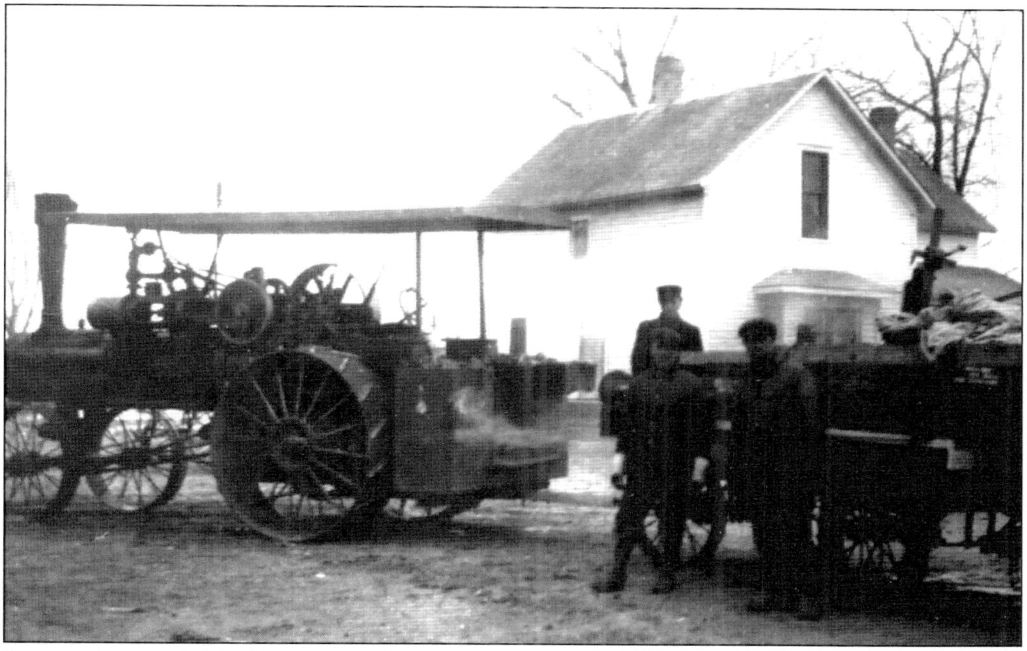

Louis Belz owned this Case tractor. It was steam driven, and here it was used to power a sawmill, then to haul the load of lumber home on a wagon bed. The men in this picture are not identified. There were many cottonwood trees along the Elkhorn River, which flowed near the Louis Belz farm. This was taken in the early 1920s. (Courtesy of Larry Belz.)

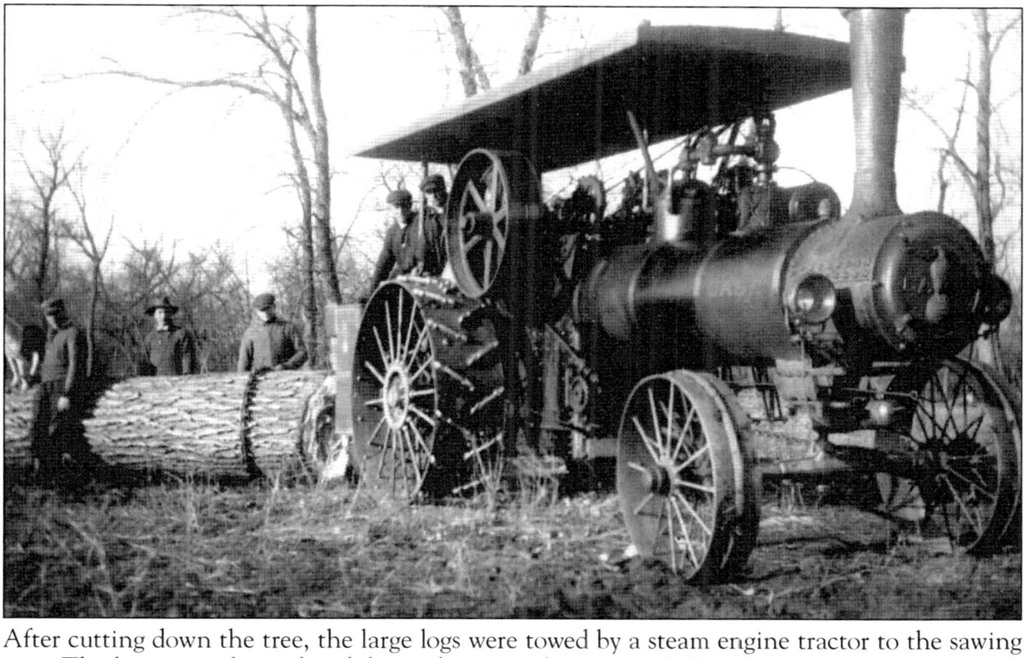

After cutting down the tree, the large logs were towed by a steam engine tractor to the sawing area. The logs were chained and dragged over to the sawing sled. A Case steam engine tractor was used, and the process required a number of men to handle every phase of the lumber milling process. (Courtesy of Larry Belz.)

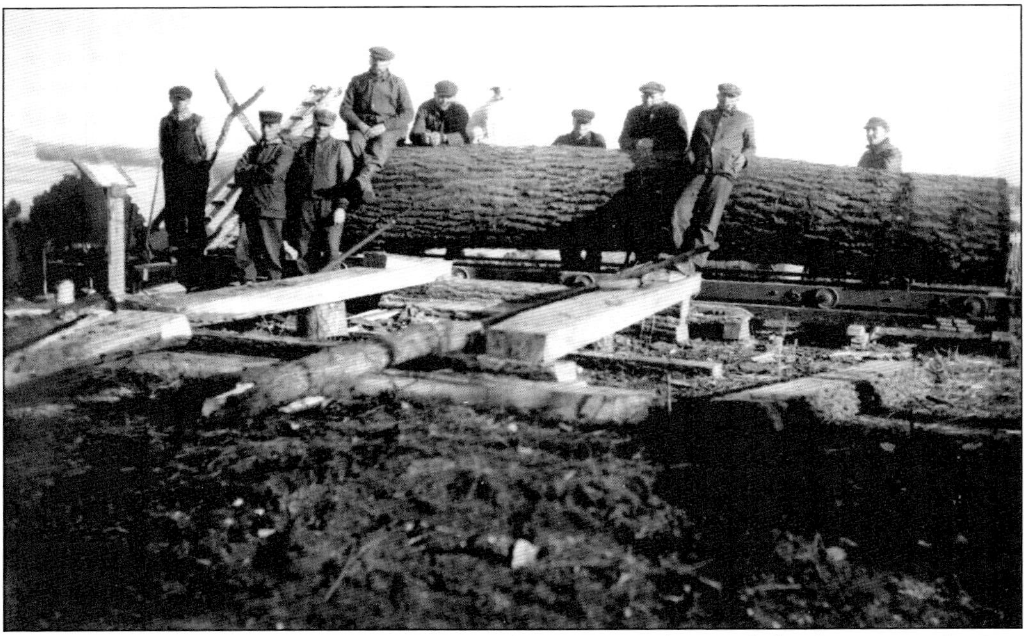

The Louis Belz sawmill crew maneuvers a very large tree trunk on a sled to be cut into lumber. The lumber had to be milled for building barns, sheds, houses, fences, and wagons. The piles of freshly cut boards are stacked on the far side of the rail on which the saw bladed through the logs. Wood was also used for cook stoves and heating fuel. A pile of sawdust is shown by the stack of lumber. This could be used for bedding in the barns. Any trees large enough to be cut for lumber were found near the Elkhorn River, which runs through Stanton County and flows close to Stanton. (Courtesy of Larry Belz.)

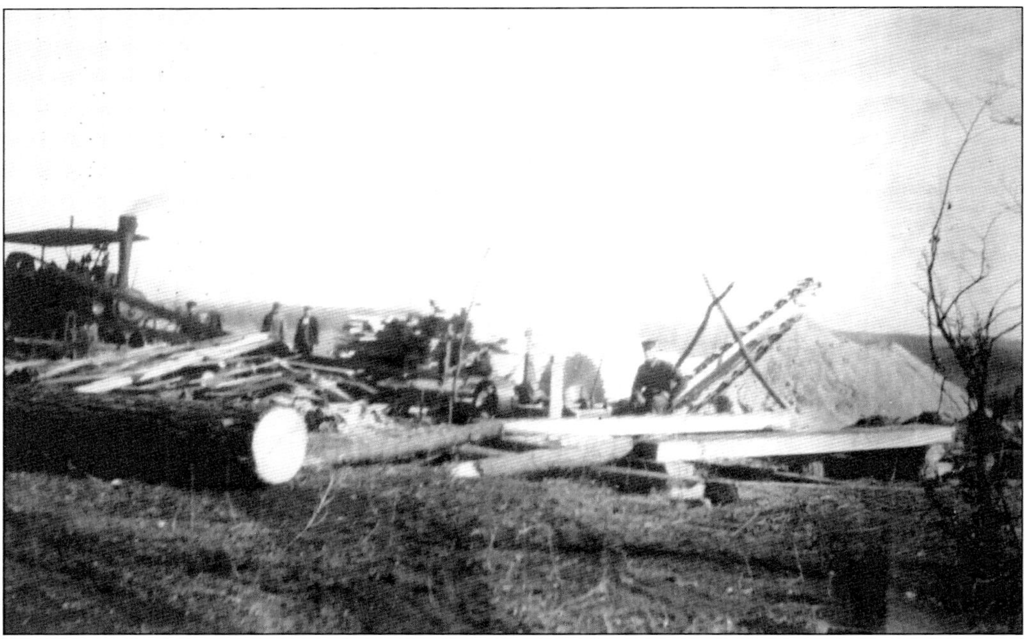

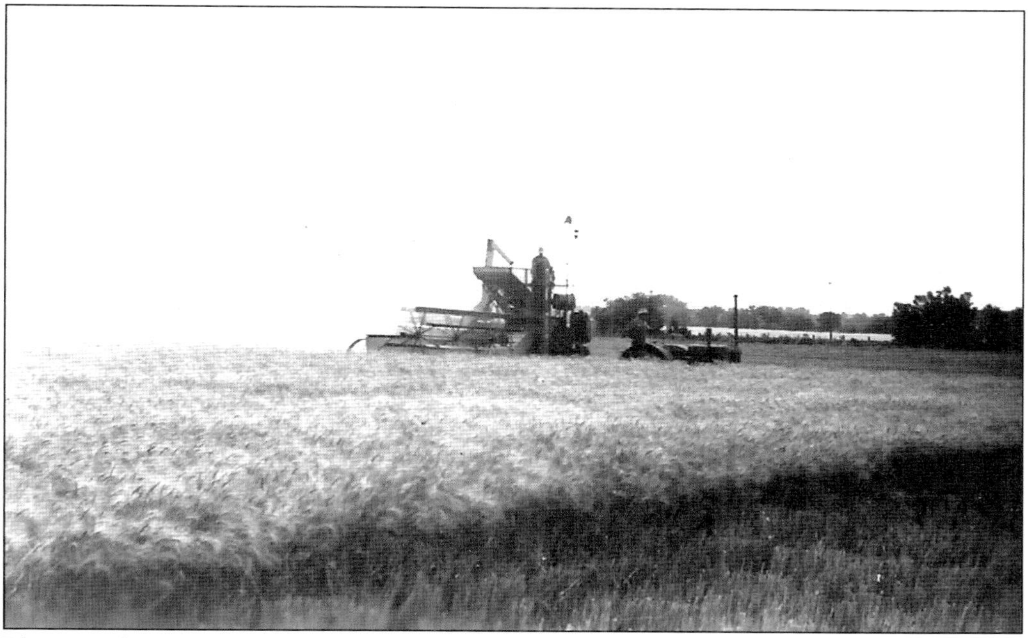

This 1936 harvest produced 50 bushels of wheat per acre. The comment written on the back of the photograph remarked "Isn't it beautiful?" Walter A. Schultze is driving the tractor, and August Seller is on the top of the binder. The Elkhorn River flows in the background. (Courtesy of Milford and Gloria Koch.)

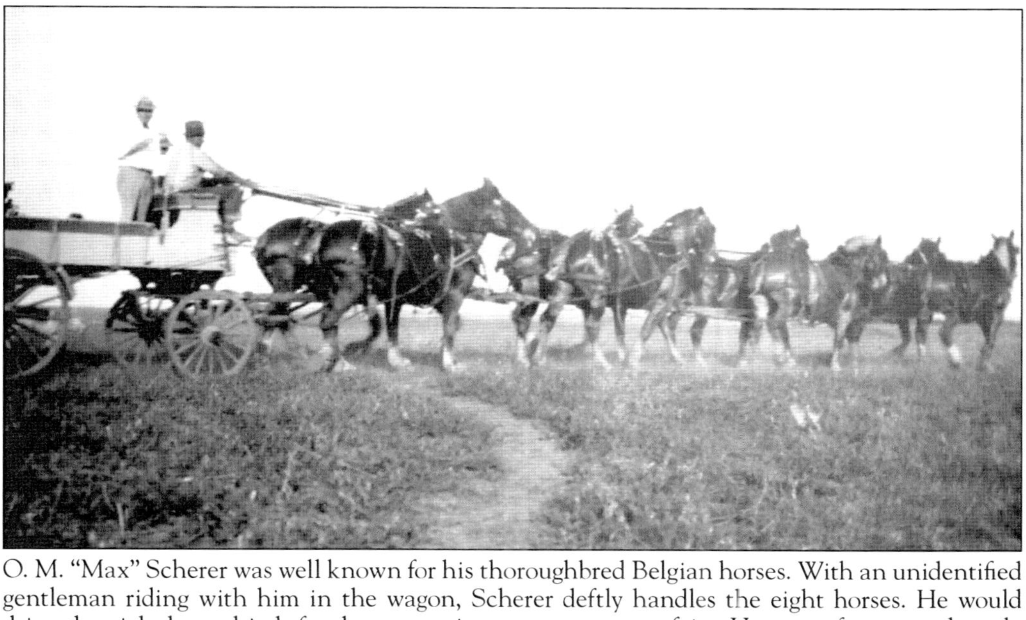

O. M. "Max" Scherer was well known for his thoroughbred Belgian horses. With an unidentified gentleman riding with him in the wagon, Scherer deftly handles the eight horses. He would drive the eight-horse hitch for demonstrations at area county fairs. He was a farmer and cattle feeder in the Kingsburg Precinct of Stanton County. (Courtesy of Marian Klima.)

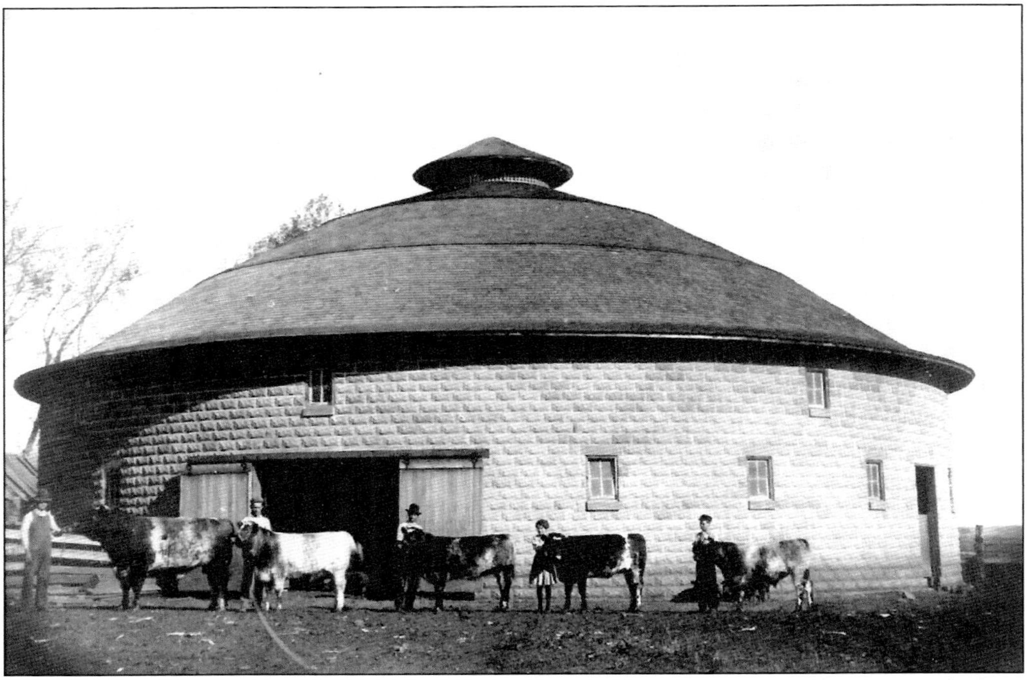

Barns played an integral part for rural homesteads. They protected the farm animals from adverse weather and roving predators. They were necessary for the storage of hay crops, birthing of calves and other farm animals, feeding, and served as milk parlors. A well-built, eye-pleasing barn was a source of pride to the family who built it and owned it. The round barn belonged to Howell Reese of Pilger. He was known for raising prize-winning purebred shorthorn cattle, which he took to show at local and state fairs. The photograph below is a very large multipurpose barn built by Henry Hawkins in 1912. It was built on his Valley View Farm, located one mile south and one and a quarter miles east of Pilger. (Courtesy of Marian Klima.)

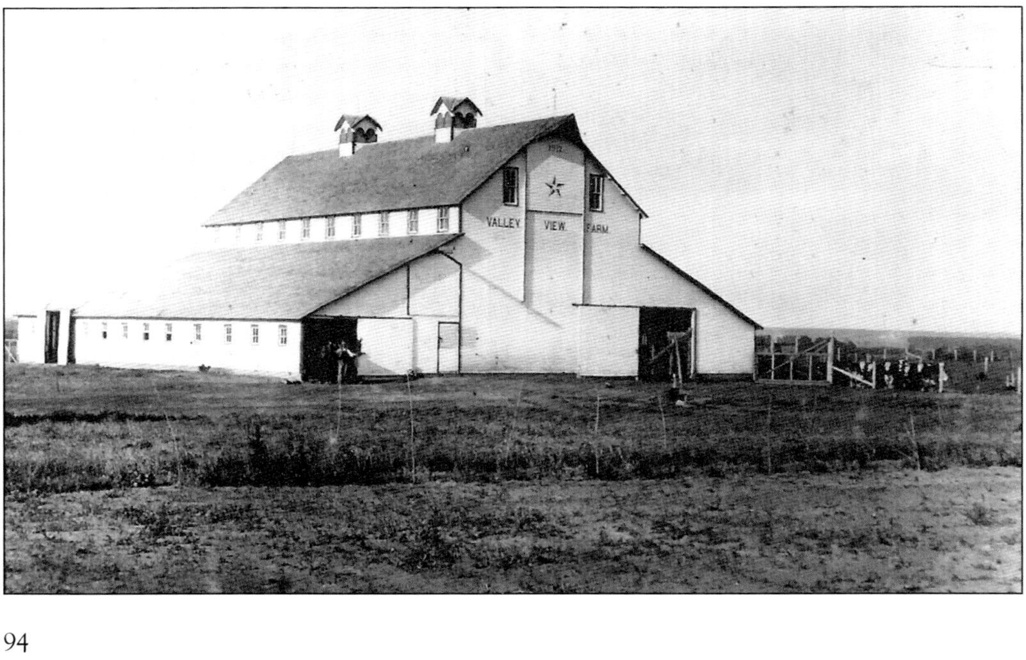

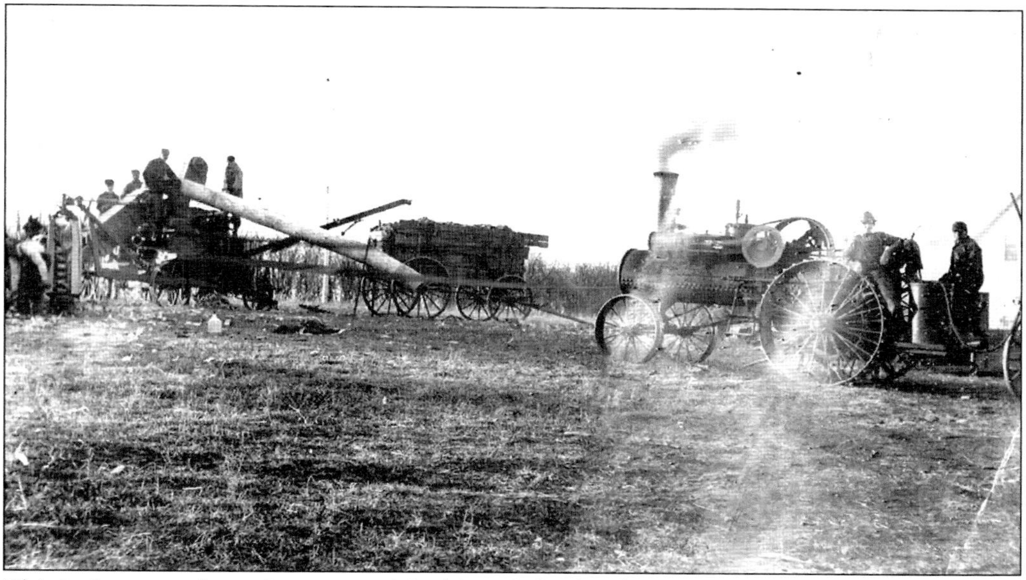

This is the time of corn harvesting. Neighbors helped with picking and hauling the crops, and then everyone would move to the next farmer's field and repeat the tasks. Here the harvested ears are being loaded from a corn picker into the wagons for transport to storage. This was the method used around 1918. (Courtesy of Art Catlin.)

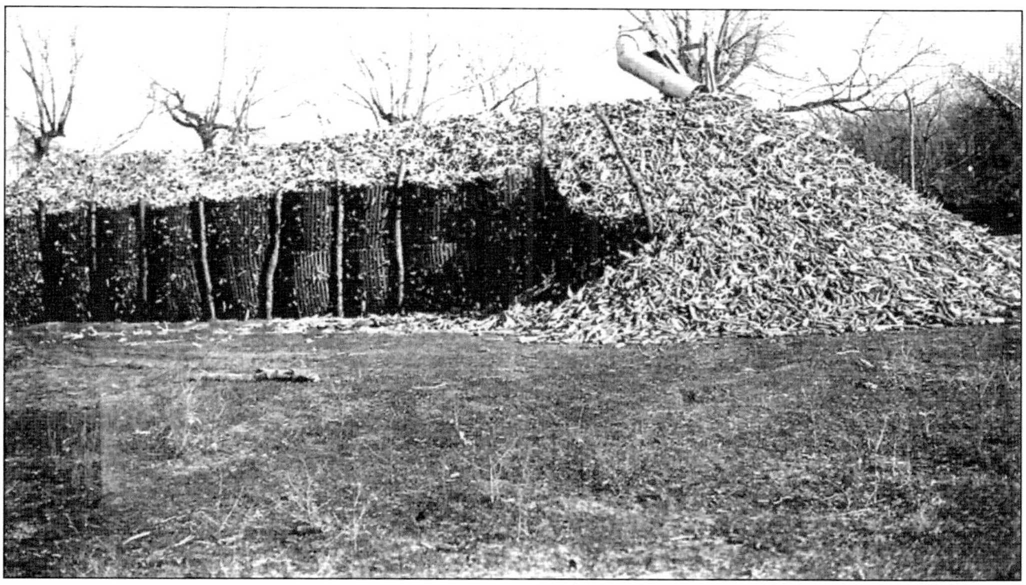

This huge pile of corn ears is only a portion of the 1918 harvest on the Walter A. Schultze farmstead. On the back of the picture Schultze wrote, "Just a part of the corn that Pat and I picked this fall." Then he simply states that there are about 4,000 bushels in the corn pile shown. The picture was signed, "Walter & Reinhart, Thanks Pat and the year 1918." (Courtesy of Milford and Gloria Koch.)

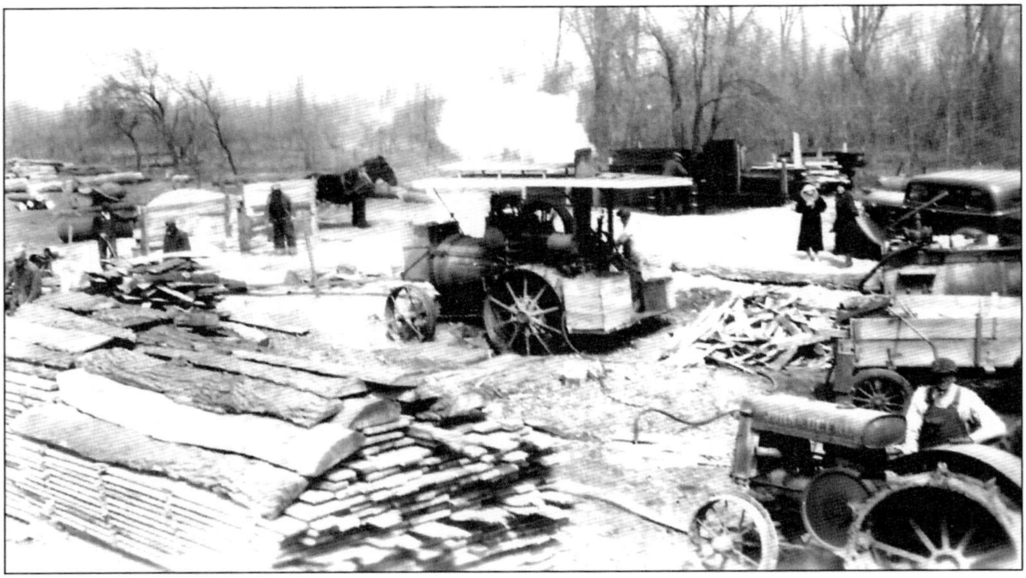

Another sawmill operation from the 1930s was active on the Walter A. Schultze farm south and east of Stanton. Thirty-eight men from the WPA program were contracted to cut the logs for firewood. A record was written on the picture that lumber cost $15 for machine, plus labor. The lumber was used to build a corncrib with a 6,000-bushel capacity and bin space above for 3,000 bushels. Some of the boards were used to build sheds, gates, and repair bunks. The dates of the piles of lumber below are March 28 through April 16, 1920. They cut 23,500 feet of cottonwood lumber and 992 pieces of ash hardwood. This WPA crew produced lumber for a corncrib that was used for 25 years and hog shelters, and it built more gates. (Courtesy of Milford and Gloria Koch.)

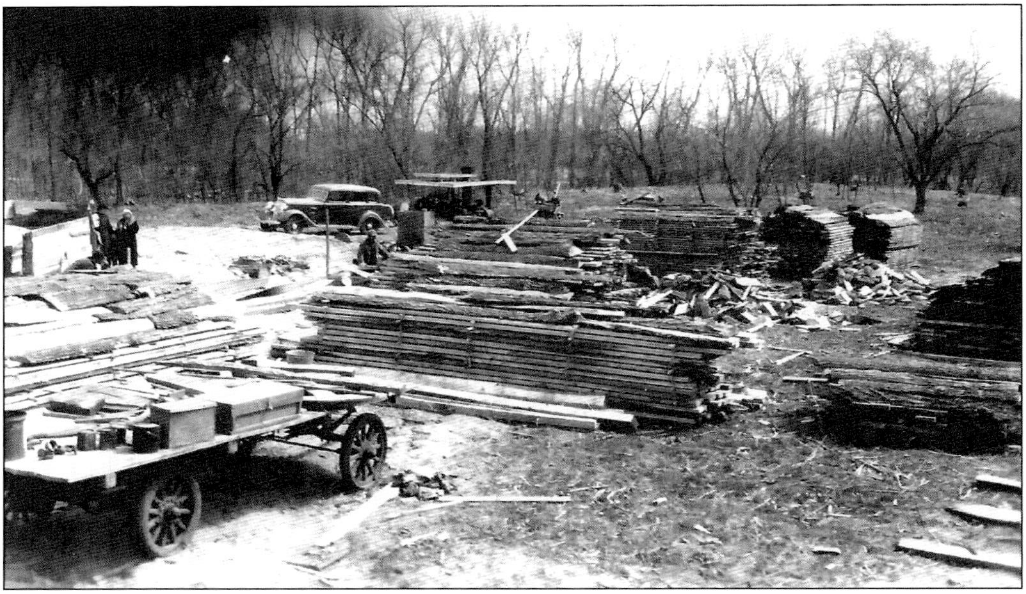

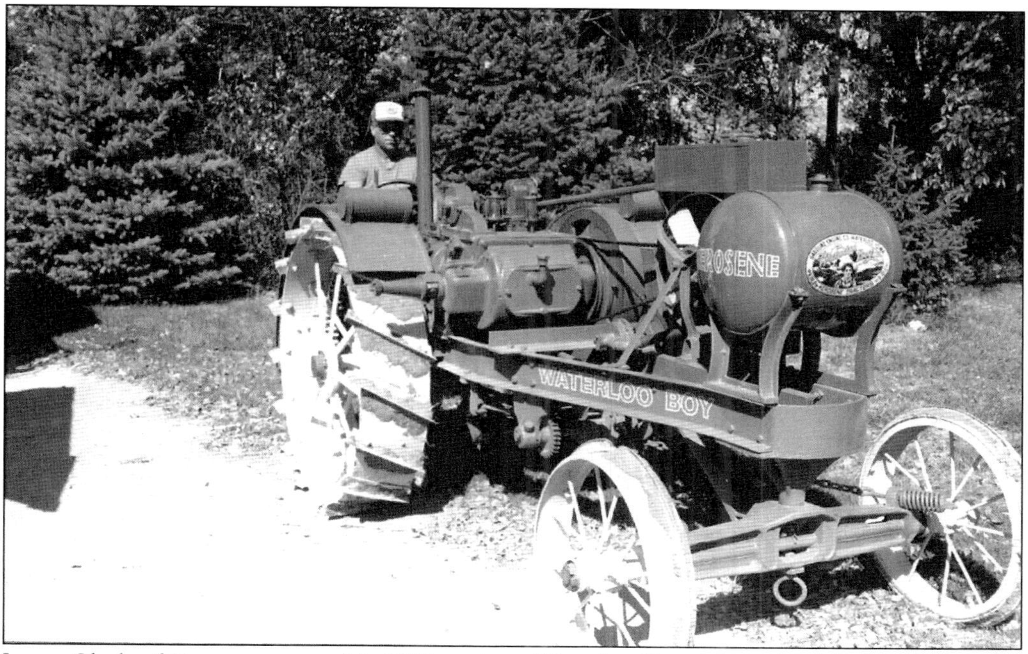

Larry Clark of Stanton owns this 1919 antique Waterloo Boy tractor. He displayed it at the Stanton County Fair in 1999. Bill Schroeder, of Leigh, Nebraska, purchased it near Cherington, North Dakota, and sold it later to Clark. It has metal wheels and operates on kerosene. (Courtesy of Larry Clark.)

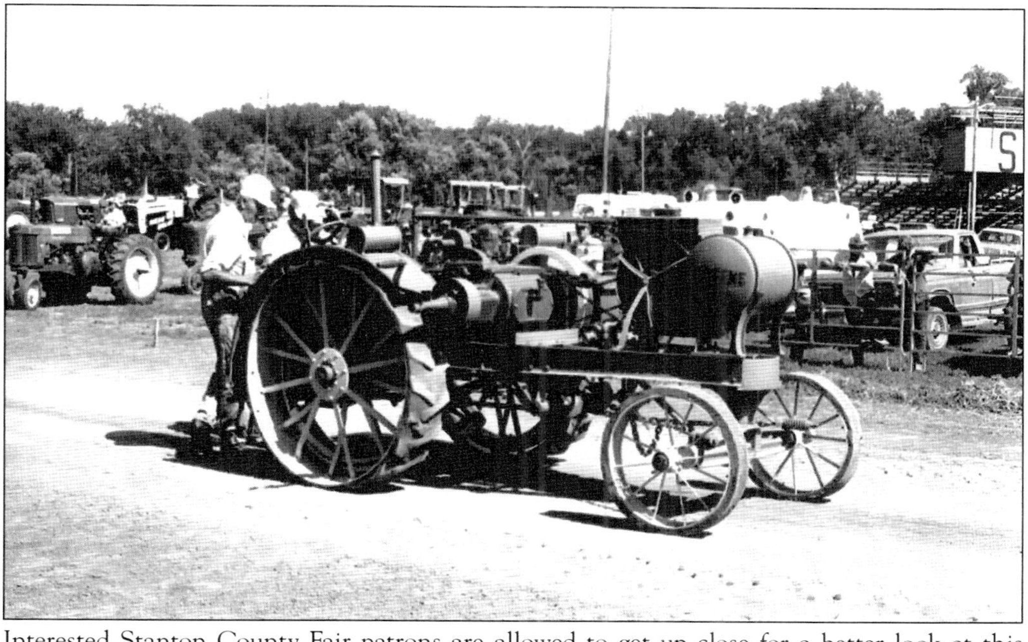

Interested Stanton County Fair patrons are allowed to get up close for a better look at this antique tractor from the same era. It also has a kerosene tank on the front and was brought for display at the 1983 Stanton County Fair. The lug wheels have a slightly different pattern, but overall it is very similar to a Waterloo Boy. (Courtesy of the Stanton Register.)

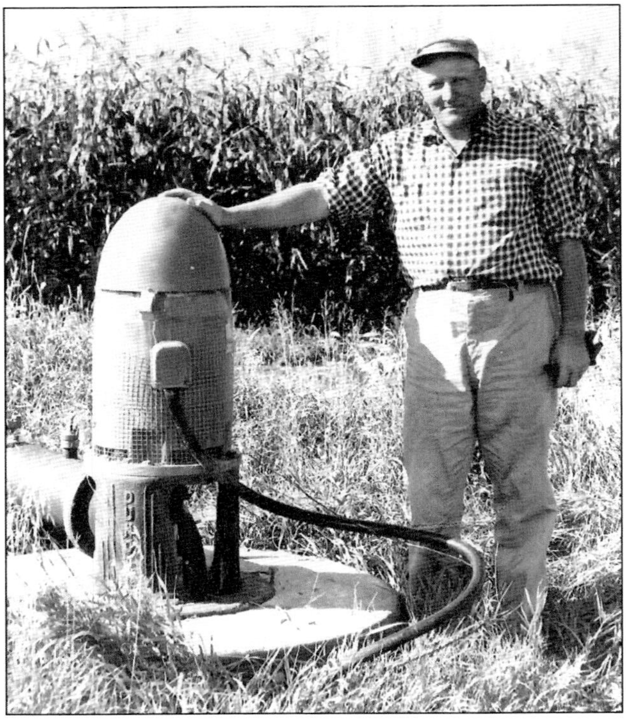

With progress and ingenuity, farmers used new technology to produce bigger and better crops. Loren Pohlman of Stanton stands next to one of the first irrigation pumps used in the county. It was a forerunner to the irrigation systems of today and required more manual handling to deliver water down the cornrows. (Courtesy of Larry Belz.)

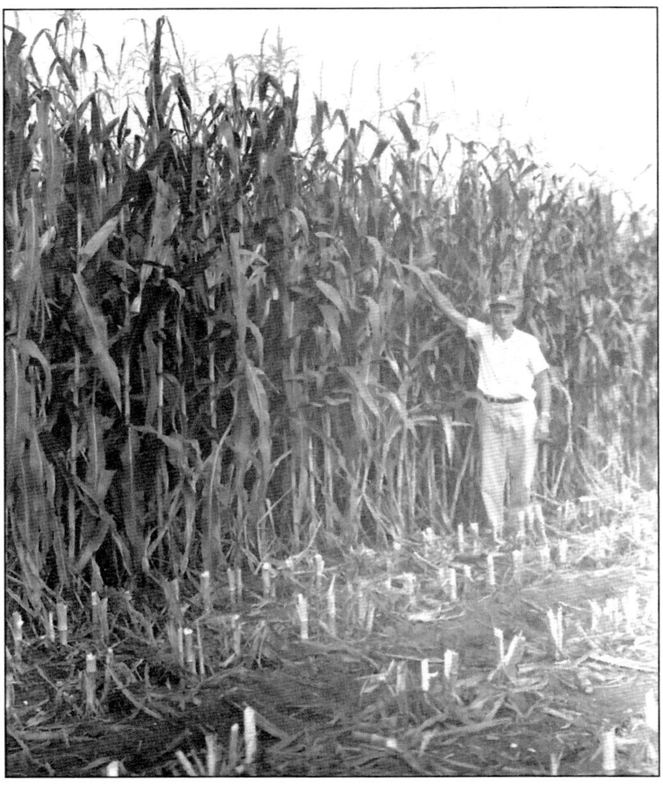

This Stanton County farmer stands proud next to his very tall corn crop. With the improvement in seed production, fertilizers, and planting methods, crop production increased and made Nebraska one of the top producing states for corn and soybeans. (Courtesy of the Stanton Register.)

Not only did improvements take place in the cornfields, the gardens produced gigantic food crops. Waldo Sonnenschein of Stanton holds his harvested turnip or kohlrabi. This giant vegetable will serve a number of people for several meals. This was taken in the 1950s or 1960s. (Courtesy of the Stanton Register.)

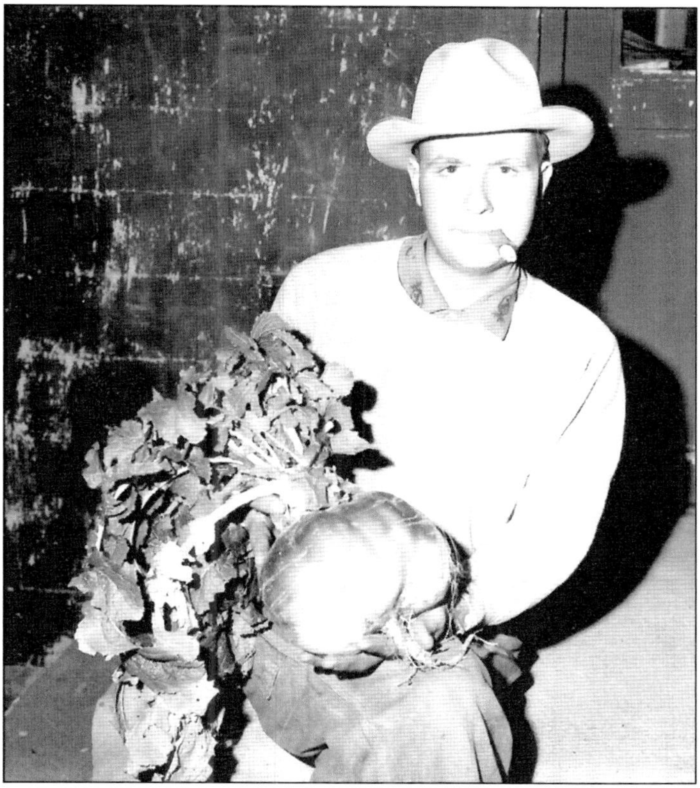

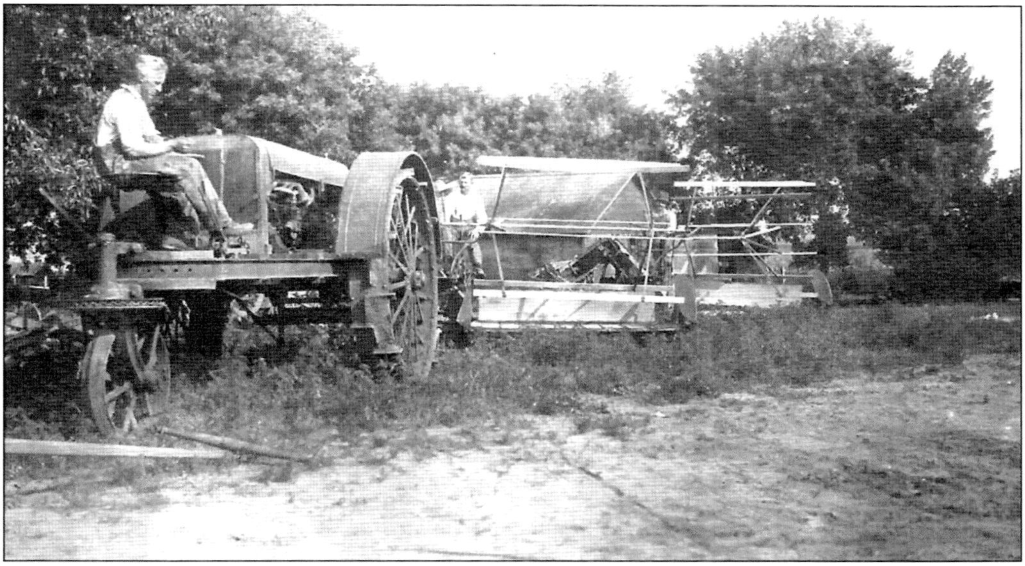

The Square Turn tractor was designed and manufactured by A. T. Kinney and A. J. Colwell in Norfolk in 1914. This innovative tractor changed the way a tractor was driven from an unwieldy steering wheel to hand manipulated levers. The tractor could make a full turn of its own length in five seconds with no clutching and no pedals. Walter A. Schultze owned and operated this Square Turn tractor. (Courtesy of Milford and Gloria Koch.)

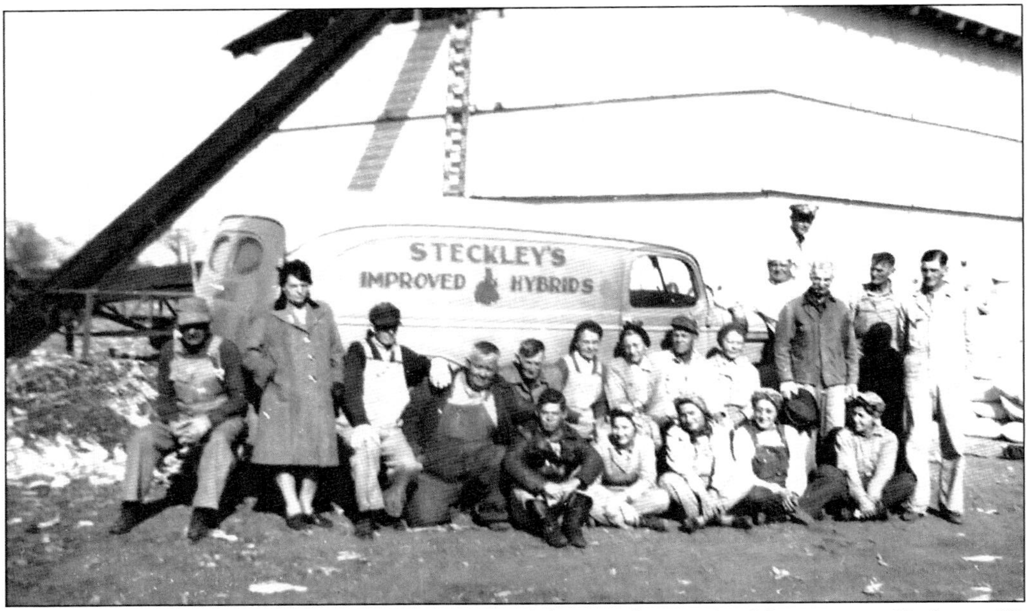

A Steckley Seed Corn Processing Plant operated three miles south of Stanton on Highway 57. It was in business for about five years. This crew detasseled, hauled, and husked the dried ears of corn for bagging as seed. Detasselers worked on foot and on machines for long hours and traveled around the county for the Steckley Company during the 1940s. (Courtesy of the Historical Society of Stanton County and Edna Mueller.)

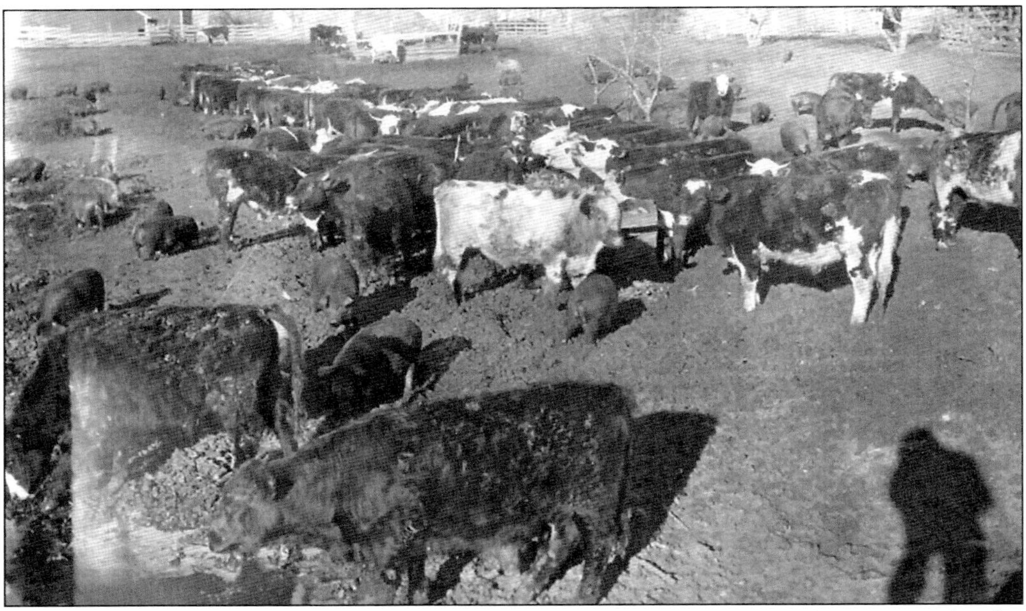

In the first fat cattle feedlots, all the chores were intensive from scooping the corn into bunks, cleaning out the bunks, pitching the hay, and cleaning the feedlot. Hogs were permissible in with the cattle in 1924, and shelter was a windbreak. Here the cattle have just been fed. Feeding cattle is much more sophisticated with technology today and thousands are in feedlots in Stanton County. (Courtesy of Milford and Gloria Koch.)

Eight

Rails and Wheels 1879

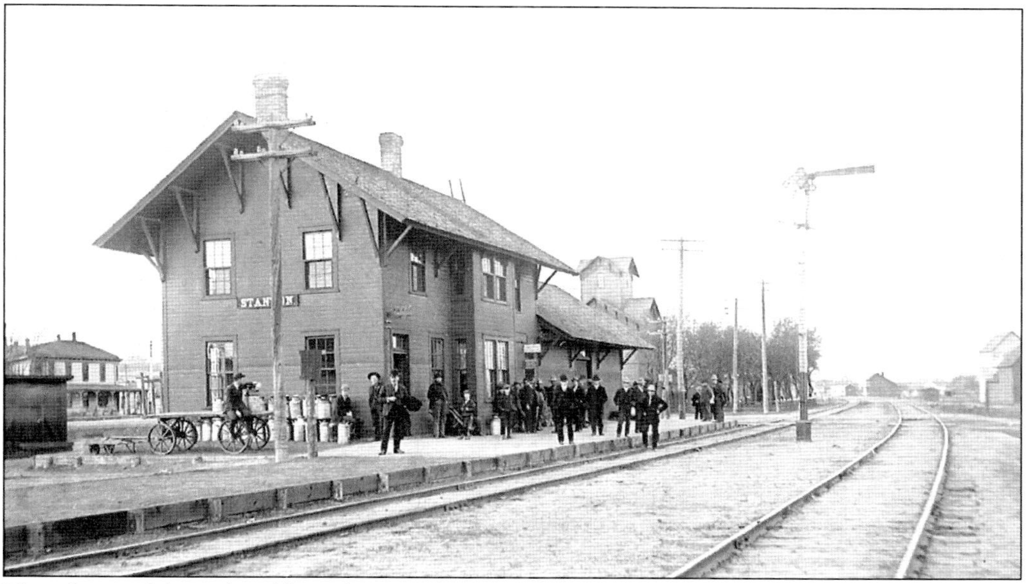

The advent of the railroad brought an increased flurry of activity to Pilger in 1879. Three railways requested permission to develop their business in Stanton County. The first train followed the tracks through Stanton County on September 15, 1879. A passenger service train was added in 1881, and by 1917, there were three passenger trains traveling east and three more traveling west daily. By 1944, due to bus service and automobile travel, the passenger trains dwindled to one passenger train at noon and one at night. (Courtesy of Art Catlin.)

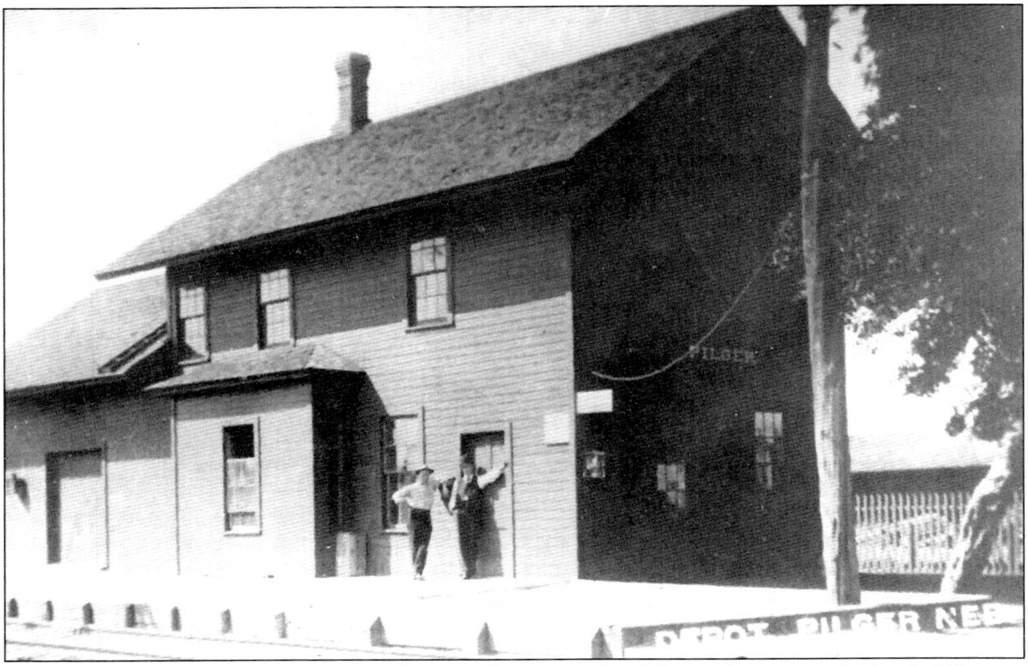

Otto Schauble and depot agent Bailey stand outside the Pilger Chicago and North Western Railway (C&NW) depot in 1908. The first railroad into the town was the Fremont, Elkhorn and Missouri Valley, but its holdings had been acquired by the C&NW system in 1888. (Courtesy of Marian Klima.)

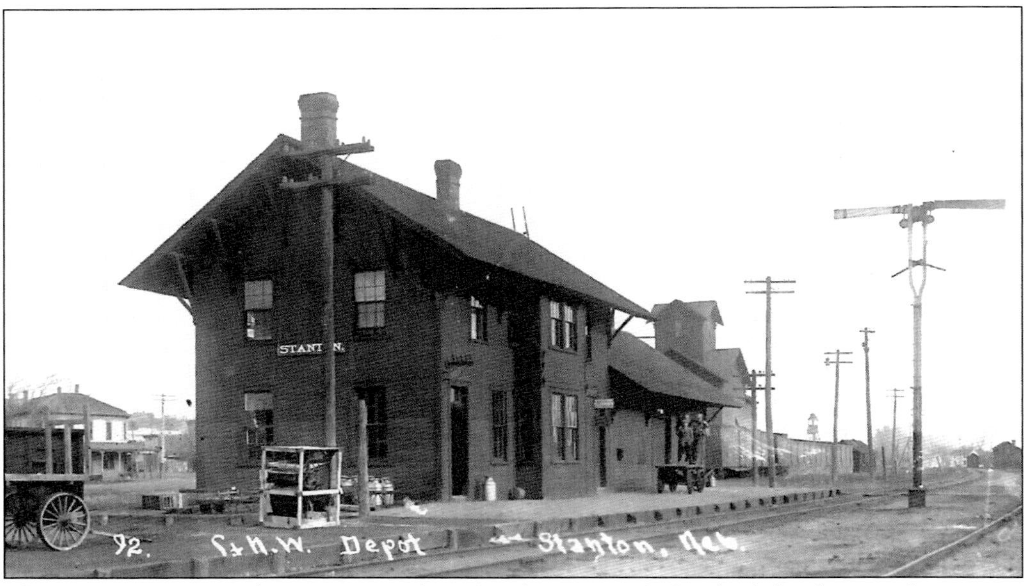

The Stanton C&NW depot is pictured on October 22, 1913. On the left side sits a dray wagon for freight delivery, and boxed freight is near the platform. The Elkhorn Hotel is partially visible on the left, and cream cans rest against the side of the depot. To the right stands the wooden Greenslit Elevator built in 1904. Beyond that, the courthouse steeple can be seen. (Courtesy of Art Catlin.)

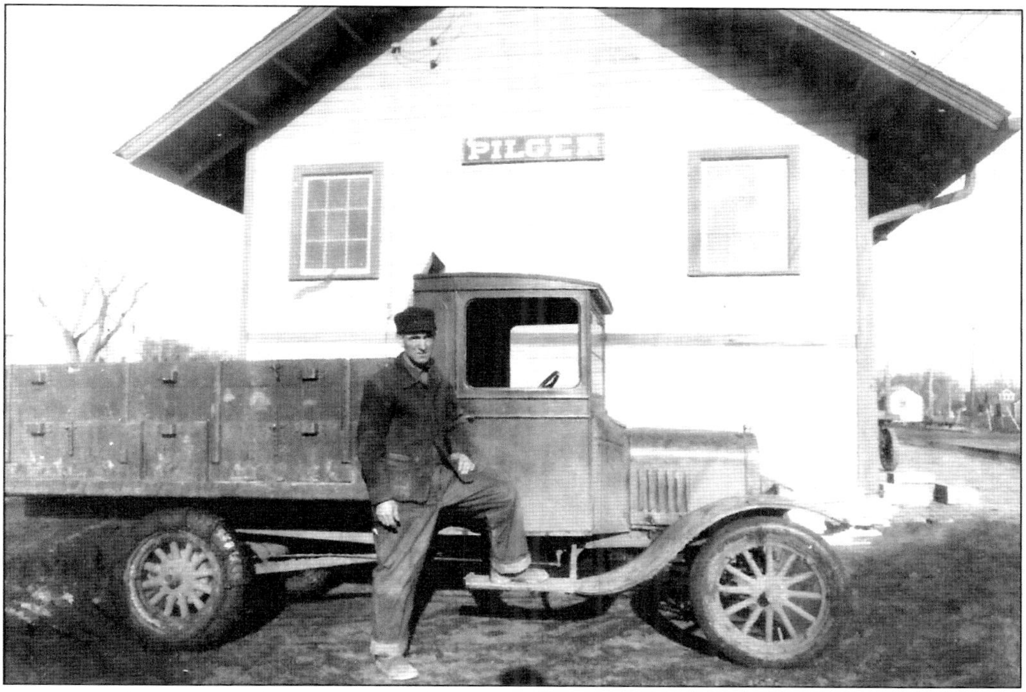

Ed Coley of Pilger waits by his dray truck at the Pilger depot. Dray trucks and wagons were used for freight pickup and delivery for train shipments and businesses. The early dray wagons were pulled with horses until trucks were available in the early 1900s. (Courtesy of Marian Klima.)

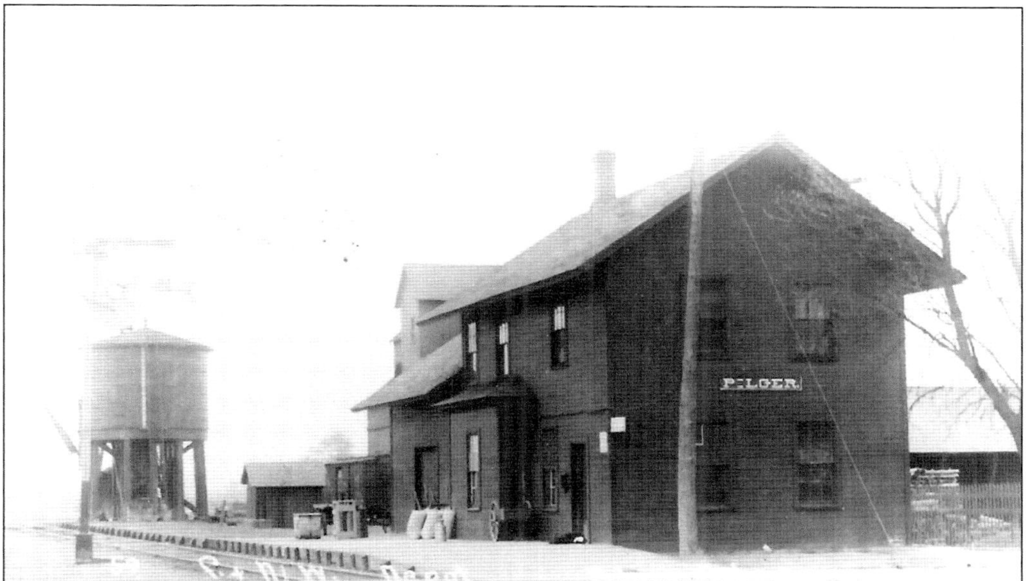

The Pilger depot and C&NW water tower are captured in this 1912 photograph. Directly behind the depot is the Nye, Schneider and Fowler Elevator. By this time there were passenger trains, with one being a "Flyer," that only stopped to drop off a passenger. A dispatcher on the Flyer grabbed the mail sack from an iron hook held out by the station dispatcher. (Courtesy of Marian Klima.)

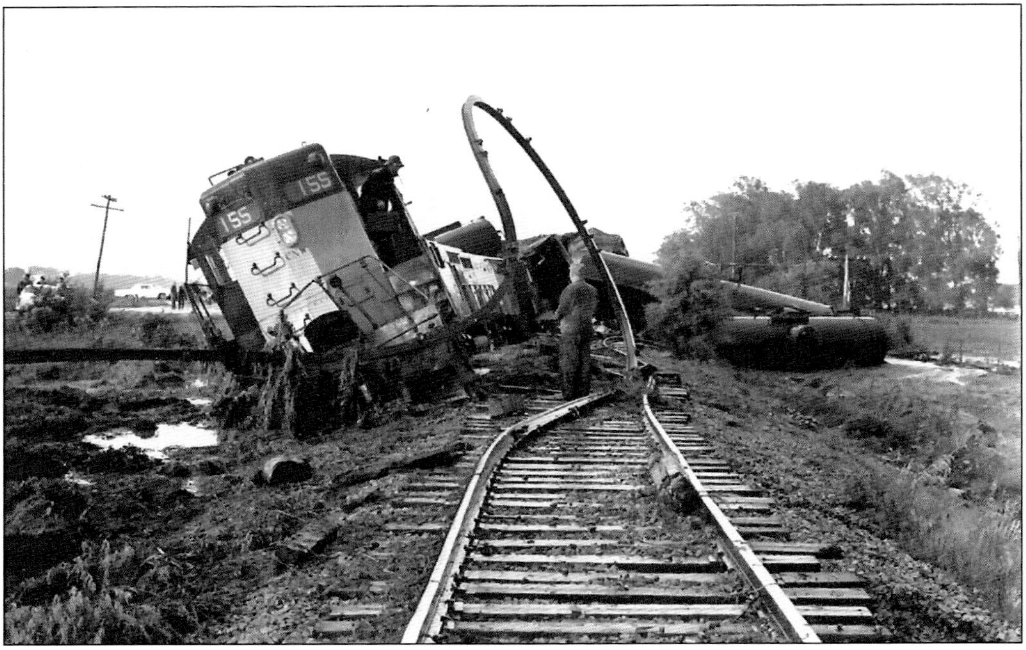

With trains and speed came train wrecks and derailments. Several derailments occurred between Pilger and Stanton through the years. The tracks would be closed for a very short time. Crews worked around the clock to repair the tracks and remove the salvage to expedite train movements. This derailment happened near the Jerome Moritz farm east of Stanton in June 1969. (Courtesy of the Stanton Register and Marian Klima.)

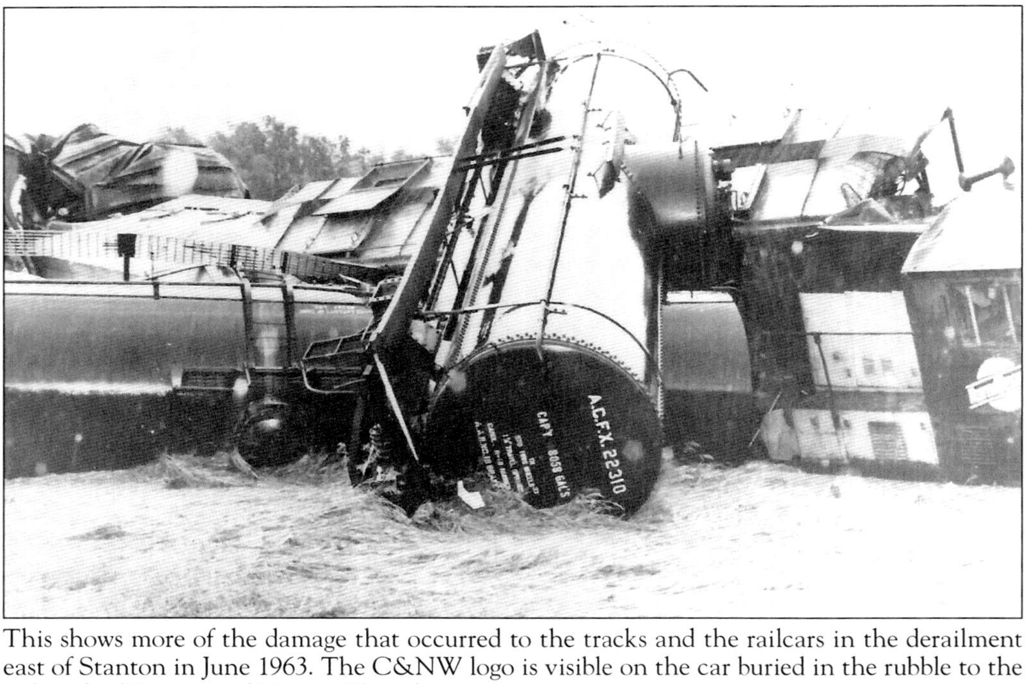

This shows more of the damage that occurred to the tracks and the railcars in the derailment east of Stanton in June 1963. The C&NW logo is visible on the car buried in the rubble to the right side. (Courtesy of Marian Klima.)

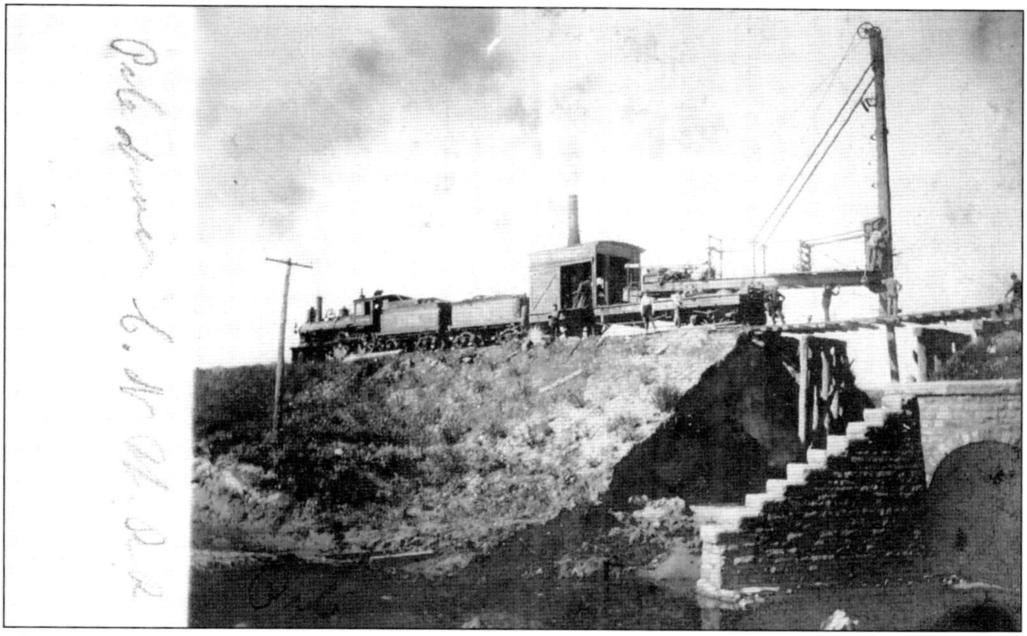

The C&NW repaired and replaced pilings across waterways with this pile driver. It is shown replacing bridge pilings on April 28, 1908. Eight railroad crew members are working and checking the equipment to run the power. (Courtesy of Art Catlin.)

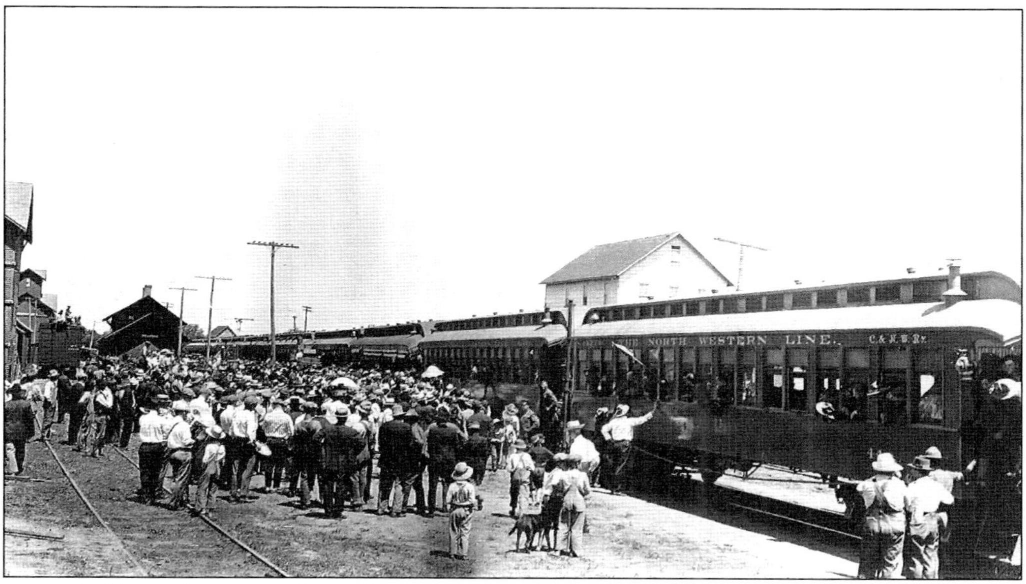

A send-off crowd waits to cheer the troops disembarking to the Mexican border in 1916. The Stanton Mill is to the right behind the train, and the elevator is to the left. Most of the troopers are on the train and lean out the windows for final farewells to friends and family. (Courtesy of Milford and Gloria Koch and the Historical Society of Stanton County.)

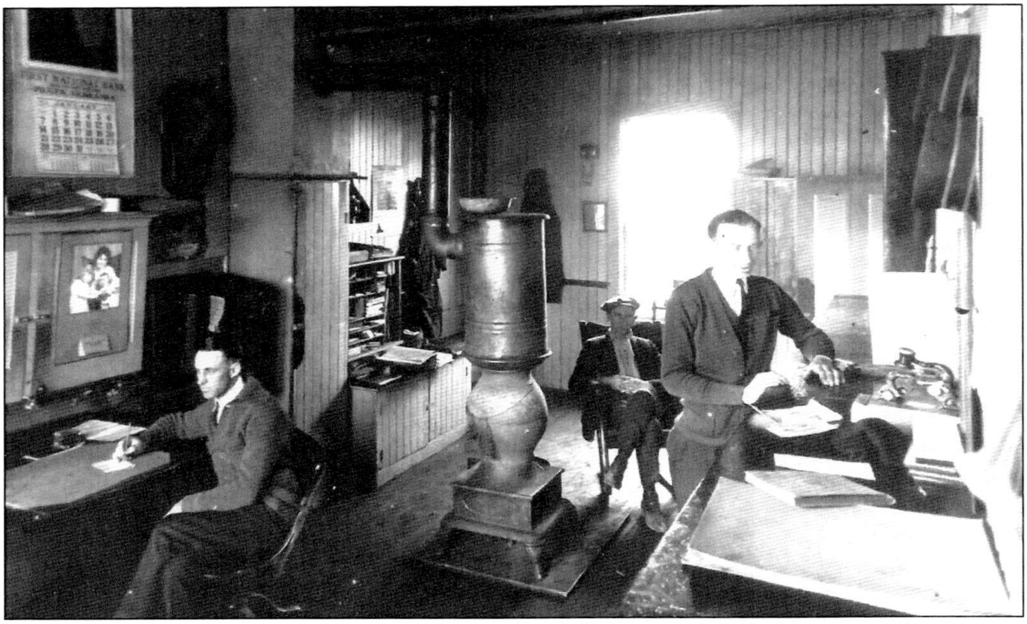

A peek inside the Pilger Depot in 1923 finds, from left to right, Frank Otradovec, depot agent from 1920 until retiring in 1957; Earl Bordner; and Oscar "Red" Schwein. A calendar from the First National Bank in Pilger hangs on the wall to the left. The telegraph apparatus is on the counter to the right. (Courtesy of Marian Klima.)

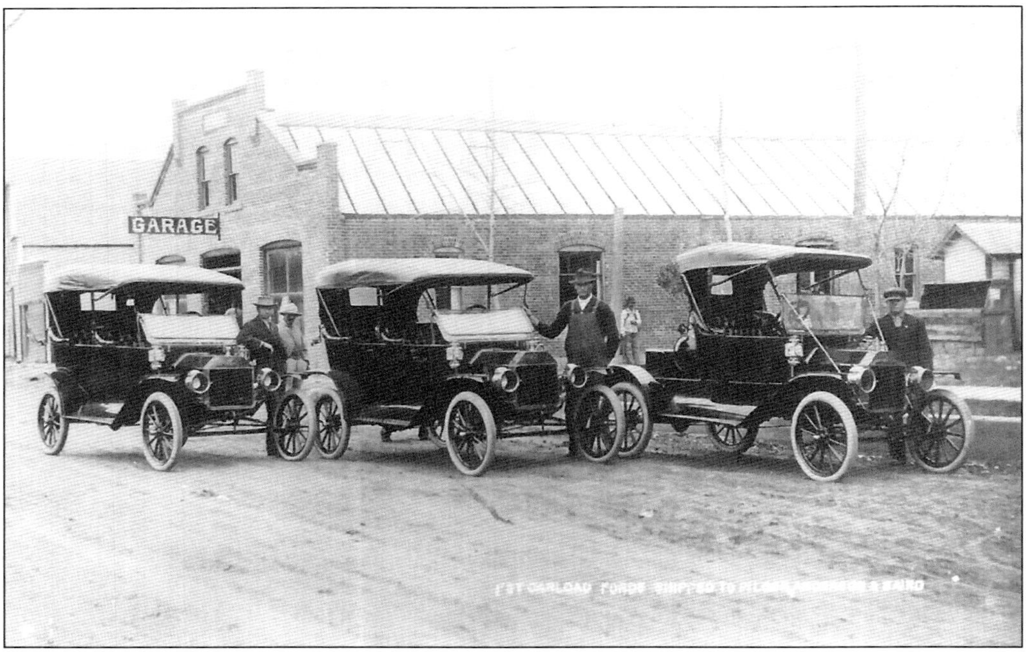

The first shipment of Ford Automobiles arrived in Pilger in 1911. The new automobiles were delivered to the Anderson and Baird Garage. Standing by the cars are, from left to right, Pete Anderson, Chris Denney, Bill O'Brien, Mitch Bourne, and Ike Baird. The Pilger livery barn is to the left of the garage. (Courtesy of Marian Klima.)

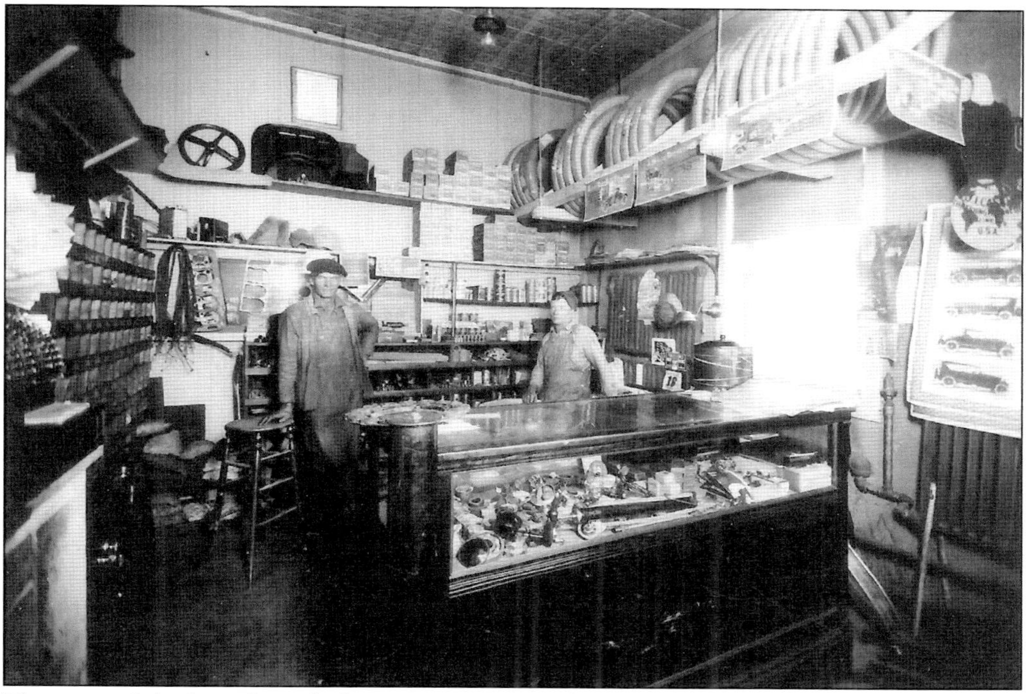

The automobiles brought with them an opportunity for a new business. The Miller and O'Brien Brothers garage carries rubber tires, a spare steering wheel, fancy horns, and gadgets are seen in the display case. Bill O'Brien is on the left and Chris Miller is on the right in their parts room in 1924. New car pictures are on the poster in front of Miller. (Courtesy of Marian Klima.)

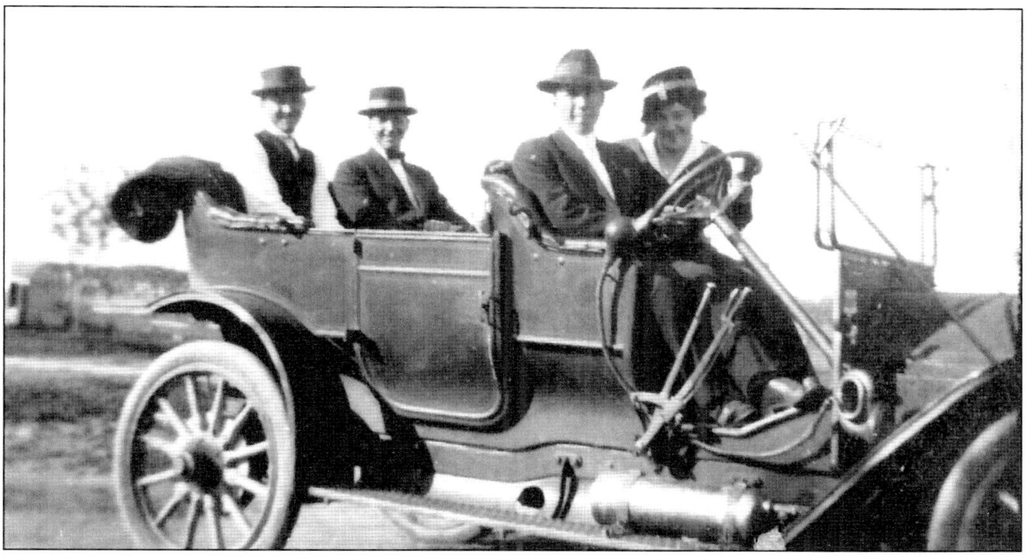

Grover Koehler and his wife, Bertie, take Harold Koehler, seated in the back seat on the left side, and Earl Bordner for a spin in their Chandler automobile. This model is adorned with gaslights. All are residents of the Pilger area. (Courtesy of Marian Klima.)

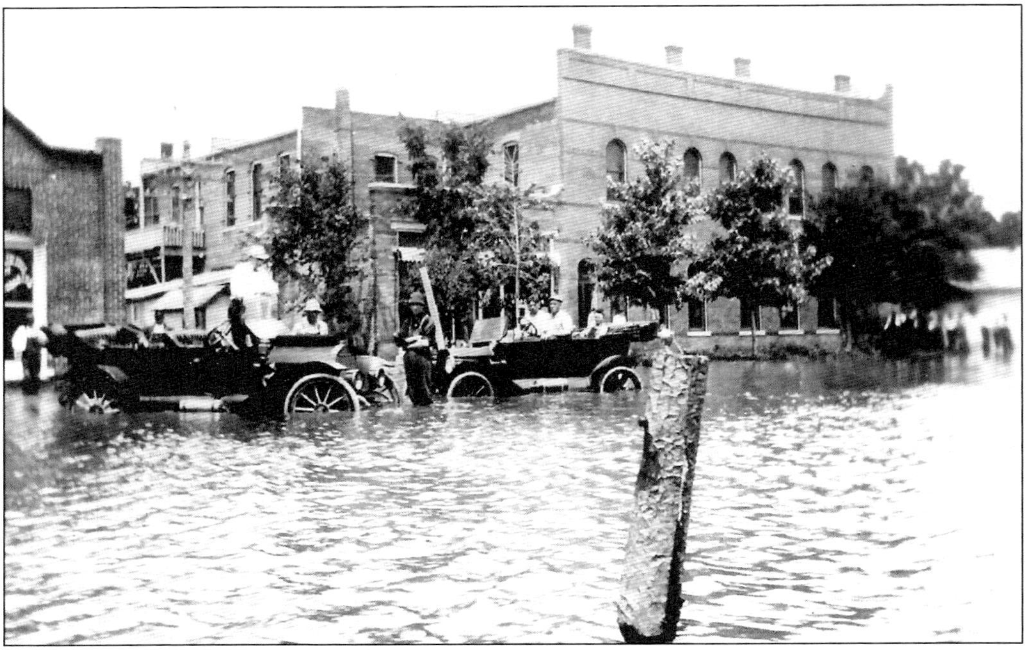

Sightseers test out their Model T Fords in floodwaters. Pilger was plagued with floods from the Humbug Creek for many years until the channel was worked on for flood control. The cars and the unidentified occupants are parked in front of the Reese Garage on a Pilger street. (Courtesy of Marian Klima.)

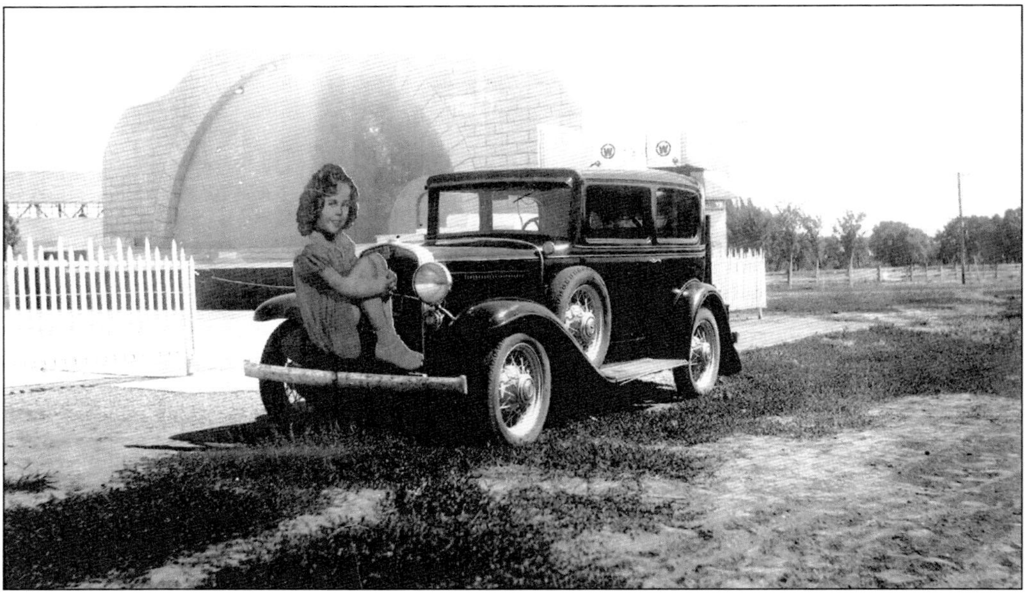

A silhouette of Shirley Temple adorns the grill on this late model car in 1936. It is parked near the Stanton band shell at the Stanton County fairgrounds. A Rialto Theater sound system is attached to the car roof and a white picket fence, which surrounded the public seating area, is on the left. Many dances, band concerts, and other entertainment took place here. (Courtesy of the Stanton Register.)

Nine

A Century of Community Spirit 1865

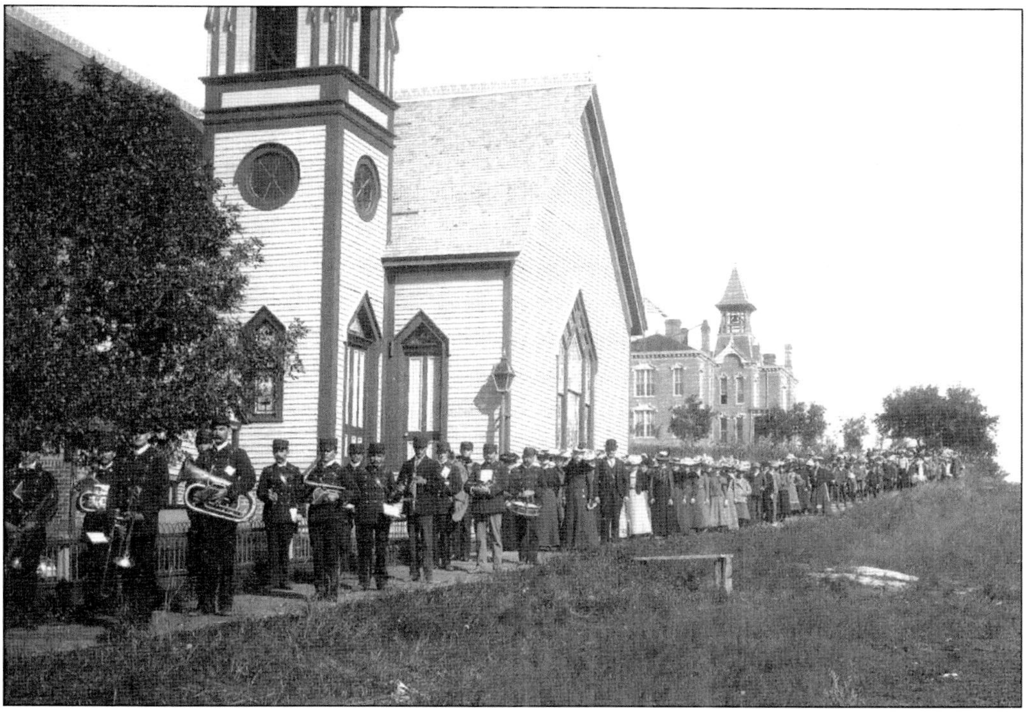

The Stanton High School Band leads a parade of students to the Stanton fairgrounds. The 1901 parade is coming down the hill from the first high school to pass in front of the Methodist church. Professor H. E. Mason, the superintendent of schools, and LaBelle Rice, principal, are leading the student body. The first brick Stanton Public School was built on the hill north of town and opened in the fall of 1885. (Courtesy of the Historical Society of Stanton County.)

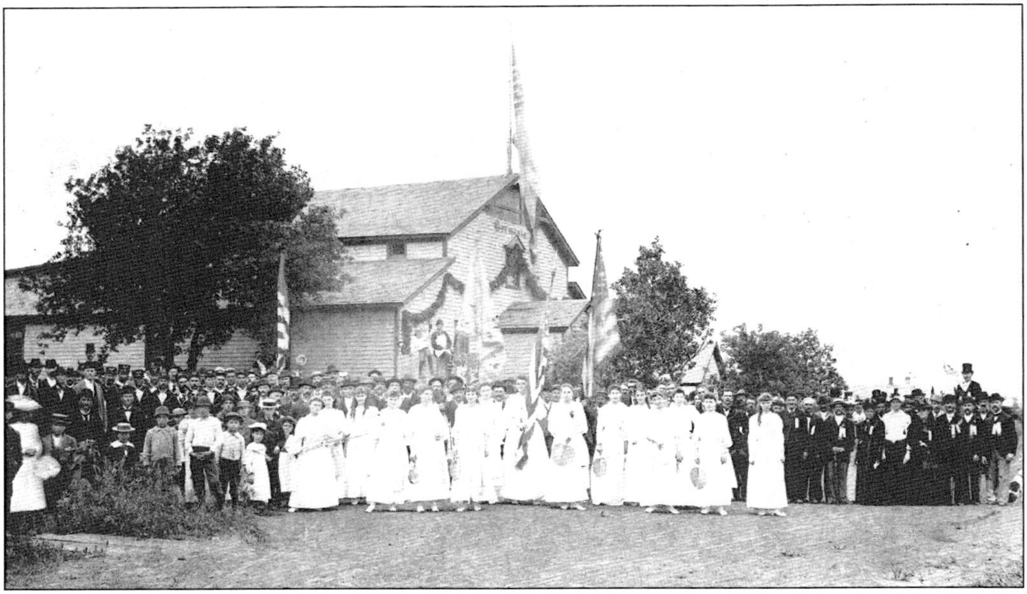

The Germania Gesangverein, or Germania Singing Society, organized in July 1884. The Germania Hall was erected in 1887 so they would have a place to practice. The hall was used for plays, dances, wedding dinners, and a commencement ceremony in 1895. The hall burned to the ground on October 30, 1919, with the destruction blamed on anti-German sentiment. (Courtesy of the Historical Society of Stanton County.)

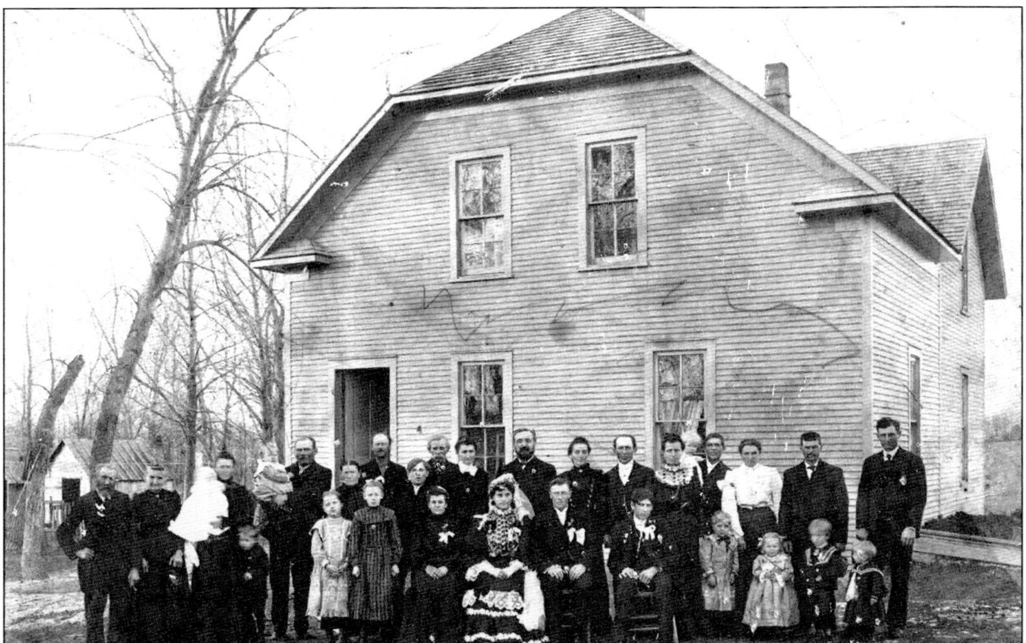

This wedding portrait was taken in the late 1800s or early 1900s at a Stanton County farmstead. Little information was available about the newly wedded couple or the family. (Courtesy of Richard Kuehn.)

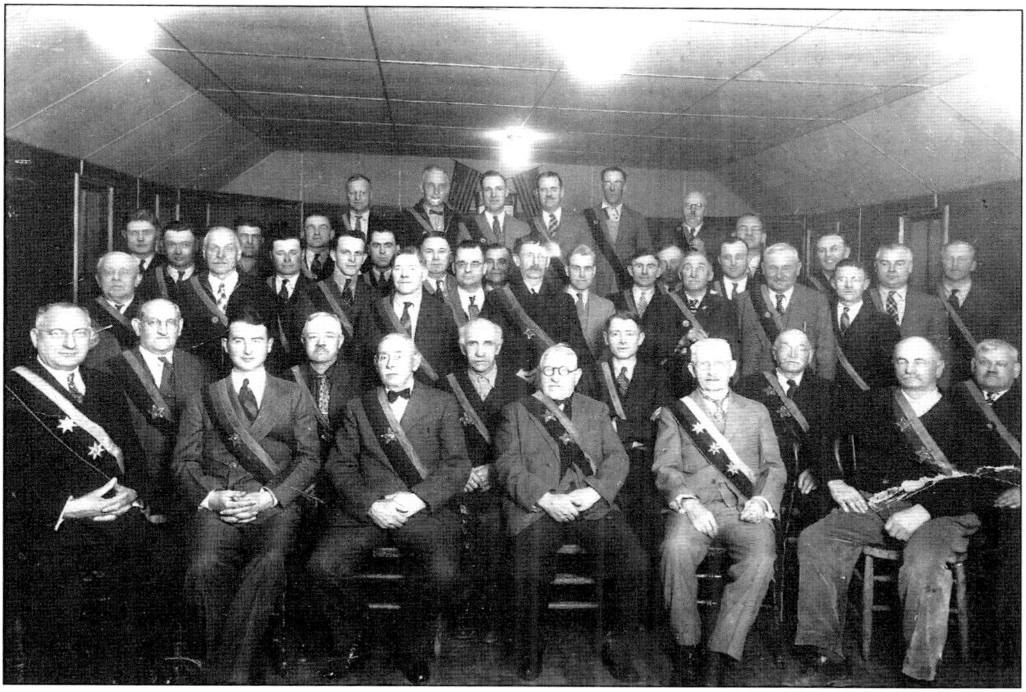

The Sons of Herman chartered its Armin Lodge No. 3 on April 6, 1898. The largest membership in the group before 1943 numbered more than 100. The Sons of Herman was a fraternal insurance organization in Stanton. (Courtesy of the Historical Society of Stanton County.)

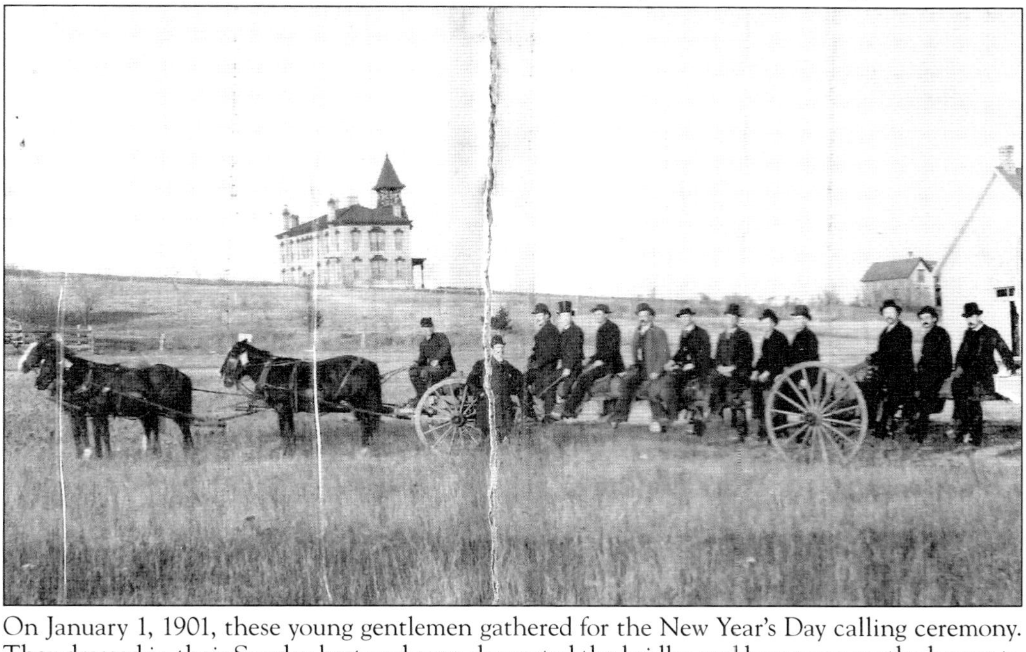

On January 1, 1901, these young gentlemen gathered for the New Year's Day calling ceremony. They dressed in their Sunday best and even decorated the bridles and harnesses on the horses to go calling on friends. A long pole was placed on wheels, which they straddled to ride from place to place. (Courtesy of Mason Moritz and the Historical Society of Stanton County.)

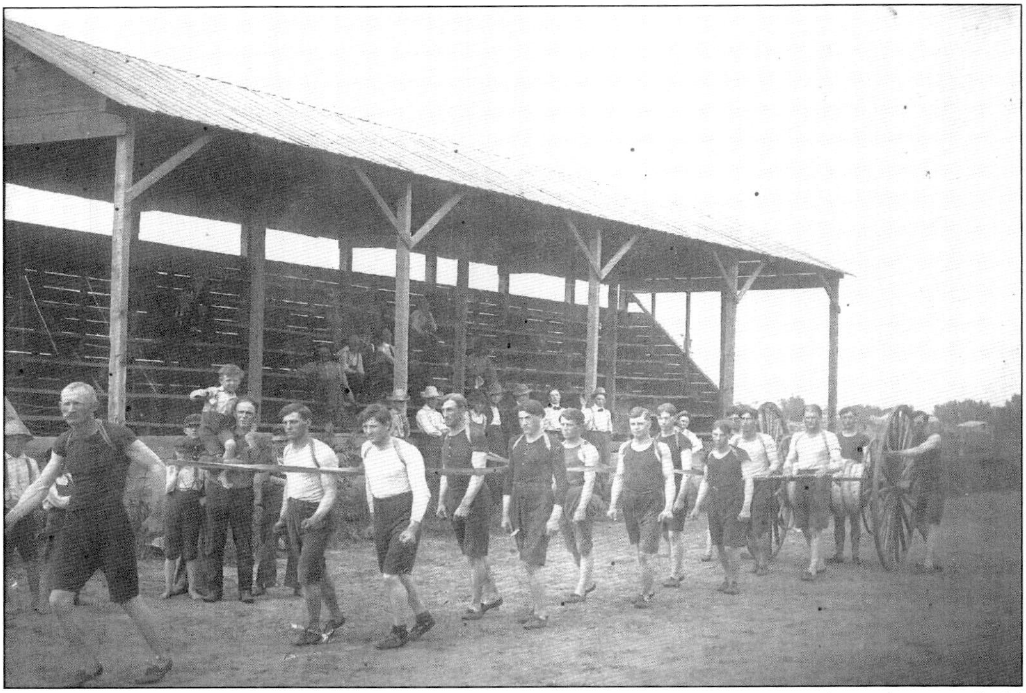

The Stanton Fire Department boasted the 1903 champion running team. Al Marks team held the Nebraska state title for the record time of 33.3 seconds for winning the competition. Team members are, from left to right, Al Marks (chief), William Zilmer, L. Poessnecker, L. Clough, J. Hollstein, William Poessnecker, W. Sonnenschein, John Hakl, Roy Sharp, Frank Mayer, Albert Felsch, W. Hollstein, Henry Zander, and L. Sonnenschein. F. Gambles was absent. (Courtesy of the Historical Society of Stanton County.)

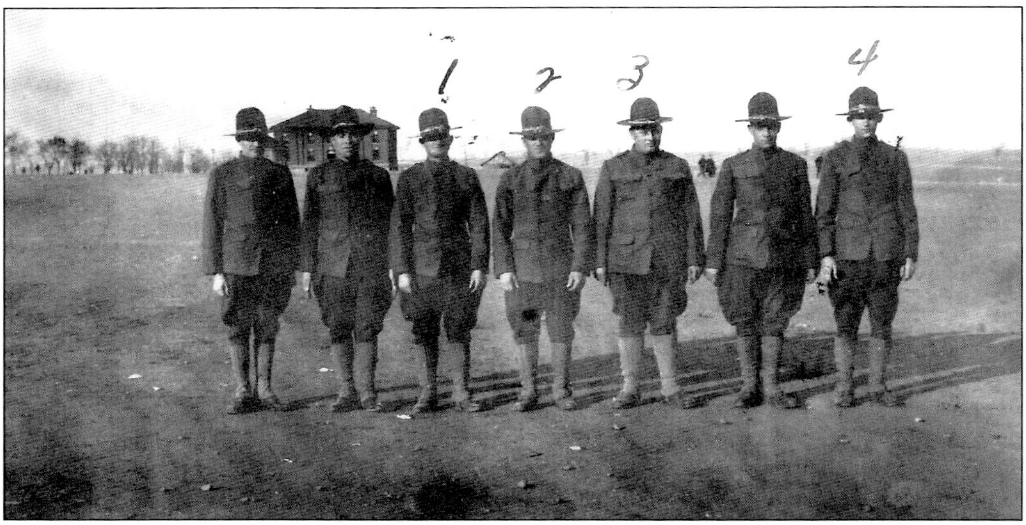

Some of Stanton County's brave young troopers line up for their photograph before leaving for duty in the early 1900s. Those Stanton boys in the group are noted on the photograph as Jay Arnold (1), Ray Hollstein (2), Ross Kinney (3), and Hugo Lueck (4). The rest are not identified. (Courtesy of the Historical Society of Stanton County.)

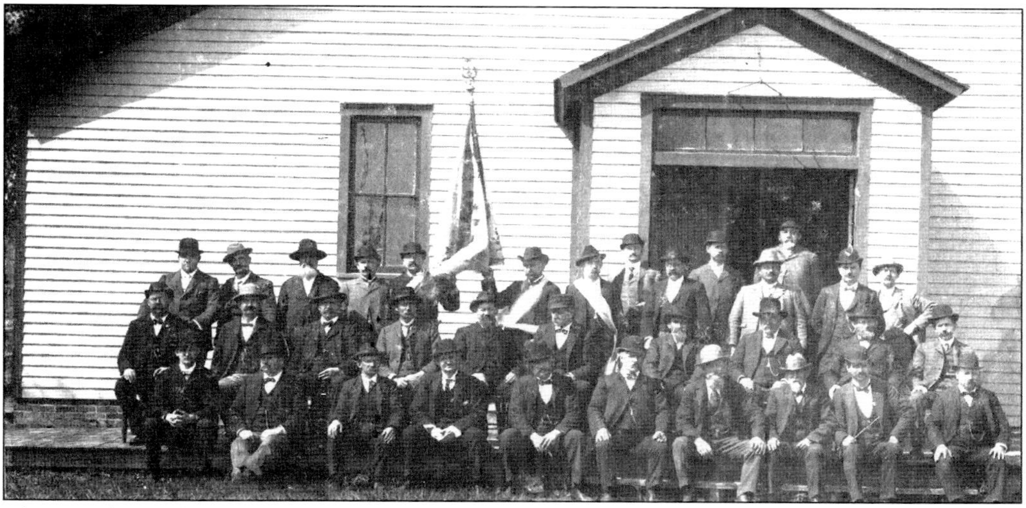

The members of the Germania Singing Society are pictured in front of the Germania Hall. When the anti-German sentiment grew in the early 1900s, the hall was burned down in 1919. The singing group continued for more than 50 years and the Stanton Gesangverein made an appearance at the 75th celebration program on October 16, 1941. (Courtesy of the Historical Society of Stanton County.)

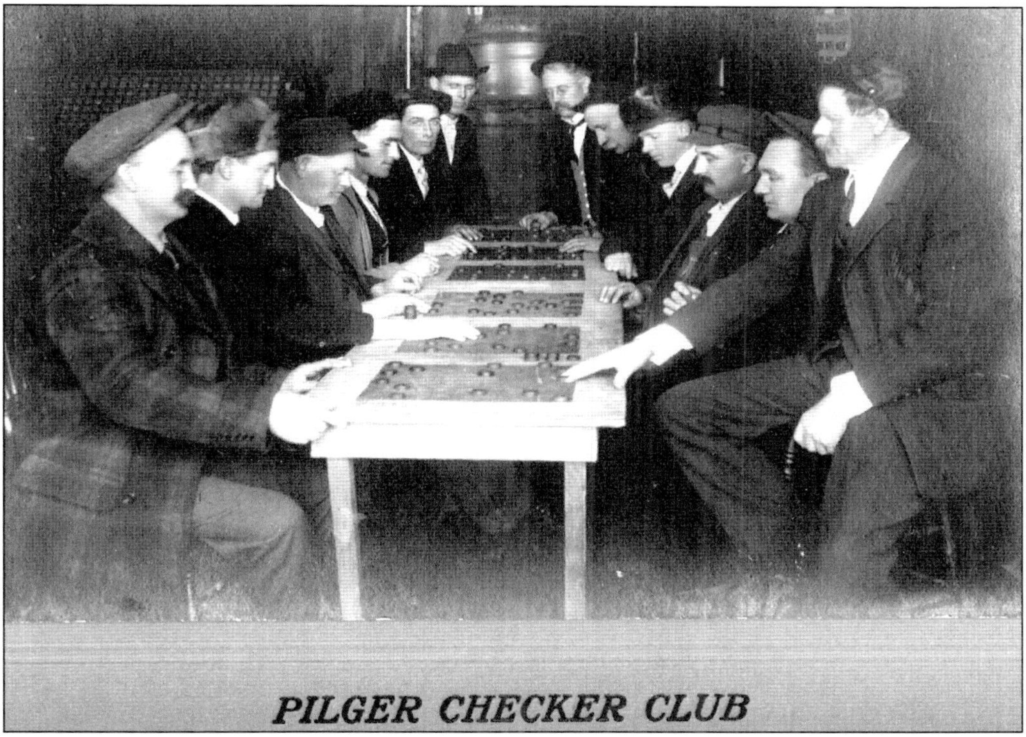

The members of the Pilger Checkers Club are identified as, from left to right clockwise, John Davis; Tom Birdwell; Henry Ellis; Carl Grogson; Brad Parody; W. C. Montgomery, editor of the *Pilger Herald*; Rev. Rex Phillips, Methodist minister; Henry Sixberry; Dr. Warren; August Grabenkamp; Bob Brandt; and W. J. Patterson. (Courtesy of the Historical Society of Stanton County.)

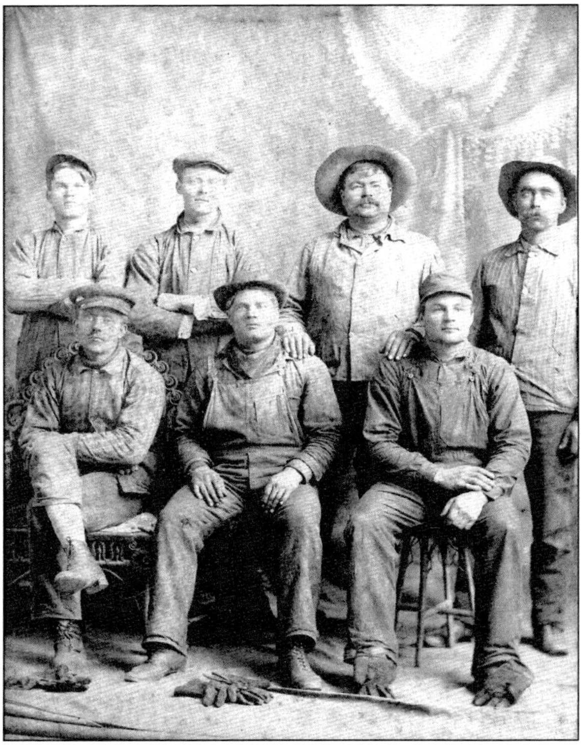

The Zander's Threshing Crew had a portrait taken as a professional group in this photograph. The workers are, from left to right, (first row) unidentified, Fred Zander, and Herman Zander; (second row) Walter Kahler, unidentified, Albert Zander, and Charles Moritz. (Courtesy of Mason Moritz and the Historical Society of Stanton County.)

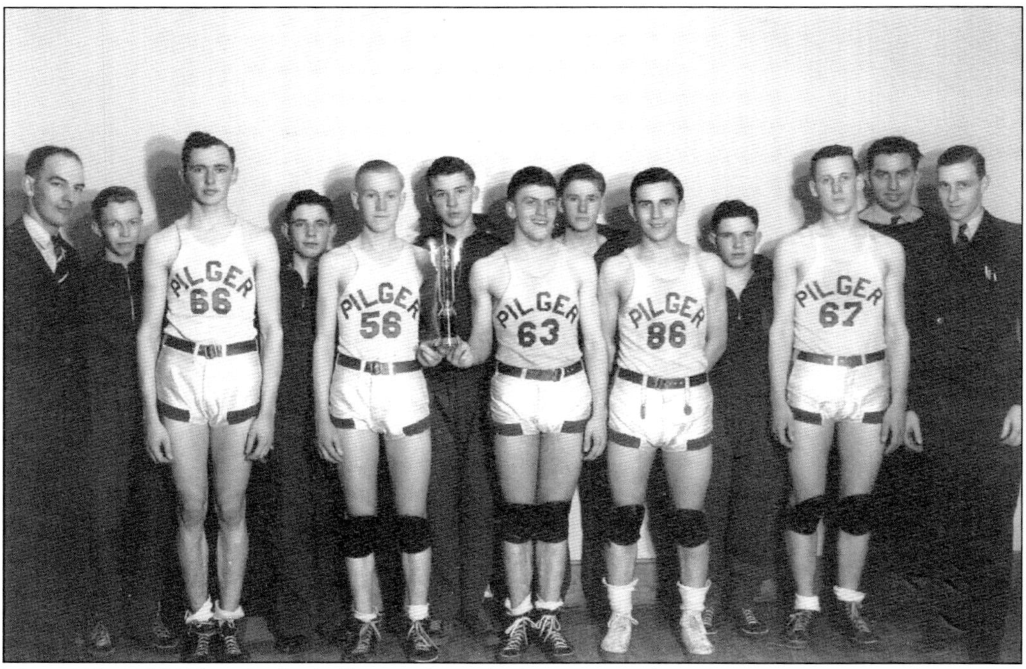

The 1935–1936 Pilger basketball team brought home a trophy. The Stanton and Pilger sports teams were always competitive, and rivalry was strong. Each had their own records to boast through the years that they competed with each other. (Courtesy of the Pilger Museum.)

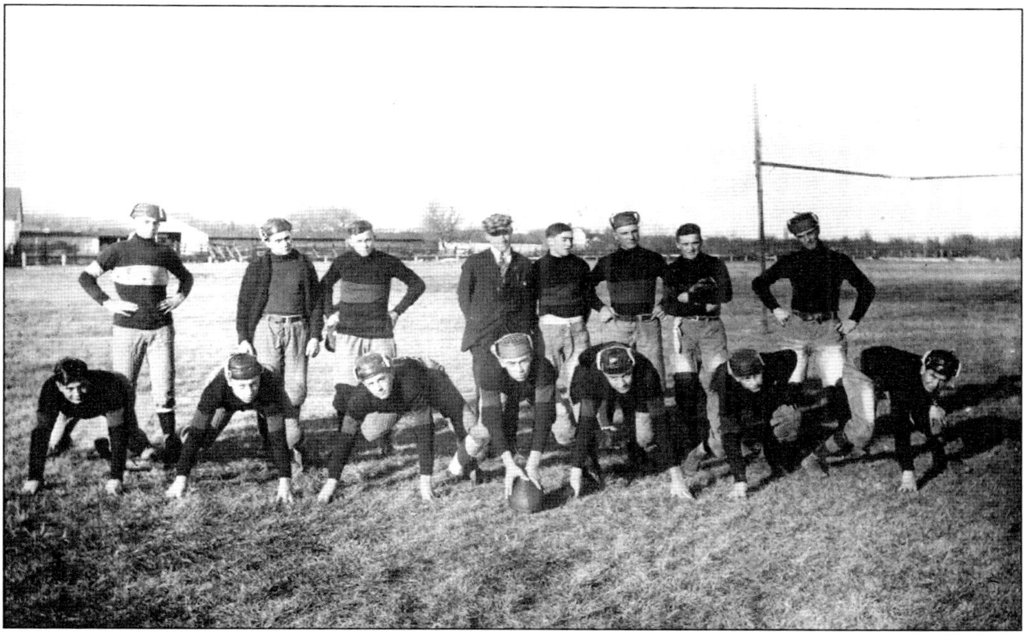

The line-up for the 1917–1918 Stanton High School Football team is ready for practice. This picture was taken at the football field at the Stanton County fairgrounds. The view is to the north where the livestock barns are used at the annual county fair. The football field is still located at the fairgrounds. (Courtesy of the Historical Society of Stanton County.)

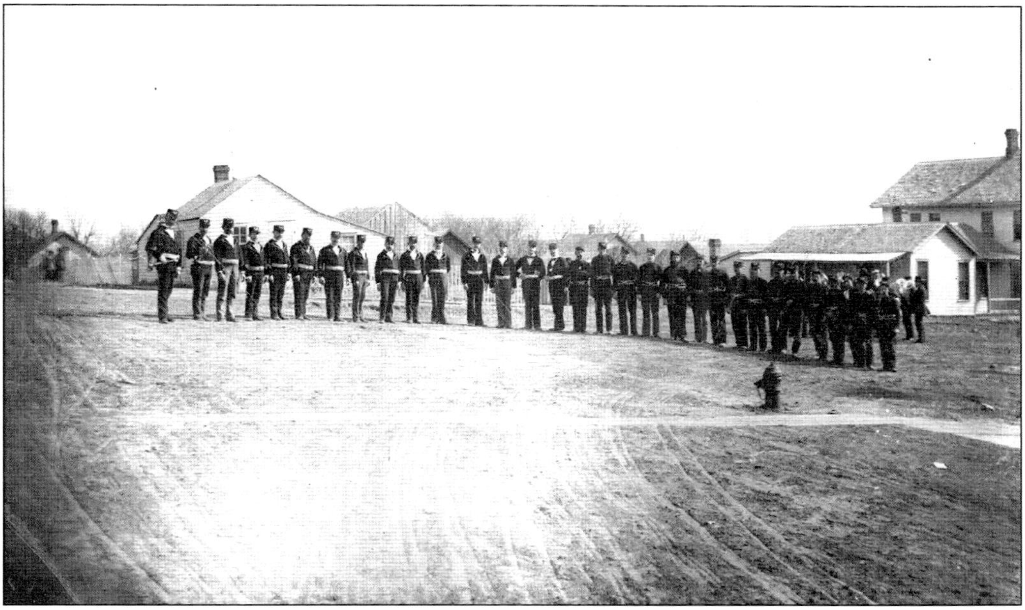

After several disastrous fires in Stanton, the Stanton Volunteer Fire Department was formed. The first elite volunteers are shown here with this photograph dating from around 1894, looking quite spiffy in their full uniforms. The town water supply was modernized with the installation of a fire hydrant, which is visible to the right. (Courtesy of the Historical Society of Stanton County.)

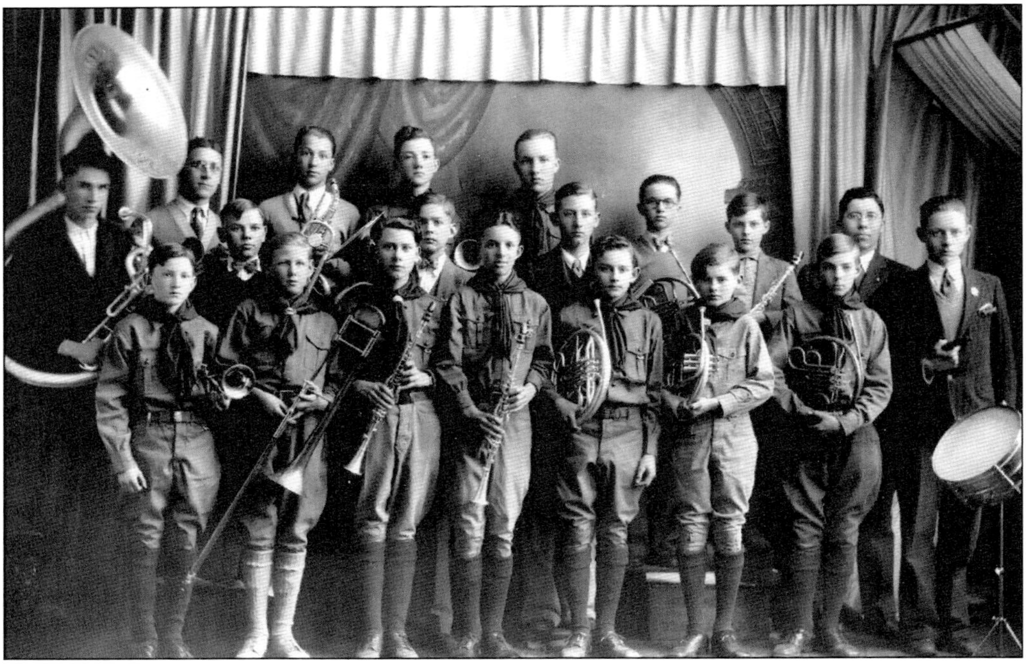

Art Greenslit directed the Stanton Boy Scout Instrumental Band in 1931. They were in competition at the Boys Scout Jamboree in Omaha at the time this picture was taken. (Courtesy of the Historical Society of Stanton County.)

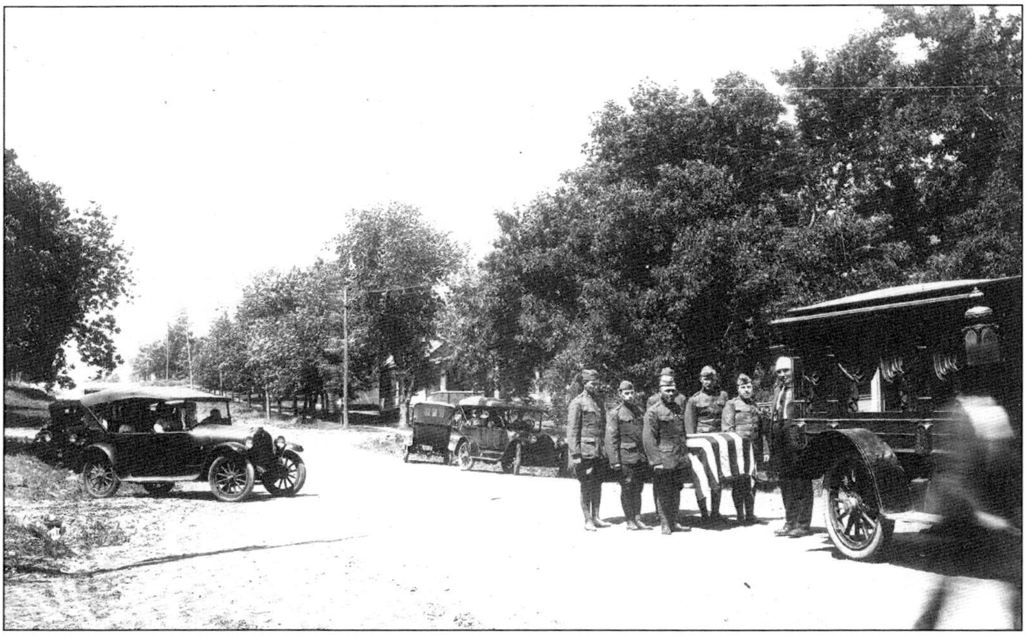

A military funeral procession is making its way down the street in Stanton. The Nicholas Mortuary hearse is waiting for the military escort to load the casket. The funeral took place sometime in 1921, but no further notation was made to indicate the identity of the dead soldier. (Courtesy of the Historical Society of Stanton County.)

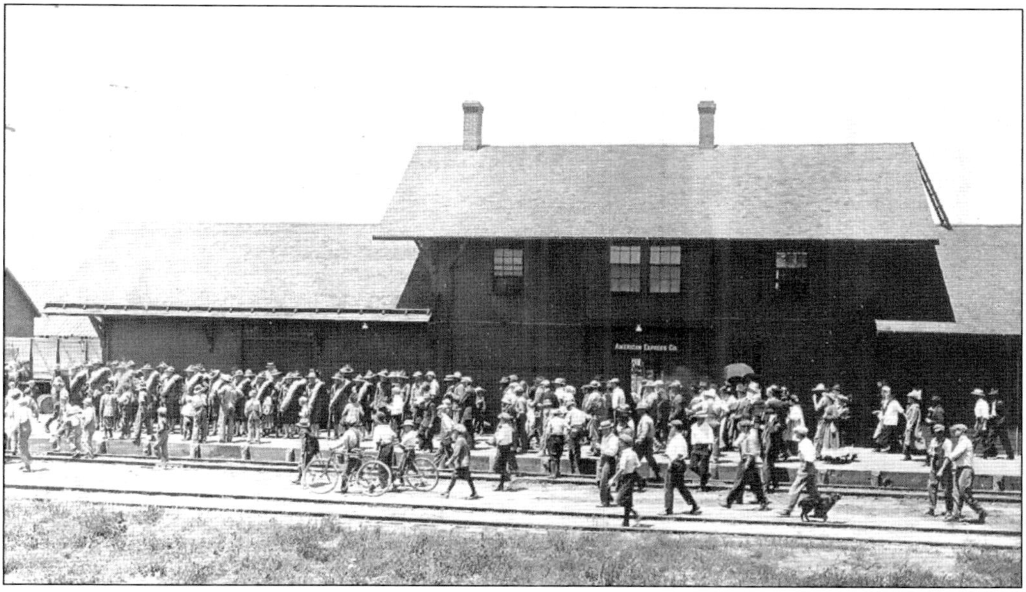

Company G of the United States Army has marched through downtown Stanton and is waiting at the Stanton C&NW depot. They are to board a train for the Mexican border. Several Stanton County boys are in the group. (Courtesy of the Historical Society of Stanton County and Milford and Gloria Koch.)

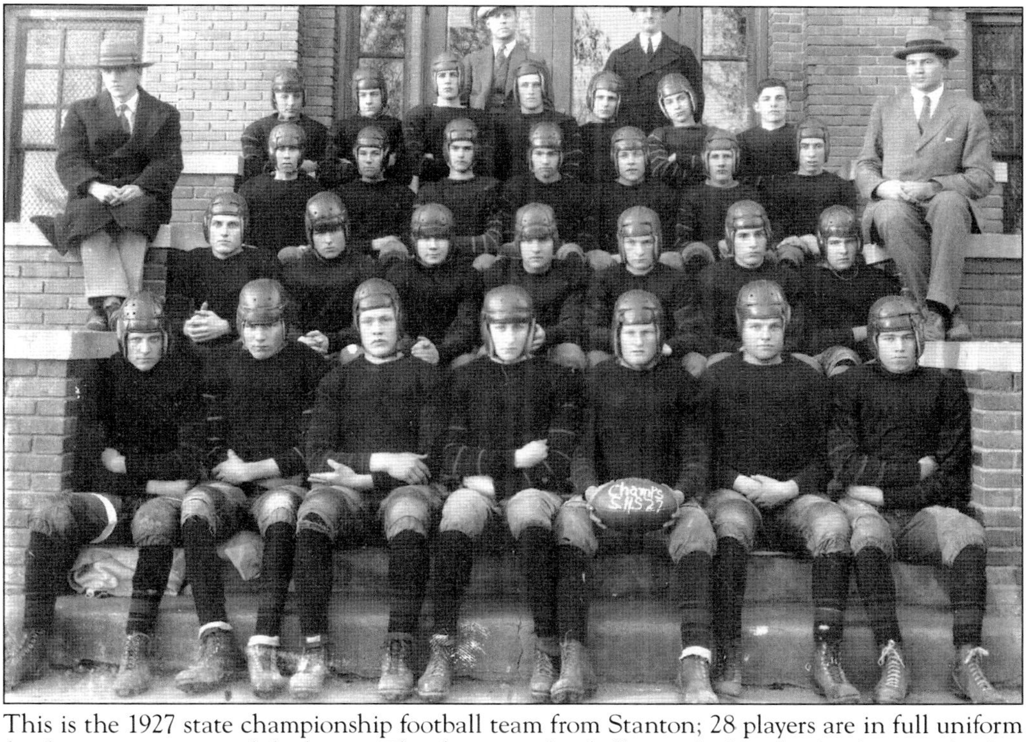

This is the 1927 state championship football team from Stanton; 28 players are in full uniform for the picture to record the honor. The championship ball is in the hands of a player in the first row. (Courtesy of the Historical Society of Stanton County.)

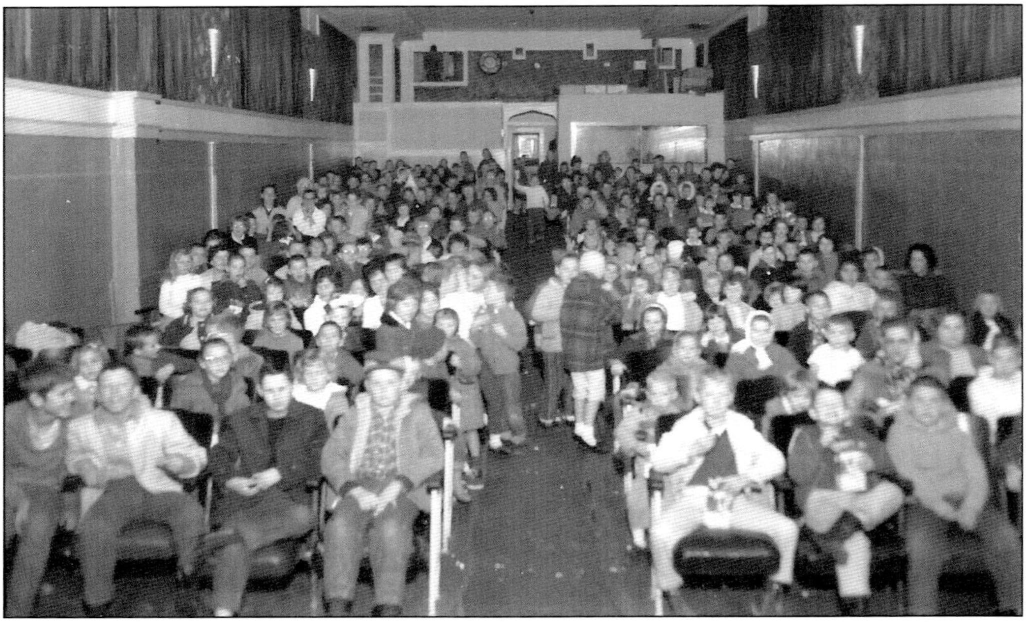

A full crowd settles in to enjoy the movie at the Rialto Theater in Stanton during the 1950s. The Rialto Theater was in operation for over 40 years. It was owned and operated by Clarence "C. J." Kremer for 35 of those years. The Rialto Theater closed up in 1963. (Courtesy of the Stanton Register.)

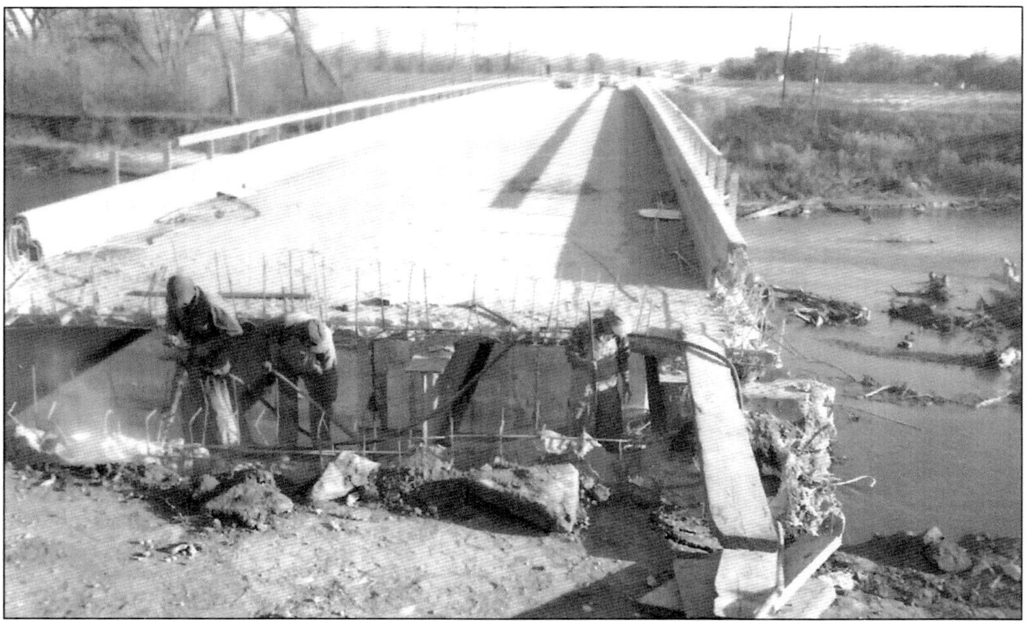

After having numerous washouts of the north approach to the Elkhorn River Bridge south of Stanton, extensive repair work was undertaken to stabilize the bridge permanently in the early 1960s. During the time that the bridge was closed to traffic, the businessmen provided shuttles for people who came across the temporary footbridge for supplies and town business. (Courtesy of the Stanton Register.)

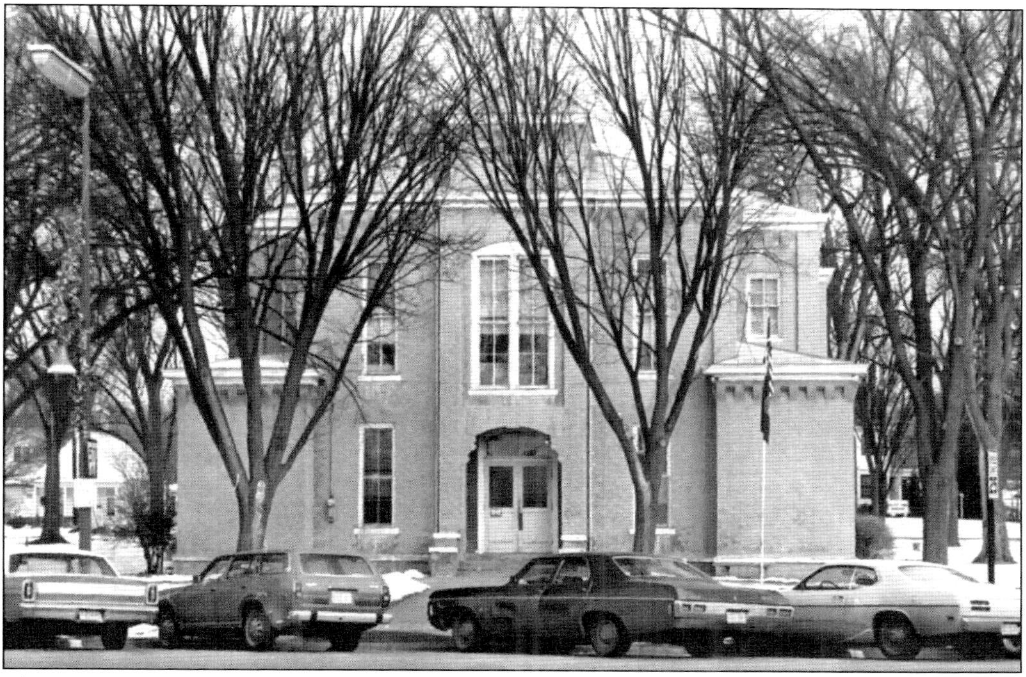

The Stanton County Courthouse was replaced with a single-story brick courthouse. This 1960s photograph shows the courthouse that served Stanton County until 1976. It was built at a cost of $10,624. The original steeple was removed several years earlier. (Courtesy of Larry Belz.)

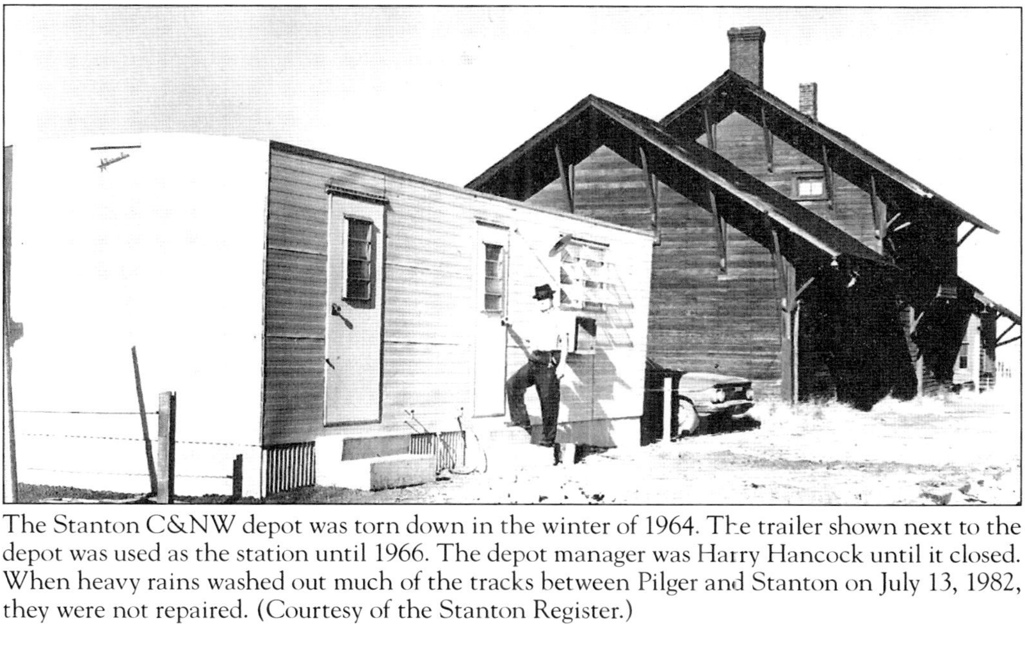

The Stanton C&NW depot was torn down in the winter of 1964. The trailer shown next to the depot was used as the station until 1966. The depot manager was Harry Hancock until it closed. When heavy rains washed out much of the tracks between Pilger and Stanton on July 13, 1982, they were not repaired. (Courtesy of the Stanton Register.)

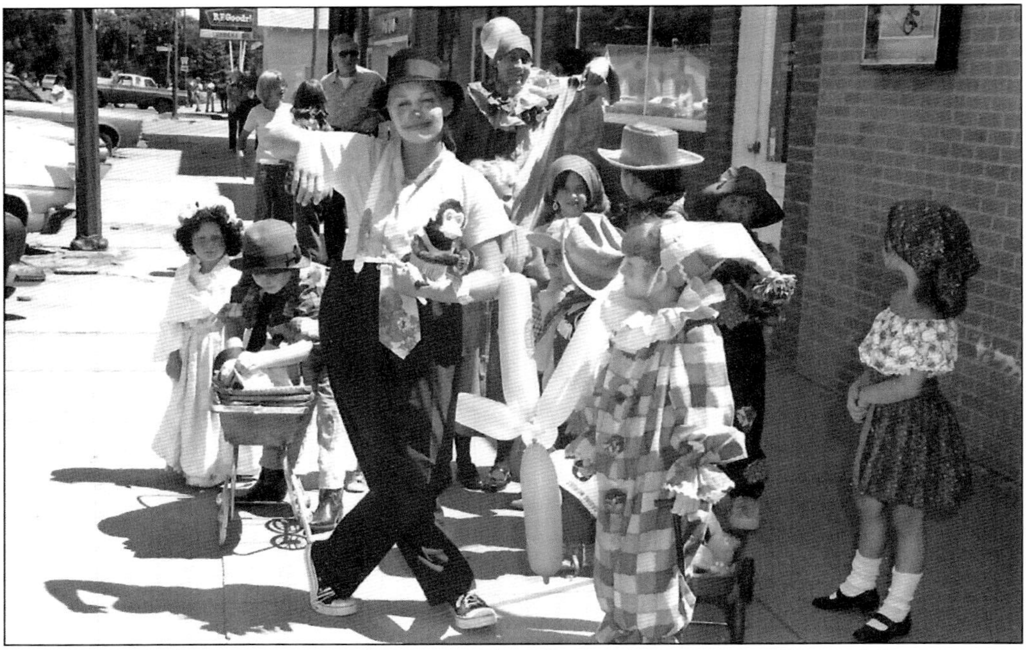

This is the day for youngsters to clown around on Stanton's main street. Even adults get to join in the fun and frolic in their clown outfits and makeup. Heidi Vogel, a graduate of Stanton High School, became a clown with the Ringling Brothers circus. She has been at Disney World as an entertainment manager for more than 20 years. (Courtesy of the Stanton Register.)

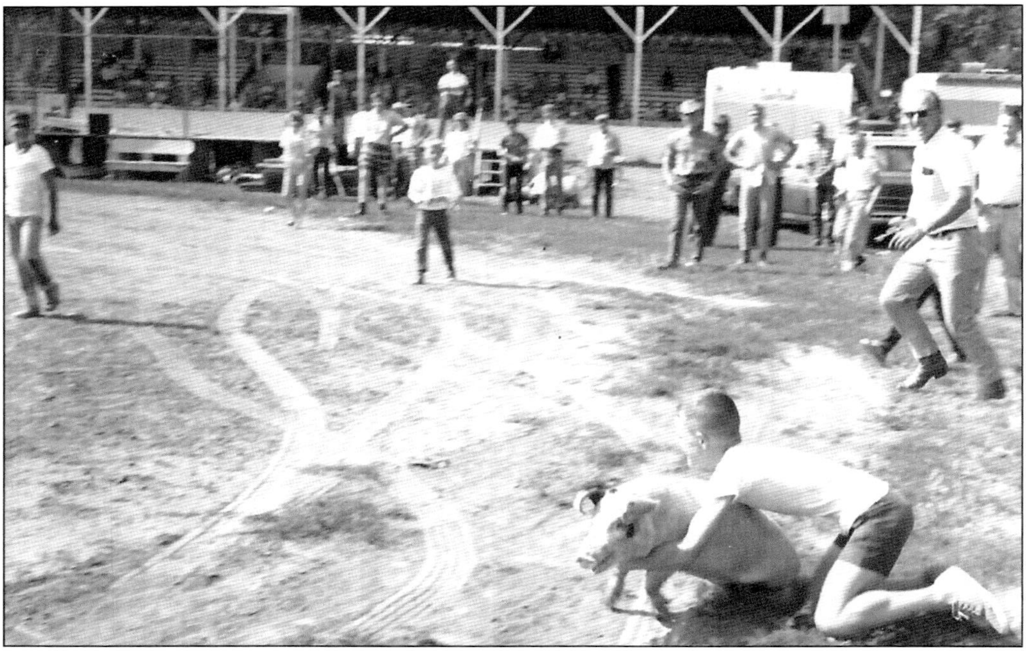

The Stanton County Fair is held every year in July or August. The activities are geared for the very young to the young at heart. In 1969, the old-fashioned greased pig contest was part of the activities. This young man seems to have captured his winning prize. (Courtesy of the Stanton Register.)

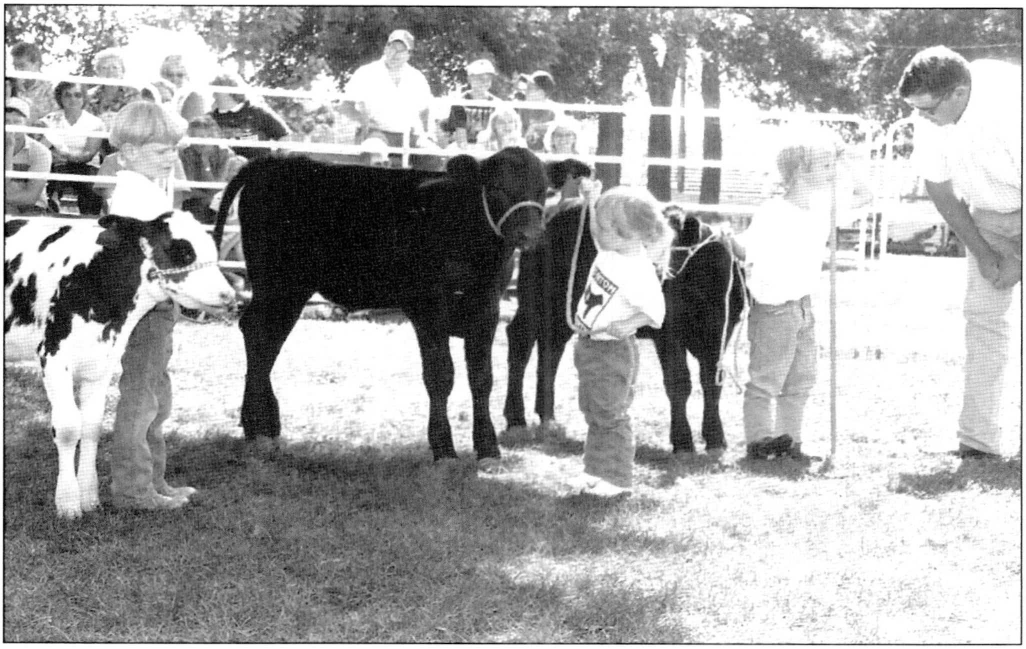

With agriculture as the major industry in Stanton County, the annual county fair is encouraging competition for 4-H members. The Cloverbuds are those youngsters who are still too young to be 4-H members, but they are allowed to show their projects locally. These three youngsters are showing off their prowess of showmanship in the judging ring. The judges are helpful with instructions and compliments to encourage the youngsters to continue. A young lady watches how her calf stands while waiting for the judge. The young lad is instructing his lamb on behavior in the show ring. (Courtesy of the Stanton Register.)

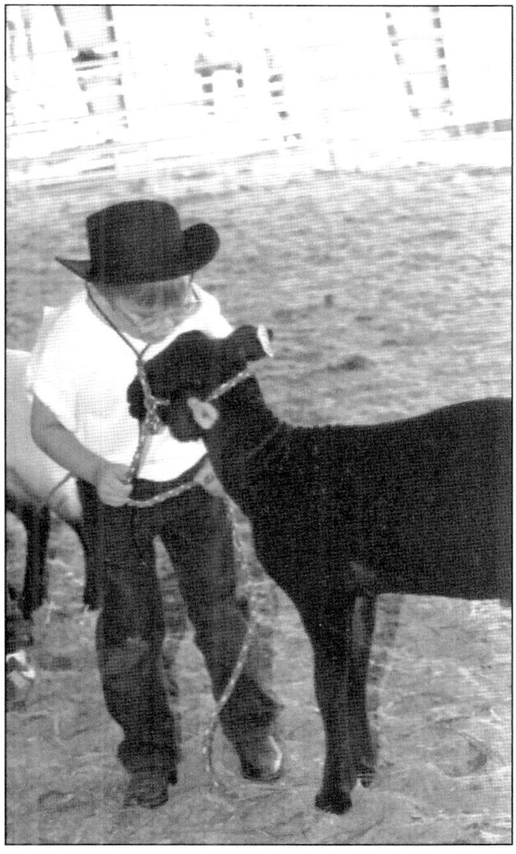

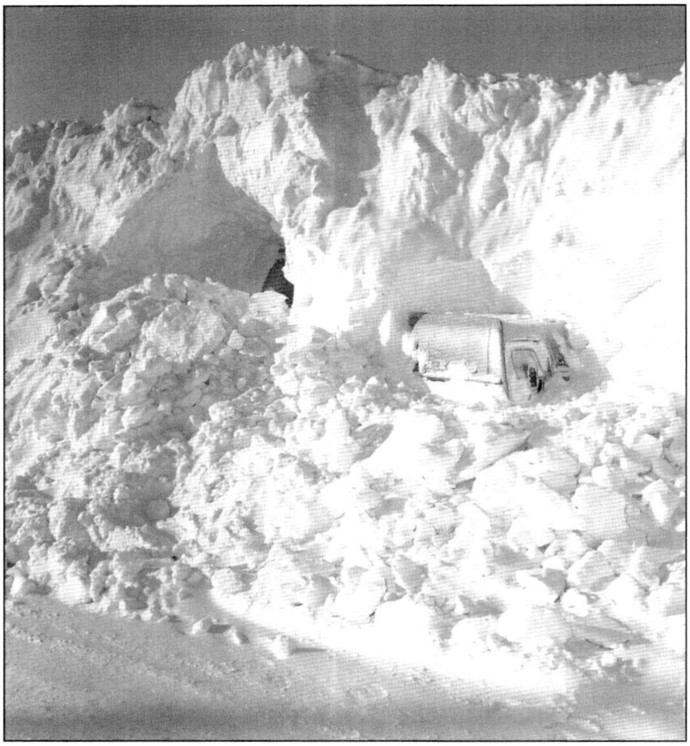

Winter weather usually brings snowstorms to the plains of Nebraska. Stanton County has experienced several blizzards one of which lasted for two days in January 1975. After the storm ended, snowplow crews were amazed to discover a vehicle buried in this huge snowdrift on the highway. (Courtesy of Larry Belz.)

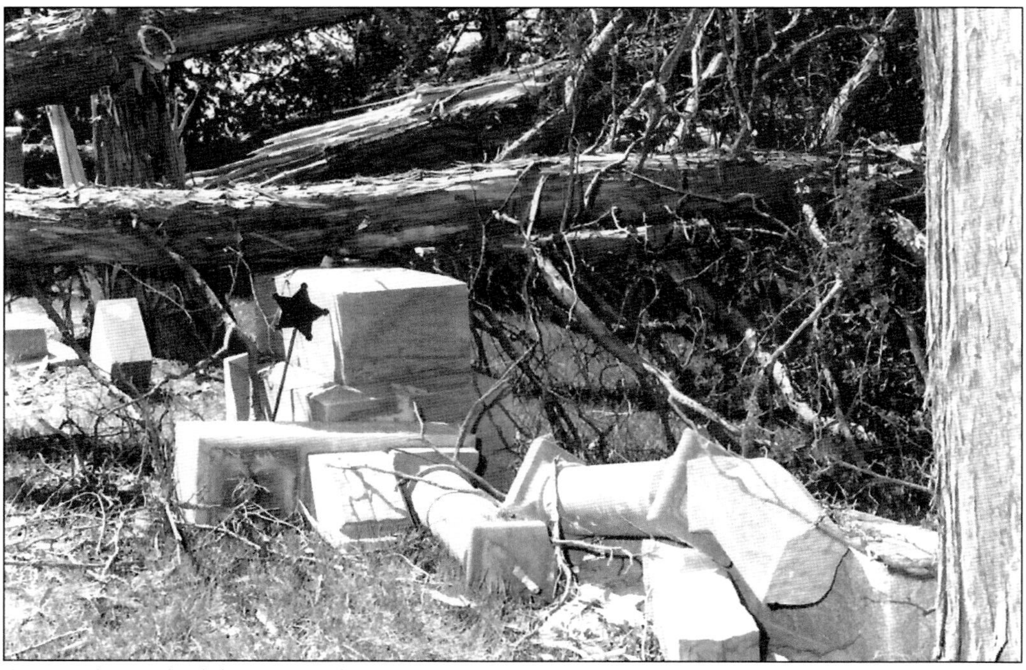

A tornado touched down in early April 1973 in Stanton County creating havoc at the cemetery. This downed tree destroyed the grave marker on a veteran's grave. No lives were lost in the storm, but considerable damage occurred in Stanton and nearby. (Courtesy of the Stanton Register.)

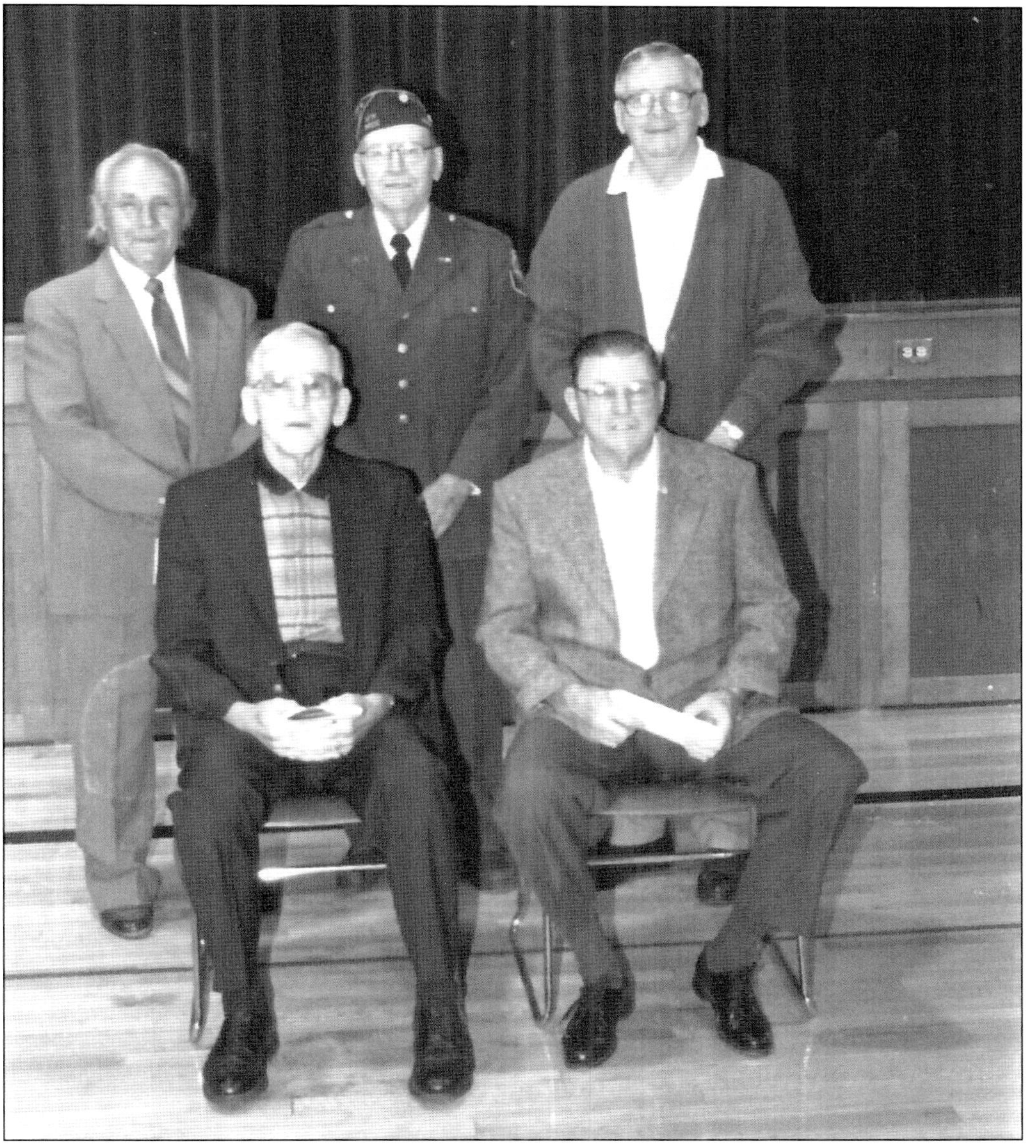

The Veterans Service office assisted in a decision to give special recognition to a group of veterans. Honorary high school diplomas were issued to veterans who left to serve their country during World War II and were not able to complete their high school education. On Veteran's Day in November 1999, the Stanton veterans who had served their country during the war were awarded their Stanton High School diplomas. Those who were present to receive their diplomas, seen here, are, from left to right, (first row) James Mandl and George Mesch; (second row) Lambert Podany, Chris Wiese, and Tom Mandl. Of these five veterans, three are deceased as of 2008. (Author's collection.)

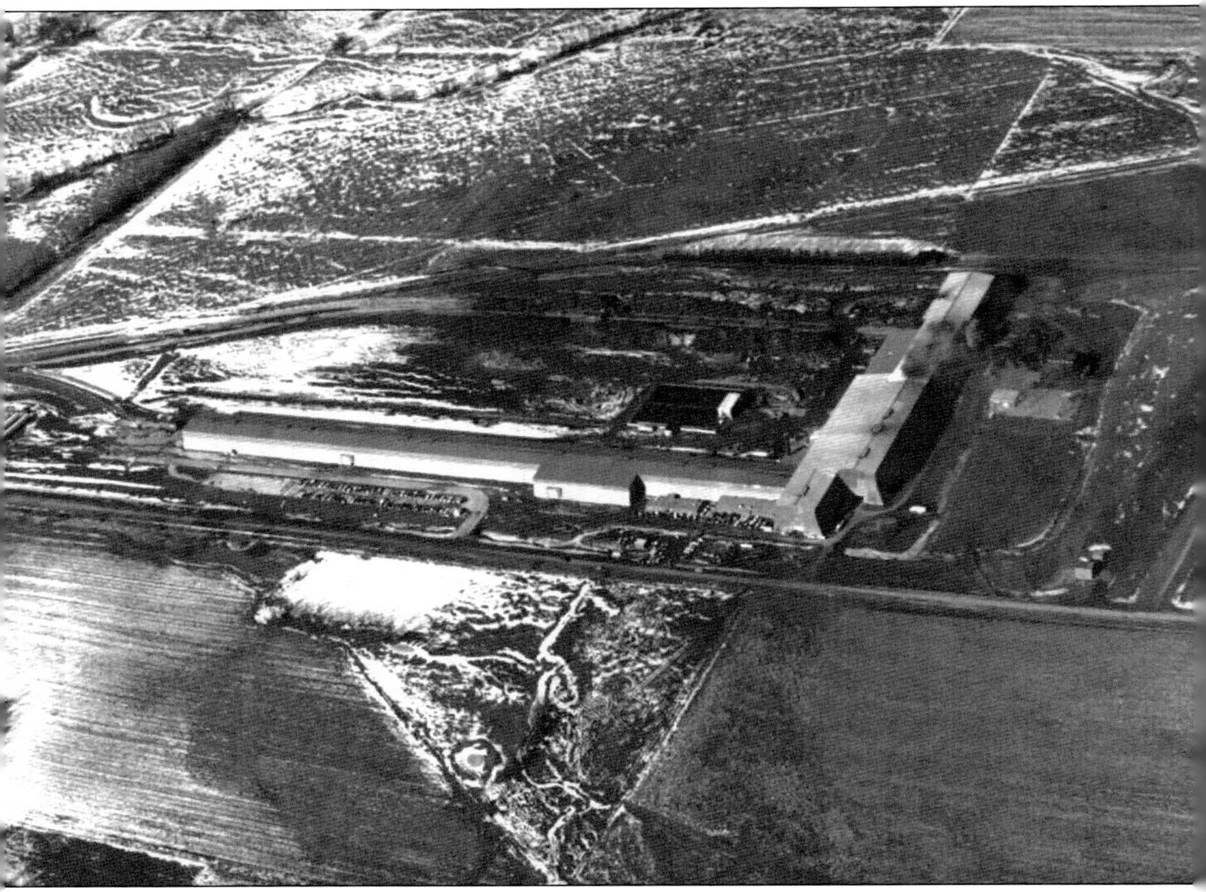

Stanton County's largest industry opened its operation 35 years ago. In 1973, Nucor Corporation built its second steel mill in Stanton County near the city of Norfolk. It included a melt and cast operation and a rolling mill. It was built on a 200-acre site with the help of 200 teammates. In 1973, it produced 160,000 tons of angles and rounds annually. By 1978, the plant expanded and built its second melt shop and rolling mill. The corporation has a joist plant, the Nucor Division of Vulcraft, located a few miles distant in the city of Norfolk. Even though Vulcraft is not located in Stanton County, the plant is beneficial to all the area. It has been operating since the mid-1960s. The two plants are separate divisions for the Nucor Corporation. The photograph was taken at the beginning of production. (Courtesy of Jeffrey Heng, Nucor.)

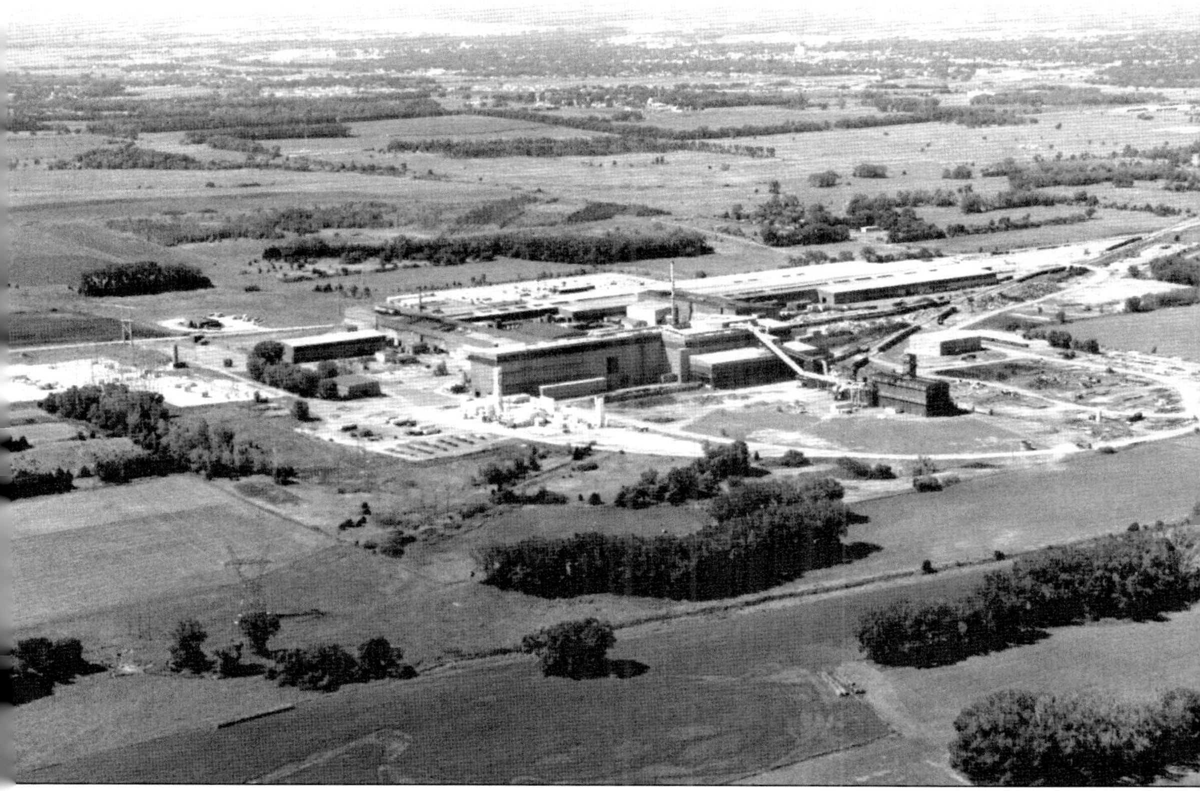

In 1997, Nucor built a new melt shop to support production in the two rolling mills. Major upgrades were made to Nucor Nebraska's No. 2 rolling mill. Nucor currently has 800 acres of land in the Norfolk plant. Of those 800 acres, 34 acres are under roof, and the division employs 410 teammates. In 2007, this plant melted and cast more than 1,025,000 tons of billets. It rolled over 850,000 tons of finished product and shipped 992,000 tons of finished product and billets. This plant is ISO9001 and ISO14001 certified. They are an OSHA Merit Site and an export processing zone (EPA) performance tract site. The Vulcraft Division plant has added a cold finish plant and a deck plant on site. The steel industry has been an important and progressive industry for the area and has one of the highest numbers of employees in the area. The photograph shows the expansion of the site since its beginning in 1973. (Courtesy of Jeffrey Heng, Nucor.)

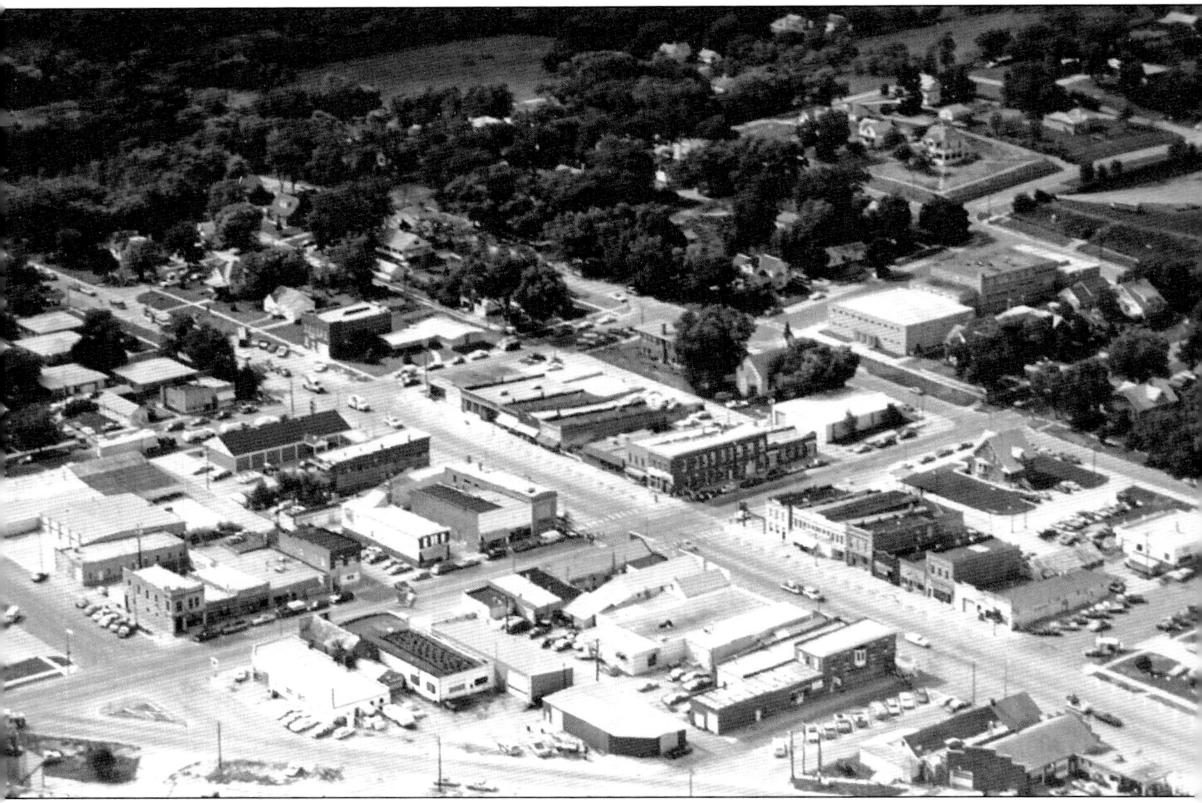

This aerial photograph of the city of Stanton was taken in 1997. Some of the buildings have changed or disappeared in the past decade. The split intersection on the bottom left shows Highway 24 heading to the north to join Highway 57. The large light colored roof to the upper right is the high school and middle school. Other buildings in town can be discerned from the placement of those streets. Although the streets and faces may have changed, the community spirit remains undaunted. New homes are built and new people come to town looking for a friendly atmosphere and a place to raise a family. The rural community remains positive and welcomes all who seek to share in a vision for the future. (Courtesy of the Stanton Register.)

This penny postcard carries a good luck wish from the community of Pilger in Stanton County. It is a memento that has printed images capturing the history of the community. Those images show how much was accomplished by the settlers who arrived so many years ago. Their accomplishments provide hope for the future for continued progress. (Courtesy of Marian Klima.)

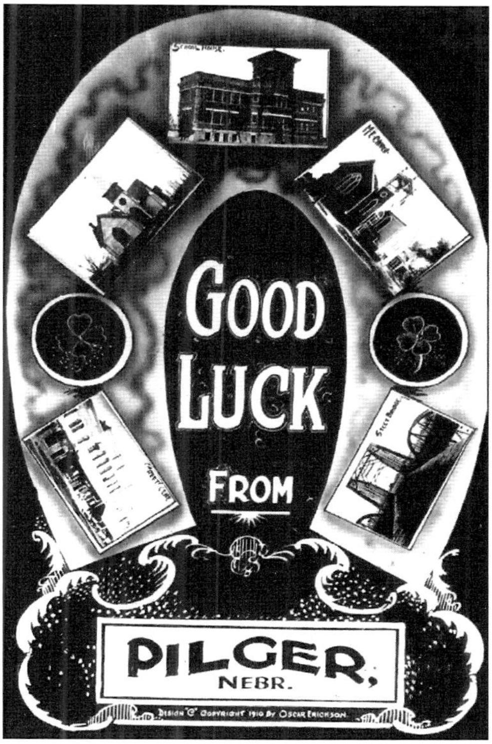

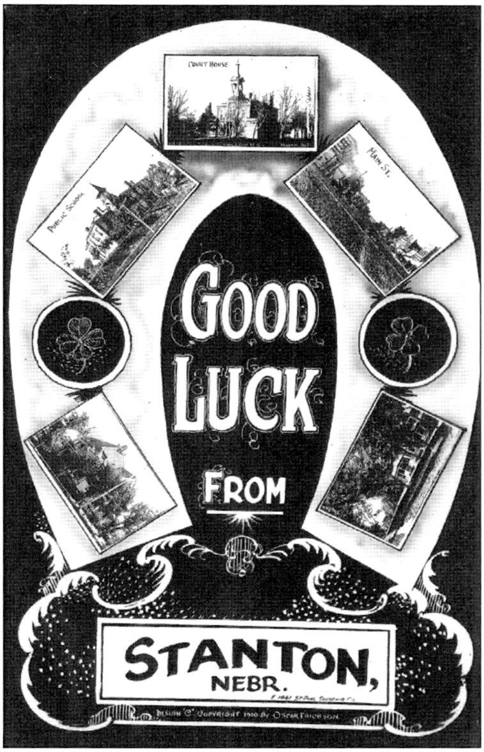

The town of Stanton remains vital and progressive. The young people have access to a good education in modern buildings. There is a recreation program for summer activities and athletics. The business community strives to provide for their patrons. The housing development is moving forward, and history is being made. (Courtesy of Art Catlin.)

ACROSS AMERICA, PEOPLE ARE DISCOVERING SOMETHING WONDERFUL. *THEIR HERITAGE.*

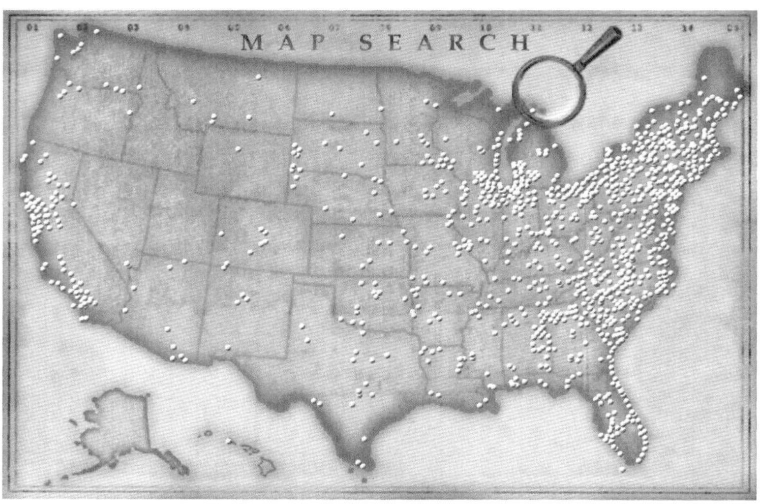